PRAISE FOR

I WAS BORN IN THE FOREST

"Otis Lee shares with us the powerful history of the 'Quilombo' of Palmares, an African state in colonial Brazil created by escaped slaves. But its importance is in his invitation to confront the legacy of slavery in both North and South America, the resilience of slaves and their determination to live freely, and the ways in which established power structures reinforced the subjugation of slaves and the marginalization—still—of those same peoples."

—*Schuyler Foerster*, Professor Emeritus, US Air Force Academy

"In this wide-ranging analysis, Otis Lee draws on evidence from a rich variety of sources to deliver an intriguing analysis of the history and relevance of quilombos in Brazil. Quilombos were communities of slaves that escaped to freedom by settling in the hinterland. Many of these fugitives boldly resisted efforts by colonial authorities to capture them. The most famous quilombo, Palmares, had thousands of settlers and fought off attackers for decades. Otis Lee relates this history of struggles for freedom to the efforts of Afro-Brazilians to draw upon this cultural heritage by establishing independent communities in modern times."

—*Robert Brent Toplin*, Former Professor of History, University of North Carolina, Wilmington

"This book should be required reading for every high school student and every undergraduate college student. In all of my 20 years of college teaching, I knew nothing about this subject."

—*Harriett F. Karuhije*, Ed.D., Former Nurse Educator, Columbia University

"This book is a grasping literary work that is at once informative and inspirational. Lee informs us with sensitivity and candor about the realities of marginalization and subjugation of a people. But it is also an equally hopeful tale of the dispossessed dignity, resilience, and indomitable quest for equity and justice, the timeless virtues that should animate us all to confront the societal inequalities we face today."

—*Sula Mazimba*, MD, MPH, Cardiologist, Former Associate Professor, University of Virginia

"This is more than a story from a nonhistorian, and it is more than creative nonfiction. [Otis Lee's] answering the question of why Africans were selected for the slave trade was astute and most likely correct. I had never thought of comparing the successful quilombos to prospering USA Black towns; a very good and informative take on the two. I didn't know that the Dutch were also guilty of attacking quilombos. . . .

"I truly enjoyed the book and learned a lot. . . . I loved [Lee's] insights into Paraty life and its beauty."

—*Alvin Foster*, DEd, Entrepreneur, Former Assistant Professor, University of Massachusetts at Boston, and Former Assistant Dean, Boston University

"Mr. Lee presents the case for a better understanding of resistance by enslaved persons to the Atlantic slave trade by examining maroon communities. He describes how escaped slaves banded together for protection and independence. Knowing more about these autonomous communities shows how social movements can promote self-determination and liberty."

—*Norman Hill*, Advisor, Ballard Center for Social Impact, Brigham Young University

I WAS BORN IN THE FOREST

I Was Born in the Forest:
A Traveler's Guide to Quilombos, the Citadels of African Resistance to Slavery in Portuguese America, and a Story of Black Spartacus

by Otis L. Lee, Jr.

© Copyright 2024 Otis L. Lee, Jr.

ISBN 979-8-88824-237-7
LCCN: 202390773

All rights reserved. No part of this publication may be reproduced, stored in a retrieval system, or transmitted in any form or by any means—electronic, mechanical, photocopy, recording, or any other—except for brief quotations in printed reviews, without the prior written permission of the author.

Published by

3705 Shore Drive
Virginia Beach, VA 23455
800-435-4811
www.koehlerbooks.com

On the cover: Three images separated by tears.

At the top, a map of the Captaincy of Pernambuco, with representation of the Quilombo dos Palmares. *Praefecturae Paranambucae pars Meridionalis* by Frans Post, 1647. Public Domain.

In the middle, an example of a palm tree forest found in Brazil.

At the bottom, a painting depicting the martial art form capoeira practiced by the inhabitants of Palmares. *Playing Capoeira, the Dance of War* by Johann Moritz Rugendas, 1825. Public Domain. Oil on canvas.

Other Publications by Otis L. Lee, Jr.:

From South Boston to Cambridge:
The Making of One Philadelphia Lawyer
A Memoir

The Last Train from Djibouti:
Africa Beckons Me, But America Is My Home

Contributing author:

"*Estate Planning for Small Business,*" to the 1980 edition of the US Department of Commerce, *"The Local Economic Development Corporation Legal and Financial Guidelines.*"

OTIS L. LEE, JR.

I WAS BORN IN THE FOREST

A Traveler's Guide to Quilombos, the Citadels of African Resistance to Slavery in Portuguese America, and a Story of Black Spartacus

VIRGINIA BEACH
CAPE CHARLES

This book is dedicated to my grandchildren: Sofia, Cristian, Ariele, Ethan and Danielle. May they continue to embrace and hold dear the love of family and read and travel extensively to learn our true history in the making of this world.

TABLE OF CONTENTS

Foreword xii

Introduction 1

Chapter 1. Traveling to Olodum 23

Chapter 2. Be Free in Paraty 32

Chapter 3. Palmares de Pernambuco, the Troy of Alagoas . . . 42

Chapter 4. Ganga Zumba and African Lineage 61

Chapter 5. Zumbi: From Kongo to Porto Calvo 70

Chapter 6. Zumbi of Palmares 83

Chapter 7. Quilombos in North America and the
General of the Swamps 89

Chapter 8. The Advent of Black Towns in North America . . 103

Chapter 9. Indians and Maroons: An Alliance
of Convenience 109

Chapter 10. The Role of Women in the Quilombo 123

Illustrations 136

Chapter 11. The Children of God's Fire and the Role of
Christianity in the Quilombos 143

Chapter 12. The Bouleversement 165

Chapter 13. The Negro Numantia 187

Chapter 14. Sesmarias and the Law of Good Reason 203

Chapter 15. The Legacy: I Was Born in the Forest 209

Chapter 16. Present-Day Quilombos: The 1988 Constitution, the Endowment 219

Conclusão. A Perspective 228

Acknowledgments 246

Appendix A 247

Appendix B 252

Appendix C 255

Glossary 258

Bibliography 266

Index 275

FOREWORD

In 1988, Brazil ratified Article 68, a constitutional provision that recognizes the collective property rights of *quilombolas*, who are the descendants of formerly enslaved Africans, many of whom had escaped slavery. Article 68 ushered a dramatic transformation in the racial politics of Brazil, one of the most unequal societies in the world. Brazil—the last country in the Americas to abolish slavery, in 1988—became the first country to constitutionally guarantee the territorial rights of the descendants of enslaved people, in 1888. In so doing, the framers of the "Quilombo Law" undertook to redress profound, longstanding inequities in the ownership of real property—the byproducts of more than three centuries of enslavement, land concentration, and racial capitalism in Brazil—through the prism of race, redistribution, and reparative justice. However, while more than 6,000 quilombo communities have petitioned the Brazilian government for collective land rights as quilombo descendants (*remanescentes de quilombos* in Portuguese) under the constitution, only two dozen have obtained full title to their territories. Today, like their ancestors, quilombolas face threats to their lands and livelihoods, from developers, ranchers, multinational mining companies, hydroelectric dams, a space launch center, and the Brazilian State. "Brazil waited almost 500 years to recognize quilombos," Aurico Dias, a quilombola activist from São Paulo's Vale do Ribeira told me some years ago. "Now it feels like we will have to wait another 500 years for the government to enforce its own laws."

Otis Lee's *I Was Born in the Forest* explores the histories and enduring legacies of the people of Palmares, Brazil's most famous quilombo. Tucked away in the arid hinterlands of the Brazilian Northeast, the 20,000-strong Quilombo dos Palmares (1600–1694)—originally known as *Angola Janga* (Little Angola) by its Bantu founders—was not merely a sanctuary for fugitive slaves. Palmares—a society organized around collective labor, communal land ownership, agroecological mastery, and trade—presented an African alternative to the slave-plantation-monoculture industrial complex of the European New World. It is little wonder, then, that the Portuguese and Dutch colonists in Brazil sought the quilombo's ultimate demise. After repelling the assaults of slave catchers and their militias for nearly a century, Palmares, and its fabled warrior-king Zumbi, were finally extinguished on November 20, 1695.

However, as Otis Lee observes, Palmares—and Zumbi—never really died. On the contrary, the so-called African Kingdom in Brazil and its occupants evolved into powerful myths and symbols of resistance that inspired oppressed Brazilians across time and space. To chattel slaves, Palmares—and the quilombo, generally—represented an emancipatory alternative to plantation slavery. Although Palmares was destroyed, hundreds, if not thousands, of quilombos dotted the vast Brazilian landscape in its wake. To immigrant and Afro-Brazilian laborers toiling in São Paulo's factories during the 1920s, Palmares presented a model of a worker's paradise. Decades later, during the 1960s and 1970s, the Afro-Brazilian intellectual Abdias do Nascimento brandished the Quilombo dos Palmares as a challenge to Brazil's vaunted reputation as a racial paradise. Finally, beginning in the 1990s, Zumbi and Palmares became symbols of a rural Black social movement demanding land, reparations, and recognition in Brazilian society: the one-million-strong Quilombo Movement. As Otis Lee writes, "myth and history are not necessarily mutually exclusive, and in some circumstances, may be inseparable."

Many have written about Palmares. Few have considered the subjectivities and lived experiences of Palmares's inhabitants. *I Was*

Born in the Forest grapples with and interrogates surviving historical accounts of Palmares—written by the very men who sought the quilombo's destruction—to consider Zumbi's particular vision of freedom. In so doing, Lee reminds us that history is shaped by the actions of ordinary people who undertake extraordinary things. As a lawyer and historian who has researched and supported the Quilombo Movement for more than a decade, I am reminded by *I Was Born in the Forest*—and indeed, it should remind all of us—about how much we can learn about freedom, justice, and equality from the lived experiences of quilombolas who still fight for land and liberation more than 400 years after Palmares.

Edward Shore, PhD, JD
Author of *A Dream Deferred: The Emergence and Fitful Enforcement of the Quilombo Law in Brazil*, 101 Texas L. Rev. 707–48 (2023) and *Avengers of Zumbi: The Nature of Fugitive Slave Communities & Their Descendants in Brazil* (PhD Diss., The University of Texas at Austin, 2018)

INTRODUCTION

The history of people of African descent is riddled with the notion that Africans enslaved in the Americas were docile, accepting, and unassertive in their condition of enforced servitude—that they benefitted from and at times embraced aspects of it. The concept of *quilombo* and, specifically, the Quilombo of Palmares is consequently important because this maroon society, one formed by escaped slaves, demonstrates that Africans fought against their enslavement successfully for a sustained period and transported much of their native culture to the settlements they created in Brazil.

As a result, descendants of these communities—along with Afro-Brazilians in general, African Americans, and others of African descent in the diaspora—have learned enduring lessons regarding the mentality needed to press on in the fight for equal justice and humane treatment at all levels of society. It is my view that quilombos were the precursors of Black towns founded in North America. The genesis of these communities and of most religions emerged from the struggle to attain mental and physical freedom.

I have attempted to frame Quilombo dos Palmares, the principal quilombo, along with the characters in this book—its leaders, Ganga Zumba and Zumbi—and their struggles, in the context of today's world, drawing upon the work of noted historians, my research, and my travels. My journey into the world of Palmares and its many components starts with my initial observations about certain aspects of Brazilian culture during my first trip to the country, when I visited the quilombo that was the catalyst for this book.

The colonial era in the Americas lasted from the fifteenth century through the eighteenth century and ensnared countless Africans in the institution of slavery. Various colonial powers also attempted to colonize the mind of the African and the public at large by use of the available media to shape the narrative about enslaved people and to denigrate their humanity, all to rationalize the cruel treatment of enslaved people. We begin our discussion of the quilombo with an overview of this colonial state of mind that still resonates in today's world. We will discuss these issues in relation to Palmares and its symbolism in each of the succeeding chapters, finding many lessons to apply to the fight for freedom for African-descended people.

So much of what we think about ourselves, our society, and our culture is influenced by the media, which includes television, the arts, newspapers, books, museums, movies, festivals, and other forms of mass cultural transmission. Even the well-read are unwittingly influenced by biased reporting and a historical record that often reflects a colonial mentality. This results in a fictionalized history built upon synthetic heroism, constructed and deconstructed for political purposes. Unbiased history, also known as historicity, is rare if it exists at all. The story of the Quilombo of Palmares and their most famous leader, Zumbi—as well as quilombos in general—is a classic example of this observable fact.

In the absence of travel, physical inspection, and research, everything we see and hear about culture (ours and others') is filtered through the lens of the purveyor, typically to achieve political or propagandistic objectives such as the "orthodoxy of White-isms": the culture of White supremacy and the sinews that underpin it. The pillars of these polarizing objectives include the hypocrisies of democracy and Christianity and the politicization of religion; the rapacious impersonality of capitalism fueled by the engine of technology; and the administration of law, especially criminal and civil law, in ways that enforce cultural norms. Law has always been politics by other means, comparable to what Carl von Clausewitz has said of war. In our family, we say, "Color shades justice."

These are only a few of the methods used to sustain the edifice of White European ethnocentrism. This view has been iterated by sociologist W. E. B. Du Bois, who said all art is propaganda.[1] And Edward Said, the late public intellectual and former professor at Columbia University, opined in *Culture and Imperialism* that Western culture has imperial objectives and purposes and seeks to denigrate, replace, or otherwise make irrelevant the culture of the "other."[2]

Brazilian historian Gilberto Freyre,[3] in his seminal 1986 work *The Masters and the Slaves*, makes the point that this subjugation of the other occurs "chiefly because the conqueror means to impose upon the subject people the whole of his own culture, in one piece, without any compromise to soften the imposition." Regarding the mechanism of Christianity, he adds, "From the sixteenth century to the present day the missionary has been the great destroyer of non-European cultures, his activities in this respect having been more dissolvent than those of the layman."

The colonial state of mind is transcendent; it suffuses the tentacles of society. This ongoing political mentality inculcates certain cultural norms that promote the economic, racial, hegemonic, and doctrinal objectives of those seeking to dominate the social landscape. Some societies promote racial stereotypes and miscegenation to dilute the genealogy of Africanness and Indigenous groups—and, in furtherance thereof, remove from the social marketplace tens of thousands of African-descended males by way of the criminal justice system.

Palmares, the subject of this book, was the African state in colonial Brazil. It was a reality, not a fiction, built by a community of African slaves. However, the history of Palmares as reflected in the

---

1. W. E. B. Du Bois, "Criteria of Negro Art," *The Crisis* 32 (October 1926): 290-297.
2. Said, Edward. *Culture and Imperialism*, 1994.
3. Gilberto Freyre, *The Masters and the Slaves: A Study in the Development of Brazilian Civilization* (Berkeley: University of California Press, 1986).

writings of the colonial authorities that describe the slaves who built it—men and women imported from Kongo and Angola to work the sugar mills and coffee plantations of Brazil and who fled the dungeons of enforced servitude—does not reflect historicity or the facts. The use of bias to frame references to people of color is exhaustingly prevalent in Brazil, North America, and most of the modern world. These writings, the mass media of the time, are nonetheless essential to understanding that era.

Then, as now, those who own the book publishing and newspaper publishing businesses, those who own television and radio stations, record producers, and those who own recording studios and other forms of mass communication are the brokers of what is seen, read, and heard. They decide what the news is, when and how much to report, and who appears in it. Everything is scripted, edited, censored, contrived, or synthesized. Nothing appears in print or film without being scrutinized for its content and the messages it delivers.

Anthropology professor Julio Cesar de Tavares[4] reaffirms one essential point, among many others, when discussing mass media in prior slaveholding countries: "Images produced by the communications media reflect the ways that those in control of the editing equipment and other technical aspects of image production see the world." The writer, the historian, the editor, the control room technician, the cameraman, the judge, the prosecutor, the executive producers, and the directors reinforce stereotypical images of African-descended and Indigenous people and disseminate these negative representations, such as in the film *Birth of a Nation* from 1915. The old *Amos and Andy* TV show and the film *Gone with the Wind* were shown throughout the forties, fifties, and sixties in the South and throughout the United States. The minds of innocent Black children and uninformed White and Black adults are affected by this design.

---

4. Julio Cesar de Tavares, "Deconstructing Invisibility: Race and Politics of Visual Culture in Brazil," in *African Diaspora in Brazil: History, Culture and Politics*, ed. Fassil Demissie (London: Routledge, 2014), 5-14.

Noted psychologist Kenneth B. Clark testified and presented data in the 1954 case of *Brown v. Board of Education* on the psychologically toxic effects these negative portrayals have on the minds of young Black children, causing them to favor Whiteness over representations that looked like them. I mention de Tavares in this context because he has written insightfully on this subject. He asks,

> Is it possible for a transmission uncontaminated by subjectivities to guarantee the audience a vision capable of showing the value of black culture and reinforcing the self-esteem and self-confidence of the black citizen? The struggle for the right to self-esteem and self-confidence should be considered a struggle for justice, a struggle for the presentation of the image of the world and way of life of populations that are not necessarily of Western origin. This is the struggle for self-determination and for citizenship and, simultaneously, for breaking the chains of Western domination.[5]

De Tavares relates that the "growing movement of subaltern consciousness"[6] is responsible for this unshackling of Western cultural domination, a task in its infancy—manifesting in Black power movements, Black Lives Matter, Indigenous movements, the civil rights movement, and the National Council of La Raza, to name a few examples.

Related to the colonial state of mind reflected in mass media portrayals and transmissions is the concept of "heroism" and the making of "heroes," an artistic artifice in Western media image-making. This correlates with biased reporting and biased historical writing. In Western culture, anyone can be a hero, unless they have a Black face. In that respect, the larger question regards who the hero is. Why does the media bombard us with heroes of a certain

---

5. De Tavares, "Invisibility," 9.
6. De Tavares, 8.

type? Is it to perpetuate a myth? According to de Tavares, "the hero is a social construction"[7] and is essential to how we see ourselves in the broader context of society. Our heroes make us want to be like them, and if we do not look like them, how do we frame the heroic reference? Our heroes become our alter ego identity.

There are authentic heroes and fictive heroes. Some examples of authentic heroes are Jesus Christ, the hero of Western Christianity; George Washington, the hero of American democracy; Mahatma Karamchand Gandhi, the hero of nonviolent civil disobedience in South Asia; Nelson Mandela, the most prominent hero of African liberation; and Dr. Martin Luther King Jr., the hero of the civil rights movement in North America. Examples of inauthentic or fictive heroes are Superman, the hero of adventure, defeating evil so that good can survive; James Bond, the modern epic White hero, the personification of English virility—suave, cunning, a woman's man, always a winner, and he does it all without putting a wrinkle in his tuxedo; and Elvis Presley and Marilyn Monroe, musical and cinematic personalities that never die.

Rarely do we hear in the mass media about genuine African heroes, such as Patrice Lumumba, first prime minister of the Democratic Republic of the Congo; Jomo Kenyatta, first president of Kenya; Kwame Nkrumah, first president of Ghana; Medgar Evers, civil rights activist and first field secretary of the Mississippi NAACP; Ralph Bunch, a diplomat and winner of the Nobel Peace Prize for his work on the Israel issue; George Washington Carver, a prominent agricultural scientist and inventor known for his success with the peanut; Fannie Lou Hamer, a voting and civil rights activist and cofounder of the Freedom Democratic Party; Dorothy Height, civil rights and women's rights activist and long-serving president of the National Council of Negro Women; and many others of African descent.

True heroes are not created. They emerge naturally by circumstance, and their sacrifices transcend their lives and redound to

---

7. De Tavares, 8.

the substantive benefit of society over time. Certain heroes, especially the authentic ones, have been killed or endured significant losses from the forces they fought to overcome. Zumbi, the last leader of Palmares, fits into that group but has purposefully remained unheralded.

Fictive heroes are creations of the media elite, who are thus also responsible for the invisibility of other potential heroes. When the media decides to make someone a hero, they become a hero in the minds of many. De Tavares cites Joseph Campbell[8] and Sigmund Freud as postulating that "important analysts of heroes in Western mythology did not consider the hero with an African face. They only considered the Greek myths as symbolic ancestors of European narratives, recognized as repositories of heroes." He adds that "in Brazilian history, as well as in the apparatus of state machinery (law, education, medicine, etc.), the leading roles have been assigned to the Indo-European places and agencies, ignoring the place of the hero with a Black face."

Zumbi has emerged as a hero in Brazil after centuries of deliberate obscurity. Previous descriptions of Zumbi and Palmares and all the key players in this maroon colony were constructed by the powers that sought to destroy him and it. Zumbi is a symbol, a source of identity for Afro-Brazilians, and both the sword and shield in their fight against racial irrelevance and subjugation—a tool to change the narrative from "victim to valorization," as Ana Lucia Araújo,[9] professor of history at Howard University, puts it.

Professor of romance languages Robert Nelson Anderson[10] states, "The last leader of Palmares has enjoyed an 'apotheosis' as an ethnic hero. . . . Zumbi is viewed as an ancestor, antecedent in what the

---

8. Joseph Campbell, *Historical Atlas of World Mythology* (New York: Harper & Row, 1998), as cited in de Tavares, "Invisibility," 8.
9. Ana Lucia Araújo, "Zumbi and the Voices of the Emergent Public Memory of Slavery and Resistance in Brazil," *Comparative* 22, no. 2 (2012): 95-111.
10. Robert Nelson Anderson, "The Quilombo of Palmares: A New Overview of a Maroon State in Seventeenth-Century Brazil," *Journal of Latin American Studies* 28, no. 3 (1996): 545-566.

outsider might see as a fictive lineage. . . . [H]is spirit is inherently divine and immortal, and thus worthy of respect from those who consider themselves his descendants." Author Yvonildo de Souza[11] likewise writes that Zumbi is today considered to be the "first great Negro of Brazil."

De Tavares[12] asserts:

> Recognition and respect make it particularly urgent to embark upon an immediate decolonialization of the mind by the contaminating influence of the Indo-European cultural and imaginary supremacy. This would make a significant contribution toward expanding the reach of democracy and toward curtailing mental colonization. Thus, in Brazil and indeed all over Latin America, to resurrect the hero with a black face to defend his/her space in the pantheon of historical symbols, to identify the importance of his/her presence, and the reasons for his/her erasure, might be a necessary component in the task of deconstructing the invisibility that has long been promoted by social institutions, especially the state.

Araújo,[13] writing on this subject in the context of Afro-Brazilian culture, talks about the competition for "public spaces" in Brazil—spaces that the public can use to understand and be educated about its culture: museums, libraries, festivals and celebrations, government agencies, charitable institutions, and social activist community groups. She argues that in Brazil, the public spaces have essentially failed the Afro-Brazilian community by inaccurately portraying the nation's history of African slavery. This failure has led to decades of inactivity and dormant Black activism to elucidate and secure essential freedoms and dignities.

---

11. Yvonildo de Souza, *Grandes Negros do Brazil* (Livraría São José, 1963), 15.
12. De Tavares, "Invisibility."
13. Araújo, "Zumbi."

Compare this judgment with the debate in the United States about teaching "critical race theory" in public schools. Opponents of critical race theory decry teaching about slavery and the reality of racism in the United States of America and cast aspersions on the *New York Times*'s 1619 Project. Does this mean the United States is failing its Black citizenry?

Both de Tavares and Araújo reaffirm the same point: that in Brazil, and certainly in North America, the absent portrayal of the Black hero denies African-descended people space in the public domain and adds to their invisibility and irrelevance within the host culture. The strategy of "alterity"—specifically, making races of color invisible—is a product of the media elite.

De Tavares substantiates my earlier observation when he expounds upon the phenomenon:

> In general, television orchestrates fantasies representing the worst aspects of humanity.... It then projects them onto black people claiming these to be their defining characteristics. This perpetuates notions of a racialized profile of black people that includes: inferiority, indigence, laziness, and incompetence according to the work of Gislene de Santos.[14]

The foisting of these negative traits onto the backs of Africans and African-descended people has been accomplished by the strategic use of imagery for political purposes, ever since the dawn of colonialism in the fifteenth century.

Images promote stereotypes and stigmas of subaltern groups and people of color; these images usually emanate from an aggressive, suffusive, and pernicious colonial state of mind. De Tavares[15] goes on to say:

---

14. De Tavares, "Invisibility."
15. De Tavares, "Invisibility," 10.

> Identities construct and proliferate concepts about a given group and also disseminate the stereotypes imputed to them . . . denoting aspects of a certain gesture, movement, or image. And this has certainly been a universal process under capitalism. . . . [T]he more multiculturalism is discussed, the more intense the expression of racism and stereotypes has become.

In contrast, heroes with Black faces give "direction to black lives"[16] where there otherwise is none, provide role models, and help promote a sense of community where it is lacking. In essence, then, the construction of "heroes" fills those voids where they exist in society.

According to scholars, multiculturalism does not diminish the onslaught of negative images but rather increases it. Professionals, the intellectual elite, and the media occupy unique positions to control public opinion, and this is especially true where capitalism is the underlying economic system. As de Tavares notes:

> The educated middle and the upper classes of society . . . [are] heir to the traditional elite's worldview. . . . In the end, when the media is a vehicle of culture, in all its polyvalence, the media reproduces the old colonial frameworks: it places value on knowledge stemming from its own cultural referents.

Sociologist and activist Roderick Bush[17] quotes Henrick Clarke: "The Europeans not only colonized most of the world; they began to colonize information about the world and its people"—thus the example of Palmares, Zumbi, and other cultural icons of subaltern people.

---

16. De Tavares, 9.
17. Roderick Bush, *The End of White World Supremacy: Black Internationalism and the Problem of the Color Line* (Temple University Press, 2009), 3.

One goal of this book is to share the viewpoints of historians who have studied the postcolonial era, a potpourri of opinions that provide different perspectives on the establishment of Palmares and the meaning of its survival. The research and opinions of these scholars act as a counterpoint to the colonial narratives. Another goal is to give the tourist, the traveler, a starting point toward understanding the significance of the quilombo and the role maroon societies played in African history.

Various scholars have referred to Palmares as a state, republic, confederation, or kingdom. Regardless of these political classifications, according to archaeologist Charles E. Orser Jr.,[18]

> Palmares was without doubt one of the most important maroon settlements in the history of the New World. It is said that all "literate Brazilians . . . know of Palmares, the great slave hideaway" and that Palmares represents "the first dawn of independence" of an African nation. Palmares, the largest, longest occupied, and most tenacious runaway slave society in the New World.

Just as importantly, in a paper published in the *Journal of African History*, R. K. Kent says:[19]

> The most apparent significance of Palmares to African history is that an African political system could be transferred to a different continent; that it could come to govern not only individuals from a variety of ethnic groups from Africa, but also those born in Brazil, pitch black or almost white, Latinized or close to Amerindian roots; and that it could endure for almost a full

---

18. Charles E. Orser Jr., "Toward a Global Historical Archaeology: An Example from Brazil," *Historical Archaeology* 28, no. 1 (1994): 5-22.
19. R. K. Kent, "Palmares: An African State in Brazil," *Journal of African History* 6, no. 2 (1965): 161-175.

century against two European powers, Holland and Portugal.

The advent of this African society in Brazil destroyed the canard that Africans could not govern themselves or maintain an operating society or did not have a worthwhile cultural underpinning.

In researching the maroon colony of Palmares, I came upon one historian's conclusion that "Palmares was a community at war, fighting for its very existence, and the state of continuous warfare strongly influenced every aspect of life in the villages."[20] In reflecting upon this statement, it occurred to me that this "community at war, fighting for its very existence" is the mindset that African-descended peoples find themselves in throughout the Western world. We are in a constant state of agitation, fighting to emancipate our rights; it is a perennial struggle.

So then, what does Palmares stand for as a cultural heritage icon in the Black diaspora? It signifies the value of fighting for existence—our existence as free Black men and women—and resistance to subjugation and cultural subsumption. What Palmares stands for, what it evokes in the minds of informed African-descended people, is the fight! That is the message, indeed an inspirational one that has been archaeologically and historiographically verified.

One should note that Palmares lasted longer than the enclave Black people established in Tulsa, Oklahoma, in 1899, which was incinerated by Whites in 1921, killing hundreds. Palmares also outlasted the Black residents who established themselves as a majority in Wilmington, North Carolina, starting around 1860, which was destroyed by Whites in 1898, also killing hundreds. The Quilombo of Palmares was a success by any measure.

Historical archaeologist Terry Weik[21] explains that in Palmares

---

20. Charles E. Orser, Jr., and Pedro P. A. Funari, "Archaeology and Slave Resistance and Rebellion," *World Archaeology* 33, no. 1 (2001): 61-72, p. 67.
21. Terry Weik, "The Archaeology of Maroon Societies in the Americas: Resistance, Cultural Continuity, and Transformation in the African Diaspora," *Historical Archaeology* 31, no. 2 (1997): 81-92.

(and in quilombo settlements throughout the Americas), we find "African cultural continuity"—a cultural continuity transferable in a palimpsest that neither colonialism nor centuries of slavery could erase. The fight against slavery gave Africans great incentive to cooperate with one another. An African state of mind is one of being in the majority, with no discrimination based on color and with a communal sharing of things essential to life; this, among other things, is what the quilombo symbolizes.

Anthropology professor Jan Hoffman French[22] develops several noteworthy concepts in her discussion of Palmares. She says of the Quilombo of Palmares, "It came to symbolize the privileged space of an ideal of freedom by means of which the slaves preserved their human dignity, inserted themselves into a sociocultural memory, and organized forces to challenge the system that oppressed them." This same coalescence and defiance manifested in the galvanizing struggle for civil rights in the United States and the unshackling of African countries from centuries of European colonialism.

In the same vein, Orser and archaeologist Pedro Funari write:[23]

> Many of the developing civil rights movements around the world were anchored in traditions of resistance that often had long-standing historical roots . . . revealing the history and social character of the conscious efforts of enslaved men and women to forge freedom on their own terms.

Professor and researcher Aline Vieira de Carvalho[24] confirms this view by asserting, "The colonial quilombo no longer represents just a historical event, but now symbolizes the struggles of our present;

---

22. Jan Hoffman French, "Buried Alive: Imagining Africa in the Brazilian Northeast," *American Ethnologist* 33, no. 3 (2006): 340-360, p. 342.
23. Orser and Funari, "Archaeology," 62.
24. Aline Vieira de Carvalho, "Archaeological Perspectives of Palmares: A Maroon Settlement in 17th Century Brazil," *African Diaspora Archaeology Newsletter* 10, no. 1 (2007): article 5, p. 7.

once described as a symbol of 'black weakness and inferiority,' the quilombos have moved to the level of a concrete example 'of African richness and power.'"

One of the questions that always puzzled me, and which I was challenged to answer while researching for this book, is why were Africans, among all the other peoples of the world that the Europeans had exposure to during the fifteenth century and the middle of the sixteenth century, chosen to be the bastard child for enslavement by the Europeans and their descendants?

To summarize, I have come upon some plausible but not necessarily definitive explanations. Europeans saw Africans as their mirror opposites in skin color, religion, geographic location, and culture. Because of these stark differences, Africans were seen as creations of a lesser god than the one that created Europeans or other colored peoples who looked more like Europeans, providing a rationale to treat them inhumanely. James L. Walton[25] posits that Africans were captured for enslavement because they were "a pastoral people"—simply farmers, tillers of the land, folks who were content with their lives, tribal conflicts notwithstanding. Moreover, there was no consistent, concerted resistance by force from an organized army or kingdom that sought explicitly to end the capture of Africans.

As you likely know by now, Africans themselves fought each other in tribal wars, captured each other, and made slaves of some prisoners. But in these intertribal wars, the victors did not seek to destroy the captives' cultures, change their names, or permanently remove them from their families and homelands. And the captives' duties were not limited to labor but also included service in the captor's army or household. In some instances, slaves could inherit the property of their owners.

European slavery was aided and abetted by some African kings and by the political machinations of the colonizers. Journalist and

---

25. James L. Walton, ed., *Asian & African Systems of Slavery* (Berkeley: University of California Press, 1980).

historian Basil Davidson[26] notes that the nation-state system of land ownership was introduced to Africa by the Europeans. Africa was a communal society prior to slavery and colonization. This shift led to all types of rivalries, wars, and enhanced tribal conflicts. Recently, the UN ambassador from Kenya, Martin Kimani, said that Africans had accepted the arbitrary boundaries imposed on their continent by Europeans to avoid further war and conflict.

Historian Laird W. Bergad[27] sheds additional light on the subject: "It was only in the Americas that slavery developed as an institution based upon race. . . . [B]y the 1500s, only those of African descent could be enslaved according to legal codes." Bergad asserts:[28]

> Scholars have debated why race-based slavery developed in the Americas. . . . They have arrived at the generalized conclusion that European colonial powers became reluctant to enslave people who were racially similar to themselves, even though this had been the case for centuries within nearly all European cultures. Africans were so unlike Europeans from racial, religious, and cultural perspectives that it became morally and politically acceptable to enslave them.

So, physical, religious, and governmental dissimilarity in addition to perceived overall cultural inferiority—as seen by the Europeans—were the predicates. We were enslaved because we were different.

Every movement has philosophers, poets, and academics who bring perspectives that enlighten our views on important issues, and the evolution of the "Black Movement" in Brazil is no different. Scholar and politician Abdias do Nascimento, a singularly important

---

26. Basil Davidson, *The Black Man's Burden: Africa and the Curse of the Nation-State* (New York: Three Rivers Press, 1992).
27. Laird W. Bergad, *The Comparative Histories of Slavery in Brazil, Cuba, and the United States: New Approaches to the Americas* (New York: Cambridge University Press, 2007).
28. Bergad, *Comparative Histories*, xi.

philosopher within that movement, developed the "quilombismo" ideology to relate modern Black activism to the spirit of resistance of the ancient quilombos.

Nascimento is to Afro-Brazilian culture what W. E. B. Du Bois is to Afro-American culture. His concept of quilombismo is in the vein of psychiatrist Frantz Fanon's and Du Bois's "double consciousness" concepts regarding Black people in America and people subject to colonial oppression and assimilation everywhere. Dawn Duke, a professor of Spanish and Portuguese, mentions the following:[29]

> The construction of Quilombismo as a contemporary philosophy of identity and nationhood mirrors the establishment of Negritude in the way poetics (the Arts) and politics (the ideological struggle) combined their strengths to force society toward those positive cultural transformations that erode injustice and inequality. As occurred with emergence and consolidation of Pan-Africanism associated with W. E. B. Du Bois, Jomo Kenyatta, and Kwame Nkrumah, as well as Negritude associated with the politics and poetics of Léopold Sédar Senghor, Aimé Césaire, and Leon Damas, it is clear that Quilombismo emerged in the post-World War II era.

It is important to note that the concept of negritude "emerges as a cultural flashpoint in the Afro-Brazilian struggle for cultural direction."[30] Quilombismo is the integration and merger of the above movements. Abdias do Nascimento made this convergence in his writings. The quilombo is the actualization and representation of consolidated community pride, evidencing bravery, tenacity, and

---

29. Dawn Duke, "Beyond the Quilombo? The State of Zumbi's 'Palmares' According to the Poets," *Obsidian* 13, no. 1 Special Issue: Afro-Brazilian Literature (2012): 37-60, p. 40.
30. Dawn Duke, "Beyond the Quilombo? The State of Zumbi's 'Palmares' According to the Poets," *Obsidian* 13, no. 1 Special Issue: Afro-Brazilian Literature (2012): 37-60, p. 40.

strength, signifying that the fight is not over. All these guys form segments of my collage of heroes.

It all ties together. The struggle of African-descended people has remained the same throughout the diaspora. A nucleated experience in the Western world, evolving around survival techniques and strategies that seek to hold on to the essence of our culture—our Blackness, our Africanness and everything it encompasses—while borrowing as need be from the White world, is vital to our population.

Two additional concepts are interesting and relatable: the "romanticization of Africa" and the "folklorization of blackness."[31] African Americans conjure images of Africa both good and bad, but predominantly positive, despite media presentations. And we imagine a continent where the racial animus we encounter in South and North America and Europe is muted and nonexistent. So, we romanticize Africa and seek to claim an idyllic culture of the past to incorporate into our future—remnants of what we imagine once was. But Africa is not idyllic in all its dimensions, although it has offered African Americans a place of refuge, mentally if not physically, for those brave enough to live there or interested and adventurous enough to travel there.

Together with that is a desire and need for folklore about Blackness, because for North American Black people, the relationship to Africa is more removed, and folklore can bridge this gap. We need stories and histories about our ancestors and their way of life, the "remnants of Blackness." As French says, this has aided Afro-Brazilians in their quest to gain recognition for quilombos. In Brazil, however, a closer nexus to Africa enables folklorization. Perhaps a more intimate relationship with Africa would help Afro-Americans to integrate aspects of African culture. On the other hand, perhaps there is enough folklore stretching from the sixteenth century in North America up through the latter half of the twentieth-century civil rights era to supply the need if Afro-Americans are sufficiently informed about their history.

---

31. French, "Buried Alive."

Culture is a large part of this fight—the ability to claim, apply, and maintain it, not so much via assimilation but through acculturation; this is what the *quilombolas*, descendants of African slaves in Brazil who established quilombos, are fighting for.

The preservation of culture is the pursuit of all people who have been subject to European cultural hegemony. This is especially important to people who have suffered under this domination: largely the colored peoples of the world—the Incas of Peru, the Quechua of Peru, the Aboriginal peoples of Australia, the Torres Strait islanders, the Māori people of New Zealand, and, of course, Africans from Africa and those enslaved in the Americas, as well as other Indigenous groups and subaltern folks.

One way of looking at this struggle in America is through the Civil Rights Act of 1964, coupled with the Brown decision of 1954, which for the first time opened the front door to the "house of America" for the African American masses rather than only a select few. However, many rooms in that White house remain unavailable to people of color. Some rooms are walled off, while others offer admission only intermittently. African Americans enter not as owners but as tenants. Examples of this restricted and tenuous access are legion.

As you will read, the Portuguese and the Dutch were the relentless pursuers, attackers, and ultimately destroyers of Palmares, the runaway slave community in seventeenth-century Brazil. These colonial powers desired to erase Palmares from history or to distort the record they left behind. Historians, archaeologists, anthropologists, and ethnographers have managed to unveil the existence of this maroon community—to the chagrin of many—despite the lack of primary source material to prove the community's existence and answer the following questions: How did it work? Who established it? Who occupied it? Who led it? And how did it prevail for almost the entirety of the seventeenth century?

While there is no paucity of scholars and historians interested in Palmares, they have, according to Professor Anderson, "struggled with a dearth of sources, either primary or secondary. The situation is acute for the English-speaking public: of the few primary and major secondary sources published in Portuguese, Dutch, or Latin, almost none have been translated into English." As a result, Anderson[32] opines, "activists, artisans and intellectuals have made a bounty of a poor man's charity." In other words, they have written much about the little that is known. The writings have been exhaustive on the subject; much of it, however, relies upon the colonial authorities who sought to destroy this community.

For nonhistorians like me, this situation requires reliance on the work of other scholars and writers about Palmares. But my approach has been different. I present a synthesis of opinions using segments from the work of numerous scholars on Palmares and other quilombo communities. Relying on any one of these scholars might be enough, but I have chosen to spread the work over an array of viewpoints and issues concerning maroon communities. I have sought to provide a factual basis, as much as can be provided, for the discussion about Palmares, and I have compared Palmares to other movements and similar situations common to Brazil and to regions in North America.

The historians Kent and de Carvalho seem to agree with this all-inclusive approach. Kent[33] says, "Important gaps in knowledge persist, but enough primary sources have been found and published to trace the development of Palmares, to examine it as a society and government, and to suggest its significance for both Brazilian and African history." And de Carvalho[34] surmises, "One can conclude that there is no consensus in historical studies of this past community and culture, and, most importantly, that choosing and celebrating one of the historical accounts over others entails certain political positions." Control of the narrative has always been the purview of politics.

---

32. Anderson, "Quilombo of Palmares."
33. Kent, "Palmares," 163.
34. De Carvalho, "Archaeological Perspectives," 1.

This book is not intended to be a definitive history of quilombos, nor an academic treatment of the subject. I wear many hats in this book. I am at times a travel writer, empiricist of culture, informed critic, and student of the cultural history of places in which I live and have traveled. Predominantly, however, I am a student and an empiricist. This book's purpose is to introduce those who are unaware or unfamiliar—the average traveler, in many respects—to the concept of quilombo in the history of slavery in the Americas and its place in the retention and preservation of African culture by African Brazilians, all Africans, and persons of the African diaspora.

Freyre,[35] for example, makes this observation while riding on a train across New Mexico and into the Southern states:

> One begins to lose the feeling of a Brazilian backlands . . . the place of which is now taken by the landscape of the old slave-holding South. This impression reaches a peak as the transcontinental express enters the canebrakes and swamps of Louisiana, Alabama, Mississippi, the Carolinas, Virginia—the so-called "deep South," a region where a patriarchal economy created almost the same type of aristocrat and of Big House, almost the same type of slave and of slave quarters, as in the north of Brazil, and in certain portions of our own south; the same taste for the settee, the rocking-chair, good cooking, women, horses, and gambling; a region that has suffered and preserved the scars (when they are not open and still bleeding wounds) of the same devastating regime of agrarian exploitation. . . . Every student of the patriarchal regime and the economy of slave-holding Brazil ought to become acquainted with the "deep South." The same influences deriving from the technique of production and of labor—that is to say, the one-crop system and slavery—have combined here in this English-settled portion of North America, as in the Antilles and

---

35. Freyre, *Masters and the Slaves*, xxv-xxvi.

Jamaica, to produce social results similar to those that are to be observed in our country. At times, indeed, they are so similar that the only variants to be found are in the accessory features: the differences of language, race, and forms of religion.

What, then, is the essential nature of this book? I draw inspiration from and favor the position of Carlos Diegues, the Brazilian filmmaker who in an interview described his mindset in making his 1983 film *Quilombo* by saying that he sought to meld history and legend. Diegues[36] said, "I don't really believe what was written by the Portuguese.... That was the White point of view.... So I felt free to make a film based on legend rather than on the story told by the Portuguese."

I include creative nonfiction as well. The creative aspect comprises the perspectives I give Zumbi a *sub specie aeternitatis*, a perspective based upon my ethics as it relates to the gray areas and his thinking. I have imagined what Zumbi might have pondered during his travails, from his upbringing as a young, impressionable adolescent to his assumption of leadership of the Quilombo dos Palmares. One might say that this work is a homily.

My travel experiences are nonfiction, as are the history and facts of Palmares, gathered from myriad sources with their inherent fallacies as discussed above, though filtered through my evaluative lens. As Diegues has shared, and I agree, no one knows what really happened, so why not imagine what Zumbi might have thought or done? We have "a record" to reference but no actual unbiased facts; neither do the historians, academics, archaeologists, ethnographers, or anthropologists. In the end, they are subject to the same limitations I have encountered.

But unlike Diegues, I am not trying to tell a utopian story. Diegues[37] emphasized that *Quilombo* "is about a utopia that was

---

36. Carlos Diegues and Coco Fusco, "Choosing Between Legend and History: An Interview with Carlos Diegues," *Cinéaste* 15, no. 1 (1986): 12-14.
37. Diegues and Fusco, "Legend and History," 14.

destroyed by racism, by injustice . . . a film about a very happy way of life, and they see who destroyed it."

Rather, my vision is that of a Masada epic, an Alamo theme, a fight to the finish for a valiant cause, survival against all odds, the underdog living to fight for another day, the indomitable African spirit. As Diegues[38] explained:

> Zumbi is a tragic character. . . . He has to fight. There is no alternative for him. . . . He decides that since it is impossible for him to be a winner, at least he will leave testimony of a beautiful experience. . . . When he throws the spear up into the sky, he chooses legend. . . . He becomes a myth. He prefers to die as a myth than to become a slave again.

Dawn Duke[39] likewise describes several plays written by Elisa Nascimento in the 1970s as making "heroism, emphasis on the struggle for freedom, human dignity, and the legacy of peoples of African descent" the paramount theme.

Here, myth and history are not mutually exclusive categories—and in some circumstances may be inseparable.

---

38. Diegues and Fusco, 14.
39. Duke, "Beyond the Quilombo."

CHAPTER 1

TRAVELING TO OLODUM

Afrocentric culture in Brazil is significant because of the large importation of slaves during the colonial period. Salvador, the capital city of the northeast state of Bahia, has one of the largest populations of Afro-Brazilians. Other Brazilian states, such as Pará and Maranhão, also have large populations of African-descended Brazilians. Because of this significant presence, many of the cultural activities in these cities reflect Afrocentric values.

Kent[1] quotes an early Portuguese source as saying, "Without slaves from Africa, it is impossible to do anything with Brazil." He goes on to suggest, "If early settlement and a sugar-based economy could not have been sustained without the African laborer, neither could the Portuguese continue to hold Brazil without the African soldier." A substantial portion of the Western world as we know it owes its present economic development and success to the slave labor of Africans; clearly, "the subsequent evolution of Brazil is no less a story of Euro-African enterprise."

When I first traveled to Brazil, I had no expectations. From my research, I knew that Brazil was the "fifth largest nation in the world

---

1. R. K. Kent, "Palmares: An African State in Brazil," *Journal of African History* 6, no. 2 (1965): 161-175, p. 161.

after Russia, Canada, China, and the United States.... Its shoreline stretches for 4,600 miles, and it is as near to Africa as it is to the United States."[2] Would it be as exotic as advertised, or would it be an unwieldy amalgam of races, plants, foods, and cultures? I had heard that the largest Black state in the Americas was here, and that thought triggered my imagination. I had to see it for myself.

My youngest son, Justin, had mentioned to me years earlier a description from one of his professors at the University of Maryland, Dr. Ira Berlin, about how differently the issue of race was handled in Brazil—reputed to be "a racial democracy." I was also told that in Brazil, race was not determined by color but rather by class. This was an abstraction I had never grappled with.

I was intrigued but skeptical. All I knew of "race" was how it is treated in North America, where color, hue, complexion, hair texture, and variations thereof determine everything. Was Brazil going to be a racial utopia, the best of all possible race worlds? What would such a place be like? There was no way a person like me, with an inquiring mind in search of the Black diaspora in all its dimensions, could rest until I had experienced this Brazilian reality.

As a first-time tourist to such a vast, multiracial country, I recognized at once that more than one trip would be required to even scratch the surface of what Brazil was about. The best I could hope for on my maiden voyage would be to touch base on one or two important cultural aspects and be, as I have always been, a keen observer—a heuristic empiricist, one might say. I have always sought to journey as an informed traveler. I am in the habit of reading a book on a country's history before I visit it. I want to know as much about it as the tour guides do, though that is often impossible. I relish getting off the tourist track to experience the cultural nuances of a place: to see things that the ordinary tourist might not see, to do things the ordinary tourist would not do, to ask the tour guides hard

---

2. Robert M. Levine and John J. Crocitti, eds., *The Brazil Reader: History, Culture, Politics* (Durham: Duke University Press, 1999).

questions they did not expect to answer, and to talk to the native people about what life is really like in these places.

So, I arranged for what I called a "cultural tour" of Brazil, just as I did when my wife and I visited South Africa some years earlier. I planned our trip through a British travel agency that booked tours to Brazil and Argentina. The tour vendor I chose was famous for "off the beaten path" tours with stays in "boutique" hotels—small, trendy lodgings usually located in an urban setting. All our stays thus far had been in name-brand hotels such as the Hyatt, Sheraton, Wyndham, and the like. This aspect added an intriguing flavor to the trip because it would bring us closer to the neighborhood or city.

I also figured that we should go during the season of Carnival to experience the nation in its most celebratory style. Of course, that increased the expense across all aspects of the trip. But that was not an important consideration; I wanted to experience the fullness of Brazil's offerings, whatever the cost. This trip would turn out to be a once-in-a-lifetime experience.

Bahia was a "must-see" because I had heard so much about it. It is a large state in the Northeast Region of Brazil and the home of Afro-Brazilian culture. According to the 2010 census, although the non-White population of Brazil is the dominant one, 80 percent of the population in Bahia is Black. And it has been estimated that 40 percent of Brazil's total population can trace its roots to African heritage. Local community groups have organized to secure and promote Afro-Brazilian culture.

Years earlier, I had heard a television reporter speak about her visit to Bahia and the beautiful beaches there. This was how I first learned that Bahia was the Black state in Brazil and that Salvador, the state's capital city and the fourth largest in the country, was a treasure to behold with its colonial Portuguese architecture. Eighty percent of Salvador's population is also Black and mixed race. It is the Blackest city outside of Africa and has more African cultural foundations than any city in the Western world. But despite those numbers, the governing city council is majority White by a large margin. What does this say about Afro-Brazilian politics?

• • •

In February 2012, my wife, Michelle, and I boarded an uneventful flight to Brazil. We flew directly into Salvador, and from there, the adventure began.

Salvador is known for its tropical coastline, Portuguese colonial architecture, and Afro-Brazilian culture, food, and music—especially samba. Bahia has a long colonial slave history, and its most popular historic district, Pelourinho (which means "pillory" in Portuguese), is well known as a place where slaves were publicly punished. Salvador also has one of the world's best-known beaches, Porto da Barra.

Our tour guide was Gabriella, a woman of mixed race. She greeted us cheerfully and drove us to our hotel, the Convento do Carmo, a converted nunnery in the Pelourinho area.

The visit was an awakening; our tour was tailor-made with a particular emphasis on the history of slavery in the region, and we were exposed to so much of the African diaspora. Gabriella was jovial, talkative, and unafraid to be frank about what she showed us. For the first time, we saw favelas: housing that resembled some of the worst slums in the United States, with mud roads separating the corridors. We toured the city and shopped in the historic district within walking distance of our hotel. Our guide took us to the usual churches and buildings demonstrating marvelous Portuguese architecture. We walked where African slaves had been whipped and tortured publicly. Gabriella proudly asserted that she was "considered White" and admonished us about wearing flashy jewelry.

We celebrated Carnival, the theme of which was "the Seven Ports of Energy," with new friends: Slleyke, a tall, slim, charismatic, and gracious thirty-year-old, dark-complected Afro-Brazilian man; and Marianne, his wife of a similar age, a slender White woman from the

Midwestern United States. Carnival was one of our most memorable experiences. Our new friends and tour guides involved us personally in the culture of Salvador.

Slleyke was the leader of his *bloco* ("block") Carnival troupe, Olodum, and Marianne was a key dancer in the ensemble. Michelle, a real trooper, marched with them. The energy source that Olodum represented in that year's Carnival was "aqua." Olodum means "god of gods," much like Shango, the principal deity of the Yoruba people. Also spelled Chango or Xangô, Shango had substantial importance among the slaves in Brazil and was probably a source of spirituality and inspiration for Zumbi, a Palmares leader we will discuss later. Shango was known for his tenacity, resistance, aggression, and strength.

There is much more to Olodum than its name. Olodum is a *bloco-Afro*, one of several African community groups founded in 1979 to participate in Salvador's Carnival. There are several other blocos. The Ilê Aiyê, another Yoruba-name derivative, located in the largest Afro-descended neighborhood in Salvador, means "eternal heaven." The Malê Debalê is another, inspired by the Malê slave revolt of 1835 and acclaimed by a leading American newspaper as the "largest Afro-ballet in the world." This bloco originates from Itapuã, one of Salvador's liveliest beach enclaves. The Timbalada, an Afro-Brazilian musical group from Candeal, Salvador, specializes in Axé music, which is substantially influenced by samba reggae and African styles. All these groups are centered in and around Salvador, perform at Carnival, and expressively promote African music and culture. Their themes reflect resistance to slavery and Afro-Brazilian domination by European culture.

Distinctively, Olodum is primarily known for its fusion of samba and reggae music but has evolved into a political and social nongovernmental organization aligned with the Brazilian Black Movement. This movement's headquarters are in the historic center of Salvador in the Pelourinho district, where it conducts programs and makes presentations. Olodum promotes racial pride and self-esteem in Afro-Brazilians and seeks to combat racial discrimination and injustice through social activism. Their goal is to secure human rights for the marginalized and powerless subaltern groups in Bahia as well as in greater Brazil. The vitality of this bloco-Afro is vividly displayed and excitedly supported during Carnival in Salvador.

To start the Carnival parade, the community groups assembled at a staging area dressed in representative costumes and colors. Some of them practiced their movements and dance routines. Once the parade began, the groups marched in sequence down the central avenue of the Pelourinho.

When the time arrived for Olodum to march, Slleyke took Michelle's hand and started the dance procession. She was unprepared for this unique cultural experience but enjoyed it—albeit while carefully maneuvering the cobblestone streets lining historic Salvador. Slleyke danced and swirled down the Pelourinho. His group, both men and women (but mostly women), danced to the cadence of an African drum that enveloped the audience in the African culture—a beat so innate that we could not escape the attraction or help swaying side to side.

To me, with his svelte beauty, intelligence, and mild manners, Slleyke represented a composite of African Brazilian potential if given a fair opportunity to achieve their ambitions in Brazilian society. The grace of his movements distinguished him from the others. In fact, dance was how he earned his living. He performed and taught samba and other dances to notable personalities in the Salvador community and perhaps in the state of Bahia generally.

In a colorful outfit made of diaphanous, sheer pastels in blue, green, yellow, and white that draped his arms and legs and made him appear seraphic, his slender form enhanced the rhythmic movements of his routine as he led his group down the boulevard, pausing from time to time to take center stage for an individual dance, surrounded by his swirling entourage in their sheer outfits.

I walked quickly alongside and at times even backward, trying to keep up with the parade while videotaping everything I saw. Keeping Michelle squarely in my focus, I tried not to stumble and fall on the cobblestones. I did not want to miss a minute of this event.

The throngs, mostly Afro-Brazilian Salvadorans, were mind boggling in scope. It is hard to estimate the number. I had never seen or experienced anything like it. Not even Mardi Gras in New Orleans could rival the crowd size or the sheer exuberance flowing from the unfettered exhilaration of Carnival in Salvador.

After marching through the streets with Slleyke, we were led onto a double-decker vehicle, a truck or bus of some sort, with an open top deck. Slleyke's group, or at least those who had paid for the ride, assembled there to watch the celebration below. The vehicle ever so slowly made its way along the procession, surrounded by Afro-Brazilians packed so tightly that at times they resembled sand on a beach, crushed together on both sides of the street, behind and in front of the procession as far as the eye could see.

The people had waited all year for this celebration. This was a chance to release the pent-up frustration with racism and marginalization that ensnarls Afro-Brazilians over their lifetimes. That is not to say that Carnival does not have deeper cultural footing in Brazilian cultural history, but in Salvador, the Blackest of Brazil's cities, Carnival is a pretext of sorts, a safety valve for the authorities to allow the people, especially Afro-Brazilians, to release the pressure in a system that imposes insidious and at times blatant racial discrimination. Brazilians of the darker hue suffer inexorably under the facade of a Brazilian-style "racial democracy" that does not exist. Carnival carries a sheen of happiness and joy that allows the people to focus on something other than their plight for a few days.

As the procession proceeded apace, the music blared so loudly that I temporarily lost my hearing. A similar thing happened to me while attending a Neville Brothers concert during Mardi Gras years earlier. This time, the hearing loss was so acute that Slleyke directed me off the slow-moving vehicle and onto a side street to give my ears relief. I briefly worried that my hearing would be permanently affected by the booming decibels emanating from the trucks behind us in the caravan.

Slleyke stayed with me for protection, telling me it was dangerous to be alone on any side street during Carnival in Salvador. As I sought to regain normal hearing, he offered me handmade earplugs. The pressure on my eardrums was immediately reduced. Not long after this, Michelle and I decided we had experienced enough of Carnival for one day and asked our guides to get us back to the hotel.

During the next few days, we shared two other memorable cultural encounters with Slleyke and Marianne. First, we visited Slleyke for dinner at his home in a favela, a Portuguese word for a slum. These communities were historically populated by freed slaves. Over time, they and other poor Brazilians have sought refuge in them, but these communities still chiefly house *pretas*, Black Brazilians. Favela communities number in the hundreds and are located all over the country.

Slleyke's home was pleasant, well kept, and located in one of the better Salvadoran favelas we saw. I could not ascertain whether Slleyke or his mother rented or owned the place. It had a small kitchen on the main floor, a living room, a back bedroom on the same floor, and an elevated room a few steps up that Slleyke and Marianne occupied. Slleyke's mother was a warm and friendly brown-skinned woman named Hernilda—a *pardo*, in Portuguese, which essentially refers to Brazilians of mixed ancestry—of medium build and stature, with short black hair sprinkled with gray strands.

She gave Michelle a cooking lesson in *moqueca*, one of Brazil's favorite meals: a seafood stew made of shrimp, fish, tomatoes, onions, garlic, and lime, cooked in a cast-iron pan and served in a casserole dish. She also used coconut milk, rice, and coriander. The meal was delicious. While Michelle, Marianne, and Hernilda prepared the moqueca, Slleyke showed me how to make caipirinha—one of Brazil's favorite alcoholic drinks—with vodka instead of cachaça, the local firewater made from sugarcane. He and I consumed all we made.

We ate outside in a small area in front of their home and had a great discussion about Afro-Brazilian politics and Slleyke's plans for his future. Hernilda was concerned that he was not thinking far enough ahead and wanted us to talk to him about factors he should consider in his decision-making.

Our second cultural encounter before parting ways with Slleyke and Marianne involved samba lessons in a nearby hotel. Michelle, a member of a modern dance group in college, picked up the steps easily. But I never seemed able to control my clumsiness. It was all in fun and made for another memorable activity.

Before leaving Salvador, we visited the first of three quilombos. I did not know what to make of the settlements then, and I had no historical context with which to frame this tour. But I was impressed with what I saw, especially the discussion about the founding settlers and how the quilombo was a type of Black community found primarily but not exclusively in rural areas. The door to this new knowledge was now ajar.

Afrocentrism is alive and well in Brazilian cities with large African-descended populations. This culture is positively demonstrated in festivals, museums, and other social spaces and has spawned cultural and political movements that apply traditional African values and reinforce the active Black Movement in the country.

CHAPTER 2

BE FREE IN PARATY

One of the rewards of travel is education. My initial foray into a substantive education on the subject of this book occurred after leaving Rio, our next stop on the itinerary. Our subsequent trip to Paraty opened my eyes about quilombos and made an indelible impression on me.

We flew from Salvador to Rio de Janeiro and enjoyed what remained of Carnival. Rio de Janeiro is one of the most beautiful cities in the Southern Hemisphere. A seaside resort and Brazil's second-largest city after São Paulo, it is known for beautiful women, singer-songwriter Carlos Antonio Jobim—father of the bossa nova, whom I became familiar with in college—and beautiful beaches, nightclubs, and fine food.

While in Rio, we stayed at another boutique hotel. The Casa Marques Santa Teresa was built on the foundations of an old colonial mansion overlooking a hill in Santa Teresa, a short distance from the city. As is my wont when I visit notable places, I made sure to swim in the hotel pool. This one overlooked communities within walking distance of our hotel that were still celebrating Carnival.

We visited the typical tourist spots, namely the Copacabana and Ipanema beaches along the Atlantic shore. So well known are these beaches that they are a must-see. We ambled through the downtown area as I looked for the "Girl from Ipanema," who popularized this place.

We visited Christ the Redeemer, the ninety-eight-foot statue with arms outstretched almost as wide as its height, located on top of Corcovado Mountain, a French and Brazilian collaboration. This imposing soapstone statue is one of the New Seven Wonders of the World. I took a moment to look out over the city from a spot near the statue's pedestal and beheld the beauty of Rio.

My knowledge of the convergence of religion and slavery in Brazil was nascent. I nonetheless found it ironic that such an august, white statue constructed fewer than fifty years after the abolition of slavery in Brazil and symbolic of the Christian religion—a belief system propounding faith, healing, humility, charity, courage, self-government, virtue, industriousness, wisdom, forgiveness, and love—had been erected in a country so burdened by the plague of racism.

We also visited Sugarloaf Mountain on a nearby peninsula, taking the cable car, as most tourists do, to see the magnificent view. The remnants of Carnival's colorful floats and costumed participants were still visible across the city.

I expressed to the tour vendor that I wanted to see the "Golden Law," the document signed on May 13, 1888, by Brazilian princess Isabel that freed the slaves. The tour director informed me that the document was not in Rio but in São Paulo, which we did not visit on this trip. But it will be an important stop when we return.

Part of our Rio tour was an in-depth outing in what was touted by city officials as a "model favela community." Several White European students accompanied me. Having visited the favela community in Salvador, I was still unprepared for what I saw and was appalled at the conditions. There was no substantive difference in the level of abject poverty on display between the two locales. These habitats were as bad as or worse than any slum community in the United States—worse than any I saw in parts of Russia or China. The homes were solidly constructed of raw concrete, steel, and wood but shorn of any finishes or refinements; small retail shops and housing units, each in its own cubbyhole, abutted the steep cement steps that led to the top. The climb to the "summit" was so steep that at times I doubted I would make it. People who occupied these units had nothing. Some residents jetted in and out to run their errands as though we were not even there—life proceeded naturally. Of course, the predominant skin color was Black.

The long, winding steps up this urban mountain led to a plateau at the top. Michael Jackson filmed one of his video promotions from this very favela. One store owner proudly played VHS tape of the performance. The residents were elated that Jackson had filmed his event there. Strangely, I did not see any White folks living in this community, nor did I see many people of mixed race or Asians. Where were they? The cruelty of the hoax was on vivid display for any percipient observer. After 124 years, Brazil's "racial democracy" was still a work in progress.

Before leaving Rio, we visited another quilombo, called an "urban quilombo," of which there were twenty-nine in the city. Less than three had obtained title to their land. This fight for land title, as will be discussed later, is the same historical fight waged by rural quilombos. By now, the proverbial light bulb had switched on, but I was still largely uninformed about the significance of what I was observing. We left Rio in relatively fine spirits, satisfied that we had seen the most important sites available to us during the holiday season.

∙ ∙ ∙

Our next venture involved a four-hour car ride to beautiful Paraty, also spelled Parati, located in the Costa Verde region between Rio and São Paulo. A small city nestled near the mountains—where approximately 43,000 people live—and 150 miles to the southeast of Rio, Paraty was a beautiful honeymoon stop for Bella and Edward in the popular *Twilight* series. We drove along the picturesque coast on a highway overlooking lush green mountains and small waterfront communities, giving us one eye-dropping view after another.

Once in Paraty, we went immediately to our hotel, the Pousada do Sandi, a nondescript building close to town. From there, we walked around the area to see the old Spanish and Portuguese colonial buildings, then the shops and restaurants lining the center of town. The streets there were paved with large, almost unwalkable cobblestones. It had rained the night before our arrival, and mud was everywhere, making the cobblestones even more challenging to navigate.

Before the evening set in, we took a boat ride through the Bay of Paraty to the Saco do Mamangua beach, a location for the film *Breaking Dawn*. The water was a cross between turquoise and blue, which enhanced the beautiful panorama of pristine waters. The watercraft around us displayed economic wealth of the highest order, comparable to the yachts in opulent Newport, Rhode Island. Beach homes tucked away in the forested mountains above the shoreline gave the bay a bowl-like impression.

When we arrived at the beach, the young, White, Brazilian captain of our boat waved his arms and, pointing to the beach, shouted in heavily accented, broken English, "Go! Be free! Be free!" Perhaps he did not realize that his phrasing was pregnant with symbolism and meaning. What did it mean to "be free"? Especially while visiting a country known for its long history of slavery and its present-day invidious racism, as a citizen from a country founded amid the evils of slavery, where the vestiges of that system persist and prevent me and people like me from being "really free." Is "being free" a state of mind or a physical condition, or both?

Even Paraty, for all its beauty, with its perfectly preserved colonial architecture, colorful houses, great restaurants, little boutiques, and art galleries on car-free cobblestoned streets, held this barbaric history. In the days of yore, it was known for the Gold Trail, a road built to transport African slaves and other commodities to the nearby gold-mining regions.

The boat ride and walk on the beach were pleasurable, followed by a more extended walk through the town center on those nuisance cobblestones. We browsed briefly through various shops and scanned menus pasted on restaurant windows or placed outside. While seated at a restaurant that fronted the street, waiting to be served, I looked out the window and saw two beautiful Brazilian women waiting on customers in the shop across the street. I immediately emailed my youngest son and told him he was not to marry before he visited Brazil.

• • •

The next day in Paraty evolved into an African Brazilian history lesson whose counterpoint in the African diaspora would have great meaning to me. The adventure I experienced sent me on a yearslong research mission that resulted in the writing of this book.

Our tour vendor arranged for us to visit several quilombos and sites significant to Afro-Brazilian culture. When I booked the tour, I was unaware of the magnitude of quilombos in the history of the African diaspora, and I was certainly unfamiliar with the characters who made history during the quilombo era. In fact, I knew nothing about Brazilian slavery, the roles of the Portuguese, Dutch, and Spanish in Brazilian history, and how these European states used their concerted powers at different times to colonize Brazil and the Guinea Coast of Africa. My knowledge about the heritage I am so proud of was incomplete, ready to be enhanced and forever enriched by what lay before me.

Music can get into your head when you embark on an exciting adventure. Chopin's Étude in E flat Major put me in a calm, reflective mood, as if preparing me for a maudlin learning experience. To me, the alluring melody represented the pain my brethren had endured during the colonial era, while the crescendo represented the powerful expansion of knowledge to be gained about race and self.

There was a time in my life when none of this mattered. I had lived in a world protected by parents, innocent and unaware of the antagonisms of race. But that was long ago—decades—and today was a new day. Now ancestral history mattered. It had become my raison d'être, essential to who I was.

I thought of the cliché "Ignorance is bliss," first used by the English poet Thomas Gray in his poem "Ode on a Distant Prospect of Eton College": "Where ignorance is bliss, 'tis folly to be wise." Face it: you were better off not knowing that, weren't you?

But I disagree. Perhaps that cliché only applies in limited situations, either when one is too young for knowledge of this type or if there are no consequences to not knowing. As a Black man living in the Western world, such ignorance is dangerous and self-defeating in its pull against freedom, self-esteem, and racial pride. I am better off knowing my ancestral history, even the painful parts. Such knowledge has informed my evolving worldview and my relationship with other races.

The history of Africans in the diaspora is partly a painful one that brings tears to the eyes but also vindication as the truths about our people are uncovered. We must rise above the sorrow and find solace in the justice of our struggle and fortitude in the knowledge that we can overcome. When you know your history, your respect for the struggle of your ancestors grows, and your appreciation for where you are in life and how you got there is enhanced. As Voltaire says, "Appreciation is a wonderful thing. It makes what is excellent in others belong to us as well." History is immutable; it is a picture taken in a certain period. The facts are complete except when written for political purposes. We must learn from history to prevent its negative aspects from recurring, and we must not be ashamed. Let the headwinds of history blow in our ashen faces until cracks from the brine of lessons well learned become furrows in our brow, pathways to new knowledge.

Having traveled many thousands of miles in search of knowledge of self and African history, the Étude playing in my mind lulled me fleetingly into imagining what Black life might have been had the concept of race not been constructed out of whole cloth and imposed upon the world since around 500 CE. These moments of wistful speculation are a luxury, standing in sharp contrast to the life-and-death struggles my ancestral people endured to obtain their freedom and the fight of their progeny to secure the expansion of that freedom. As writer and civil rights activist James Baldwin writes, the goal for the Black man should be to live a life like that of the White man: uninhibited, with the world as your oyster, unbridled in imagination, potential, and scope, and unrestrained by any forces on this earth except self and nature.

After breakfast, Rege—our tour guide, a young, White, Brazilian man dressed in khaki fatigues—drove us about twenty miles outside of Paraty to the Quilombo do Campinho da Independência, a quilombo located between Paraty and Ubatuba, a coastal community. There was nothing but forest on both sides of the roadway. A sign on the right shoulder eventually announced that we were approaching our destination. There was nothing striking or imposing about the sign; it simply declared that we were near the quilombo.

Once we arrived, our White tour guide faded in importance. He was facilitative but stayed in the background. We were now in the hands of the quilombo's residents. It was their show. The lead spokesperson for this community was a thin, forty-something, Afro-Brazilian woman with short black hair and a commanding air. I do not remember her name exactly, but I recall her being called Dandara. The name had no meaning to me at the time, but it certainly would later.

We were escorted to a central meeting room, and I immediately started videotaping. The roof and walls, as I recall, were made of thatch material supported by wood posts. The floor was an unpainted cement slab with plastic chairs arranged theater style. Clearly, this was where the residents greeted their guests and told their stories. Not long after we were seated, children of all ages came along with other adults and older community members. Our hosts played songs and danced for us; they were all smiles and as cheerful as could be. We too smiled a lot, to show that we appreciated them and wanted to be their friends.

These folks were not ignorant, naked, half-clothed, or crude in any sense of the word. They were more than third-world people. Modernity was present in their dress and the lives they lived. They understood the value of our visit and others like it to their economic welfare and were keenly aware of the issues they confronted in Brazilian culture.

After the dancing, singing, and introductions were over, Michelle and I asked a series of questions, some of which we had discussed beforehand and others we thought of as we went along. We wanted to know what it was like living in a quilombo. Were they trying to hold on to their African culture in a country that was hesitant to acknowledge the contribution of Africans to its history and culture? How did they earn a living? How were the children educated? What health care, if any, did they have access to? And—though I did not know the importance of this question at the time—did they own the land their settlement was on?

Certain residents took turns answering our questions, but Dandara and another older woman took the lead. They explained that their quilombo was founded by three African women: Luiza, Marcelina, and Antonica. They and their ancestors had been slaves on the land before emancipation in 1888. After the abolition of slavery, the descendants of these women remained and continued to farm. The founders had the vision to realize their settlement's importance in asserting control over their lives. In contrast, after the slaves in the United States were freed, they had nothing except the clothes on their backs, their character, and their ingenuity.

This quilombo was one of only a few that possessed the title to their land, which Dandara explained was acquired in March 1999— only thirteen years before we arrived. Later, Dandara told us that in 2008, fifty-nine families were living in this quilombo, which covered almost 288 hectares, or 711.5 acres (see appendix A).

The Q and A session lasted an hour or more. I think the residents were especially pleased to have African American visitors and that we had an earnest interest in their well-being. This part of our meeting closed with more dancing and singing. The kids took the lead. We then left the meeting hall and walked a short distance to a souvenir shop, where we bought some items before leisurely walking a trail and taking videos and photos with some of the women who participated in our meeting. As we strolled along, they pointed out who lived where, the soccer field, fruit-bearing trees that grew in the settlement, and how the buildings were built. We walked and talked; a certain camaraderie had developed. Eventually, we ended up at their restaurant.

In the restaurant, which was constructed of similar material to the assembly room, we sat at a table with Dandara, along with another young Afro-Brazilian woman from the quilombo and our tour guide. We ordered from a sampling that included Brazil's national dish, feijoada, which is a stew made of black beans and salted pork; other native dishes; and standard fare that we were more used to eating. I did not particularly like the food, but the rice was good, and I satisfied myself. Dandara then revealed her quilombo's history in more detail.

She began in 1650, when an African slave by the name of Ganga Zumba, which means "great lord" in the Mbantu language of Angola, emerged as the leader of what would become the quintessential quilombo, Palmares, a union of runaway slave villages in Brazil. Other runaway slave encampments during the colonial period were also referred to as Palmares.[1]

Dandara was clearly uplifted by our visit and told us her version of the story of Zumbi (pronounced "Zoom-bee"), the heroic leader who succeeded Ganga Zumba. She explained that no written details

---

1. João José Reis and Flavio dos Santos Gomes, "Quilombo: Brazilian Maroons During Slavery," *Cultural Survival Quarterly Magazine*, April 28, 2010, www.culturalsurvival.org/publications/cultural-survival-quarterly/quilombo-brazilian-maroons-during-slavery/.

describe the first escapes of African slaves in Brazil but that oral tradition says they occurred around the state of Pernambuco in northeast Brazil at the beginning of the seventeenth century. They established villages and settlements and organized a community of fugitive slaves. As news traveled, others were drawn there. Hundreds and then thousands of fugitive slaves made Palmares their refuge.

Dandara tried to see if the video I had taken would play on her device, but it would not. When I returned to the United States, I made three unsuccessful attempts to ship the video to them. It is my hope, one day, to personally deliver this video to the people at the Quilombo do Campinho da Independência.

After we finished our meal, we bid our goodbyes to these welcoming folks by taking a group picture and sharing handshakes and hugs. A sense of brother- and sisterhood existed between us, though we had only met six hours earlier. We were from different parts of the world, but our commonalities as African-descended people caught in the vice grip of White society and Western culture made it seem as though we lived in the same community. Politically, we did. We shared in the struggle to retain our cultural heritage and to regain the freedoms our ancestors in Africa had and that we were entitled to as human beings. Little needed to be said. Our bond was implicit, the essence of who we were as a people, caught as we were in the throngs of white society and all that went with it. There were no reservations, only a concomitance of understanding. And so, the profound story of Palmares began to unfold.

CHAPTER 3

PALMARES DE PERNAMBUCO, THE TROY OF ALAGOAS

Enjoy yourself, Negro
The white man doesn't come here
And if he does
The devil will carry him off.[1]

"The white men would be always and essentially white and the black man inevitably black."[2]

Before coming to Brazil and especially to the city of Salvador, I was unfamiliar with the phrases "maroon society" and "Bush Negroes." I would, however, gain a familiarity with them. I discovered that in addition to the dominant population of fugitives from slavery, Indigenous people as well as poor Whites lived in the Quilombo of Palmares. I also learned that the existence of quilombos

---

1. Folk song, quoted in Roger Bastide, "The Other Quilombos," in Richard Price (ed.), *Maroon Societies: Rebel Slave Communities in the Americas* (John Hopkins University Press, 1996), 199.
2. Pedro Paulo A. Funari and Aline Vieira de Carvalho, "Palmares: A Rebel Polity through Archaeological Lenses," in João José Reis and Flávio dos Santos Gomes, eds., *Freedom by a Thread: The History of Quilombos in Brazil* (New York: Diasporic Africa Press, 2016), 288-325.

in colonial Brazil was a threat to slavery across the Americas.

My visits to the quilombos piqued my interest regarding this aspect of African history and the Black diaspora. It would be several years before that interest matured, but once I began my study, there was no retreating. The more I learned, the more I wanted to know. So, in the following paragraphs, I will share with you what I learned about these villages and maroon societies more broadly, especially in Brazil, but also tangentially in other countries, including the United States.

Historian Hugh Thomas,[3] quoting from the chronicler Gomes Eanes de Zurara (courtier to Prince Henry of Portugal), gives us the following:

> "Very early in the morning, because of the heat," a few Portuguese seamen on the decks of half a dozen hundred-ton caravels, the new sailing ships, were preparing, on August 8, 1441, to land their African cargo near Lagos, on the southwest point of the Algarve, in Portugal.
>
> This cargo consisted of 235 slaves. On arriving on the mainland, these people were placed in a field. They seemed, as a contemporary put it, "a marvellous sight, for, amongst them, were some white enough, fair enough, and well-proportioned; others were less white, like mulattoes; others again were as black as Ethiops, and so ugly, both in features and in body, as almost to appear . . . the images of a lower hemisphere."

Thus began the most horrific prolonged saga of man's inhumanity to man ever recorded in history.

Moving forward to 1502, concerning the island of Hispaniola, one of Christopher Columbus's first stops in the Americas in 1492, it is reported that "the first Afro-American slave maroon, who is anonymous, first escaped to the Indians in the mountainous interior

---

3. Hugh Thomas, *The Slave Trade: The Story of the Atlantic Slave Trade: 1440-1870* (New York: Touchstone, 1997).

soon after setting foot in the New World."[4] Perhaps this anonymous slave was the progenitor for the establishment of runaway slave encampments in the Americas—the first maroons. Sociologist and anthropologist Roger Bastide,[5] citing historian Gottfried Heinrich Handelmann, relates that "the first *quilombo* dates back almost to the beginning of the slave trade in 1575, at Bahia, and was later destroyed by Luis Brito de Almeida."

From the first arrival of Africans to Alagoas in northeastern Brazil, slaves fled to the surrounding hills and mountains. Some who managed to penetrate twenty to sixty miles into the interior without being captured established a *mocambo* (typically a smaller community than the quilombos) that grew to be known as Palmares, officially established in 1605. Historian Ernesto Ennes postulates that Palmares was established by "forty Negroes from Guinea, slaves from Porto Calvo, [who] had taken refuge in Palmares some thirty leagues to the interior of Pernambuco."[6]

Historians João José Reis and Flavio dos Santos Gomes[7] note that at the start of the seventeenth century, many runaway slaves settled in forested areas approximately fifty miles inland from the coast. They often sought refuge in places that would be inaccessible and hard to find, most notably in terrain that was dense and obscured by uncleared forest with natural obstacles to hoof and foot traffic—thick with thorns, briars, prickly stemmed plants, insects, reptiles, and uncommon beasts, as well as an unrelenting tropical climate, with periodic monsoons and exceedingly high temperatures.

---

4. Richard Price, ed., *Maroon Societies: Rebel Slave Communities in the Americas*, 3rd ed. (Baltimore: John Hopkins University Press, 1996).
5. Roger Bastide, "The Other Quilombos," in Price, *Maroon Societies*, 191-201, p. 191.
6. Ernesto Ennes, "The Palmares Republic of Pernambuco: Its Final Destruction, 1697," *Americas* 5, no. 2 (October 1948): 200-216.
7. João José Reis and Flavio dos Santos Gomes, "Quilombo: Brazilian Maroons During Slavery." *Cultural Survival Quarterly Magazine*, April 28, 2010, www.culturalsurvival.org/publications/cultural-survival-quarterly/quilombo-brazilian-maroons-during-slavery/.

Also known as the Black Troy, over the next sixty-seven years, Palmares became an existential threat to the slave bureaucracy and a manifestation of African independence and self-determination in the Americas. Ennes asserts that the "history of Palmares occupies the whole of the seventeenth century."[8] Palmares existed well before competing colonizers in the form of the Dutch, who arrived in Brazil between 1624 and 1654, by at least a quarter of a century. The first Portuguese venture against Palmares began in 1612. After 1630, "increasing *palmarista* militancy" was "associated with slaves who took advantage of the Dutch presence to escape and who eventually found their way into Palmares."[9] The political entity (or "polity," as it is often called) of Palmares continued to expand until the 1640s, when the Dutch began to consider Palmares a serious threat.

The term "quilombo" originates in Angolan culture as a word and as an institution. The African tribe known as the Imbangala, or the Jaga, which invaded Kongo centuries ago, used this term to refer to a special military group within the tribe. Quilombo means "hideout." It traditionally had not been used to refer to maroon societies. But as Robert Nelson Anderson[10] notes, it has meant roughly the same thing and gained widespread usage in the "late seventeenth century, and then only at first in connection with Palmares."

The word *"kilombo"* means "war camp," derived from the Kimbundu (a form of Bantu) language. The term also referred to "originally a male initiation camp, and by extension, a male military society."[11] Kilombo was "a unifying structure suitable for a people under constant military alert."[12] In the orthography—the

---

8. Ennes, "The Palmares Republic of Pernambuco," 200-216.
9. R. K. Kent, "Palmares: An African State in Brazil," *Journal of African History* 6, no. 2 (1965): p. 165.
10. Robert Nelson Anderson, "The Quilombo of Palmares: A New Overview of a Maroon State in Seventeenth-Century Brazil," *Journal of Latin American Studies* 28, no. 3 (October 1996): 545-566, p. 558.
11. Anderson, 558.
12. Jack Bennett, "Maroon State: Slave Community and Resistance in Palmares, Brazil," *Retrospect Journal*, 2020.

conventional spelling of a term in a language—of Portuguese, it was clearly the appropriate descriptive word, and the Portuguese spelled it "quilombo."

According to Weik, discussing the work of Kent, "the Angolan *Kilombo*, a ritual society which was central to the cohesion of the ruling warrior groups in Angola, was transplanted to Palmares, an 'African state in the Brazilian hinterland.'"[13] That is not to say that other less notable quilombos and runaway slave encampments were not established earlier, but "nothing, however, compares in the annals of Brazilian history with the 'Negro Republic' of Palmares in Pernambuco."[14]

Kent stresses the multicultural character of Palmares: criollos, mulattos, Indians, renegade Whites, and mestizos lived together. As he further[15] notes,

> All of this leads to the only plausible hypothesis about the founders of Palmares. They must have been Bantu-speaking and could not have belonged exclusively to any subgroup. Palmares was a reaction to a slave-holding society entirely out of step with forms of bondage familiar to Africa. [As I have mentioned, slavery was common in Africa. The Arabs and Africans practiced slavery *before* the Europeans, but not as it was practiced *by* the Europeans.] As such, [Palmares] had to cut across ethnic lines and draw upon all those who managed to escape from various plantations and at different times.

According to Reis and Gomes,[16] the terms and the language used to define these runaways and their communities depend upon

---

13. Terry Weik, "The Archaeology of Maroon Societies in the Americas: Resistance, Cultural Continuity, and Transformation in the African Diaspora," *Historical Archaeology* 31, no. 2 (1997): 81-92.
14. Kent, "Palmares," 163.
15. Kent, 166.
16. Reis and Gomes, "Quilombo," 4.

which continent coined the term. For example, the English used the term "maroons"; the French, *"grand marronage"* to distinguish it from the *"petit marronage"* (the latter denoting an individual escape, generally of short duration); in Brazil, "quilombos," "quilombolas," *"calhambolas,"* *"mocambo,"* *"mocambeiros"*; in Spanish America, *"palenques"* or *"cumbes."*

Palmares was a *grand marronage*, a long-term or permanent escape with the intent of becoming an autonomous community. Contrast this with African American maroon settlements in the United States, which were mostly characterized by *petit marronage*.[17]

• • •

PALMARES ENVIRONMENT

Archaeological evidence has established that Palmares was situated along a mountain range known as the Serra da Barriga, or Potbelly Hill as it is now called, in northeastern Brazil. The quilombo straddled what are now the states of Pernambuco and Alagoas. At that time, the Dutch occupied Pernambuco; later, it would be occupied by the Portuguese as a captaincy, an administrative division. The area, which formed a plateau above the adjacent land, derives its name from the Tupi Indians, one of many Indigenous tribes in that area. Topographically, it is a "hilly upland area" with deciduous trees and thorny woody bushes and is known as Caatinga, which translates to "white forest" in Tupi. Weik asserts that this community "could not have enjoyed longevity without the formidable mountains and densely vegetated hills in which they settled."[18]

Brazil has an immense amount of ocean access. The climates are milder in this region and the weather less harsh overall. The totality of these conditions favored runaway slaves in Brazil: less robust houses could provide adequate shelter, and less clothing was

---

17. Price, *Maroon Societies*; and Weik, "Archaeology of Maroon Societies."
18. Weik, "Archaeology of Maroon Societies," 82.

required. The forest floor was rich with nutrients and excellent for crops. The understory of low-lying trees and shrubs made gathering berries and fruits, among other edible plants, possible.

Compare the natural defenses afforded by forests to the swamps and wetlands where runaway slaves often settled along the southeast coast of the United States. Many areas surrounding the Southern plantations had been cleared to make room for further settlement and expansion of farms, plantations, and cities.

There were quilombos in Brazil that were not established in forests, such as in the Amazon, Cerrado, Atlantic Forest, and Pantanal regions. The Cerrado, defined as wooded grasslands, and Pantanal, tropical grazing lands, are home to the world's most abundant tropical and subtropical wetlands and one of the world's most extensive freshwater wetlands.

Palmares eventually comprised over nine separate villages. Between 1630 and 1654, after the Dutch failed to conquer Bahia, there was a high growth rate in slave trafficking, and Palmares consolidated its position as the "Black State" embedded in the Brazilian slave system.[19] The Black Troy represented the Africans' ability to build something out of nothing amid extreme adversity. They constructed it through intrepidity, endurance, and willingness to suffer greatly to escape the horrors of slavery.

The fugitive slaves from Pernambuco purposefully chose a terrain where palm trees were plentiful, hence "Palmares," the name given to the settlement by the Portuguese. The palm was the dominant tree species in this area, and the palm forest in the Serra da Barriga mountains was probably an old-growth forest. Palm trees are evergreens and do not shed their leaves at any particular time. They offered many advantages to the fugitive slaves throughout the year.

Perhaps most important to the quilombolas was the coconut

---

19. Ronaldo Vainfas, "God Against Palmares: Lordly Representations and Jesuitical Ideas," in Reis and Gomes, *Freedom by a Thread*, 56.

palm.[20] This palm tree and its various species produce coconuts and wax. Coconut milk is used as a drink and for cooking. Coconut flour is a byproduct, and cooking oil is derived from the seeds, which can also be ground up to produce a type of coffee.

The fruits of other palm trees can also be eaten and used as feed for livestock. Leaf fibers are used to make baskets, bags, and other products to sell. The leaves also make for good roofing materials and wood for construction. In addition, the maroons made salt from the palm tree ashes and grew sugar cane. They also made butter by melting and clarifying the fat of the palm tree worms.

Palm tree wine was usually available. In Kongo, the Imbangala, an African tribe that influenced and populated Palmares, drank palm wine as part of their culture. Seventeenth-century English traveler Andrew Battell, quoted by historian Stuart Schwartz,[21] notes that the Imbangalas' "chief luxury was palm wine and that their routes and camps were influenced by the availability of palm trees."

> [T]he palm-tree wine they have always in plenty; they procure it by making deep incisions of a foot square in the fallen trunk, where the juice being collected, it soon ferments by the heat of the sun; it is not only a cool and agreeable beverage but sufficiently strong to intoxicate.[22]

Palm oil and its derivatives were a favorite of the Imbangala from their early days in Angola. Journalist and writer Glenn Cheney[23] mentions that a hookah could be fashioned from the coconut shell to

---

20. Irene Diggs, "Zumbi and the Republic of Os Palmares," *Phylon* 14, no. 1 (1953): 62-70.
21. Stuart B. Schwartz, "Rethinking Palmares: Slave Resistance in Colonial Brazil," in *Critical Readings on Global Slavery*, eds. Damian Alan Pargas and Felicia Roşu (Leiden, Netherlands: Brill, 2005): 1294-1325, p. 1323.
22. Price, *Maroon Societies*, 11.
23. Glenn A. Cheney, *Quilombo dos Palmares: Brazil's Lost Nation of Fugitive Slaves* (Hanover, CT: New London Librarium, 2014).

make *fuma Angola*. The hookah, in combination with the palm tree wine, was an evanescent balm for their anxieties, soothing their war-weariness and sweetening their dreams for a few fleeting moments. The utility of the palm tree made it the élan vital of the mocambeiros' existence.

Cheney[24] quotes from the book *O Quilombo Dos Palmares* by Edison Carneiro (1958) a section attributed to a Dutch militia combatant after having attacked Palmares between February and March 1645:

> The road to this Palmares is lined with groves of palm, which is very useful to the Negroes because first, they make their houses of it and second, their beds, and third, fans with which they fan fires and so forth, they eat the inside of the coconuts, and from coconuts they make their pipes and they eat the outside of the coconut and also the heart of the palm.

Thus, the settlement of the quilombo in a "grove of palms" was not by happenstance but due to careful consideration of the environment and how to make it work for them. In addition to palm trees, the fugitive slaves found a food source in the Brazil nut tree, *Bertholletia excelsa*, common near the Amazon. These are edible nuts sold today and are known to be tasty.

Many additional factors contributed to the growth of Palmares:

> Isolation, its fastness, essential for the protection of the maroon people, the fertility of the soil, and the recruitment of new members. . . . They harvested wild fruit and practiced . . . hunting, fishing and harvesting; there was mixed farming based on corn, beans, manioc, sweet potatoes, banana and sugarcane . . . crops through horticulture, tobacco, cotton,

---

24. Cheney, *Quilombo dos Palmares*.

bananas, pineapples and sweet potatoes.[25]

Reis and Gomes[26] note that the Palmaristas did everything they could to maintain their subsistence and produce goods such as baskets, brooms, pottery, and ceramics to sell in the local markets.

The vegetation that populated the mountainous terrain was varied—and not all of it was harmless. Lessons were learned either by trial and error, which could be deadly, or by instruction from the *Indios*, Indigenous people, who were experienced in the best uses; after all, the forest was their natural habitat. According to Cheney,

> Many of the techniques for dealing with the environment clearly were learned, directly or indirectly from American Indians. . . . Throughout Afro-America, Indians interacted with slaves, whether as fellow sufferers, as trading partners, or in other capacities. Indian technologies—from pottery making and hammock weaving to fish drugging and manioc processing—were taken over and further developed by the slaves, who were so often responsible for supplying the bulk of their own daily needs. Life as maroons meant numerous new challenges to daily survival, but it was on a base of technical knowledge developed in the interaction between Indians and Blacks on plantations that most of the remarkable maroon adaptations were built. . . . Up to this point, it is not yet possible to say how many environmental adaptations had some sort of antecedents in the African homeland.[27]

One can postulate that many survival techniques were derived from Africa. Weik claims that the Palmaristas relied heavily on

---

25. Schwartz, "Rethinking Palmares."
26. Reis and Gomes, "Quilombo."
27. Cheney, 11-12.

"Africanisms, the transfer of African traits to the Diaspora."[28]

To return to the topic of vegetation, over ninety species of trees can be found in the rainforest of Brazil. The vines and trees of the Palmaristas' environs offered protection as well as harm to be avoided. Liana vines, for instance, grow abundantly in South American rainforests. They obstruct passage through the forest and consume time in cutting and removal. Humans use these vines for various purposes, including for food and medicine, psychedelics, poisons, and the erection of buildings. Thus this vine aided in defense and subsistence while also being a natural obstacle to overcome.

A variety of toxic plants in the rainforest can cause inadvertent poisoning—for example, a common species of the oleander plant. Other plants can cause paralysis, cardiac arrest, irregular heartbeats, dizziness, and numbness if ingested. One is named the "women's bane" or "wolf's bane." There is also the "Dracula flower" and the "Palm of Christ," *Palma Christi,* commonly known as the castor oil plant.

• • •

QUILOMBO CHARACTERISTICS

In *Maroon Societies*, researcher and author Richard Price[29] repeats the question of E. J. Hobsbawm: "How do casual collections of fugitives of widely different origins, possessing nothing in common but the experience of transportation in slave ships, albeit a bonding experience, and of plantation slavery, come to form structured communities?" The answer is, in effect, by establishing structured communities from scratch.

Freyre[30] explains the emergence of these habitations in the following observation about the Indian revolts during the colonial

---

28. Weik, "Archaeology of Maroon Societies."
29. In the preface to the 1996 edition of Price, *Maroon Societies*, xxvi.
30. Gilberto Freyre, *The Masters and the Slaves: A Study in the Development of Brazilian Civilization* (Berkeley: University of California Press, 1986), 157.

era and the incorporation of the African revolts therein:

> This is not to speak of those movements that were plainly slave revolts, explosions of race hatred or of rebelliousness on the part of the socially and economically oppressed class—the insurrection of the Negroes in Minas for example.... For they were something very like that, on the part of the oppressed cultures bursting forth in order not to die of suffocation and breaking through the incrustations of the dominant culture that they might be able to breathe, as would appear to have been the case with the Negro movement of Bahia in 1835.

Accordingly, various historians have given their versions of the different eras of Palmares. There was a New Palmares and an Old Palmares, designated as such by the Dutch around 1645; both were described as villages containing some 1,500 people living in 220 dwellings. Ennes[31] cites Nina Rodriguez's *Os Africanos no Brazil* (1933), which divides the history of Palmares into three epochs: "the Palmares of the Dutch period (destroyed in 1644 by Bareo); the Palmares of the restoration of Pernambuco (destroyed by the expedition of Pedro Alameida); and the final Palmares (definitively annihilated in 1697)."

According to Kent,[32] Palmares was not a single enclave but a combination of many small and two larger units (based on land area). The smaller units contained about 6,000 Negroes total living in numerous huts. The two large Palmares were deeper in the forest, some thirty miles into the mountain region of Barriga, and housed around 5,000 Negroes total. The names of the *cidades* (settlements and villages) and mocambos of Palmares were Zumbi (located in the northeast), Arotirene, Tobacas, Dombabanga, Subupuira, Osenga,

---

31. Ernesto Ennes, "The Palmares Republic of Pernambuco: Its Final Destruction, 1697," *Americas* 5, no. 2 (October 1948): 200-216, 202.
32. Kent, "Palmares," 166.

Amaro, and Andalaquituche. All were established in a radius of fifty miles or less north, east, and west of each other. Andalaquituche was the most fortified. There were other mocambos (also known as *mu-kambo*, another word meaning "hideout," in Ambundu, the language of the Bantu people living near the Kwanza River in northwest Angola) of lesser importance and with fewer inhabitants.

Anthropologist Irene Diggs[33] posits that the magnitude of the *grand marronage* could have been as large as Portugal, as much as 4,500 square leagues. The inhabitants of this rebel polity used several Bantu terms to describe their quilombo, such as Ngola Janga. The name can be interpreted as "little Angola" or the "little red polity." Evidently, the rebels preferred to think of themselves in African terms, not European ones.

During the colonial period, quilombos in many areas of Brazil were near *engenhos*, plantations where sugarcane, coffee, dried beef, and gold were farmed, harvested, mined, produced, refined, and sent to market. Slaves working on these plantations often fled to the nearest quilombo. Hence, there was an interaction between the enslaved, the *coiteiros* (free men with slaves), the quilombolas, and nearby markets.

Particular notice should be made of Oitizeiro, a hybrid quilombo that interacted with the nearby urban community of Bahia. It was known for its coiteiro culture where runaways lived with and worked for the slave-owning free men on their plantations and moved freely between both societies. The free men were protectors and employers of the runaways. There were very few coiteiro quilombos.

Professor Fassil Demissie[34] estimates up to 5,000 quilombos in more than twenty-four states across Brazil during the seventeenth and eighteenth centuries. They formed as far west as Amazonas, in

---

33. Irene Diggs, "Zumbi and the Republic of Os Palmares," *Phylon* 14, no. 1 (1953): 63.
34. Fassil Demissie, ed., *African Diaspora in Brazil, History, Culture and Politics* (London: Routledge, 2014).

southeast Brazil, and south of São Paulo, and many exist today (see appendices B and C).

The number of residents in a quilombo could be small—less than a dozen—or their numbers could swell significantly into the hundreds. Reis and Gomes[35] describe the sheer number of members in the quilombo Ambrosio, for example; located in Minas Gerais, south of Bahia, and destroyed in 1746, there were potentially over 1,000 inhabitants. The migration of new slaves plus natural reproduction over time accounted for the increase in population.

The viability of the Quilombo of Palmares proved that free African people could manage their affairs without dependency upon a slave bureaucracy. Certain officials in Palmares were designated as keepers of the law and of religion. Within their religious rituals, they worshipped venerated images in a transmogrification of Catholic and African religious deities. The maroons ensured their African religious rituals were incorporated into the version of Catholicism they reinterpreted.

Palmares developed well enough to have African blacksmiths.[36] Moreover, before colonialization in Africa, Africans had worked with iron and stone, and their cultures had surpassed Europeans' in the workings of metallurgy.[37]

The quilombo we visited, Quilombo do Campinho da Independência, was largely isolated from the modern world until the end of the twentieth century. It was not until the government enacted laws recognizing the legitimate presence of quilombos in Brazilian history that title was granted to people occupying quilombo land, descendants of the original quilombolas. The current state of Brazilian law as it relates to land ownership will be discussed in later chapters.

---

35. Reis and Gomes, "Quilombo," 123-126.
36. Kent, "Palmares."
37. Basil Davidson, *The Black Man's Burden: Africa and the Curse of the Nation State* (New York: Three Rivers Press, 1992), 77-78; and Cheney, *Quilombo dos Palmares*.

INITIAL ATTACKS

Palmares was the most emblematic manifestation of the colonial quilombo. Composed of hundreds upon thousands of "runaway slaves who were united to rebuild an African lifestyle in freedom,"[38] it resisted repressive expeditions for about 100 years, promoted attacks on sugar mills and colonial towns, and motivated massive waves of slaves to escape to the captaincy of Pernambuco. According to historian Ronaldo Vainfas, "Palmares provoked such unrest among the colonials, priests, and royal officials that the Portuguese crown, under pressure from a variety of sources, attempted at various moments to negotiate with the rebels."[39]

The strength of Palmares resided in its ability to provide security for its inhabitants. They knew how to protect themselves when war was imminent. They knew how to defend their food as well as the women and children.[40] For almost a century, the Dutch and Portuguese colonizers threw everything they had against the settlement, using every man who could walk, carry a weapon, and was willing to fight the Africans, including Indians, slaves, freed slaves, conscripts from their communities, and paid mercenaries. From the late sixteenth century all the way to near the end of the seventeenth century, the "Black nation," the "Black Republic," the citadel of an aspiring free people, continued to exist.[41]

Kent[42] reports that the first attempts by the Dutch to destroy Palmares took place between 1640 and 1645. They began with reconnaissance, followed by an expedition. The first attack happened in 1643 and captured more than 100 *indigenas brasileiros* and mulattos

---

38. João José Reis, "Slaves and the Coiteiros in the Quilombo of Oitzeiro, Bahia, 1806," in Reis and Gomes, *Freedom by a Thread*, 288.
39. Vainfas, "God Against Palmares," 54.
40. Reis and Gomes, "Quilombo," 288.
41. Cheney, *Quilombo dos Palmares*, 3.
42. Kent, "Palmares," 166.

out of over 6,000 people estimated to be living in the main settlement at that time. The second attack occurred on February 26, 1645.

One can surmise that by the mid-seventeenth century, Palmares was in an advanced state of political maturity—a "civic humanist polity." From 1645 until 1672, Palmares remained free of further interference from Dutch and Portuguese authorities, and the Palmares of 1677 encompassed over 180 miles or sixteen leagues. Unfortunately, the colonists gained more intimate knowledge about Palmares during this lull in the fighting, and the next two decades saw a sustained period of war.

Eight expeditions went into Palmares between 1672 and 1680, in addition to several *entradas* between 1676 and 1677. Kent notes that "the almost equally long years of peace and war between 1645-94 point to Palmares as a fluctuating 'peril.'"[43] Pernambucan authorities looked upon Palmares as an aggressor state. Vainfas[44] avers,

> Perhaps Palmares is, with proper cause, the greatest symbol of resistance. It lasted for almost a hundred years, and lead to humiliating defeats of the Portuguese and their defenders on numerous occasions. Palmares refused to negotiate with the colonial rulers (unlike the Tupinambá santidade), in spite of the "Recife agreement," signed by Ganga Zumba, the leader of Palmares ... in 1678.

The Recife agreement is discussed in detail in later chapters.

In the early sixteenth century, the Portuguese cash crop exported from Brazil was sugar, a rarity among commodities. Sugar had durability; it could be stored for an indeterminate amount of time and farmed and exported on a scale that made investment in production facilities, namely sugar mills and manufacturing depots,

---

43. Kent, 169.
44. Vainfas, "God Against Palmares," 53.

worthwhile.[45] But to accomplish this vast agricultural production over a landmass that stretched from the Amazon River down to what is known today as Uruguay required an immense labor force. Sugar was to Brazil in the sixteenth and seventeenth century what cotton was to the South in North America in the 1830s and 1840s: white gold in both cases.

The escape of African slaves created labor shortages for the sugar plantations during Dutch rule from 1630 to 1654, and the African slaves were considered not fully conquered until Palmares was destroyed near the end of the seventeenth century.

The maroons fought to save themselves and their mocambos. The slave revolts and the attacks by the maroons on nearby plantations were efforts by which the Africans could recover their honor, self-worth, respect, and pride; they would force the colonial authorities to take them seriously.

Palmares presented an existential threat as well. Freyre[46] says:

> The fact of the matter is that Mohammedan Negroes brought to Brazil from that African area which had been most deeply penetrated by Islamism were culturally superior not only to the natives but to the great majority of the white colonists—Portuguese and the sons of Portuguese, with almost no education, some of them illiterate, most of them semi-literate. These latter were individuals who could not write a letter or cast an account unless that was by the hand of the *padre* schoolmaster or with the brain of some clerk. Almost none of them were able to sign their names, and when they did so, it was in a broken script, like that of a child learning to write.

And Reis and Gomes[47] say:

---

45. Cheney, *Quilombo dos Palmares*.
46. Freyre, *Masters and the Slaves*, 298.
47. Reis and Gomes, "Quilombo," 5.

According to this current of thought the social organization of the quilombolas was identified with a counter-acculturation effort and as a resistance to the European acculturation of those living in the slave quarters. R. K. Kent, a North American Africanist . . . sought to redefine Palmares as a true African state in Brazil. This is the vision of quilombo as a restoration project, in the sense that fugitives sought to restore Africa on this other side of the Atlantic.

Despite the autonomy of the villages, the "Palmares Confederation" had a capital in Macaco, which, according to Silvia Hunold Lara,[48] indicates that Macaco was separated from the Serra da Barriga by tens of kilometers. Leading historian Edison Carneiro and Ernesto Ennes differ as to whether the villages of Palmares were a confederation or a republic. The differences in their analyses have much to do with the military role in the political organization of each village.

I prefer the configuration of Carneiro and others who conclude that Palmares formed the foundation for a republic, a "true African state in Brazil."[49] The fear persisted that if Palmares was not defeated—wiped from the face of the earth, its history destroyed, and its leaders plunged into the abyss of anonymity—a Black state in Brazil could become a permanent reality, a precursor to what became known as Haiti.

Reis and Gomes[50] confirm their point:

> Ngola Janga, or Palmares, represented a most successful political challenge to the oppression of European colonialism. It was an inspiring polity, grounded on Africa but open to all

---

48. Silvia Hunold Lara, "O Território dos Palmares: Cartografia, História e Política," *Afro-Ásia*, no. 64 (2021): 12-50.
49. Reis and Gomes, introduction to *Freedom by a Thread*, 31.
50. Reis and Gomes, "Quilombo," 39-41.

those fighting for political freedom.... Black African thinking is not a state (statis) but a process, an act, and, as a consequence, there is no single definition, but a proliferation process.

Contrast the longevity of Palmares with the Black towns established in the USA, the oldest being in Brooklyn, Illinois, between 1830 and 1915. The oldest Black incorporated city in the United States is in Eatonville, Florida, established in 1887, and it continues to this day. Neither of these towns was attacked with the frequency and ferocity that Palmares withstood.

CHAPTER 4

GANGA ZUMBA AND AFRICAN LINEAGE

The African country of Angola was the wellspring from which slaves were captured and transported to Brazil from the sixteenth century until the mid-nineteenth century. Consequently, Angola and Central African countries supplied much of the African culture transferred to Brazil and were the fount from which the leadership of Palmares sprang.

History reveals that Portuguese explorer Diogo Cão discovered the mouth of the Kongo River sometime between 1450 and 1500. Thereafter, the precolonial Kingdom of Kongo and Angola established trading relationships with the Portuguese. To understand the establishment of Palmares, its sustainability, governance, and even its defense, one must start with the precolonial Kingdom of Kongo and the Thirty Years' War between, among others, the Netherlands, Spain, and later Portugal, as well as the Dutch project titled the *Groot Desseyn* ("Great Design"), the object of which was to decouple the Portuguese and the Spaniards from their West African possessions centered on Kongo and Angola.

The two countries are now separate African states. "Kongo" became "Congo" via Portuguese translation, and Angola is the successor to a large portion of what was historically Ndongo. The war of the Dutch, Spaniards, and Portuguese in Africa against the kings and queens of the Kingdom of Kongo essentially ended at the battle of Mbwila, where it is speculated that the founders of Palmares were captured and subsequently sold into slavery, ending up in northeast Brazil.

Brazil was itself discovered by Europeans on April 26, 1500, by Pedro Alvarez Cabral, under the sponsorship of Dom João II, king of Portugal. After making this discovery, many of the sailors returned to Portugal. According to Cheney,[1] "they left behind a couple of Jews or criminals (the record is unclear which, or whether they were, by definition, one and the same)."

According to Freyre,[2] the Portuguese had the following adage: "There is no sin below the equator." Freyre remarks:

> It is customary to say that civilization and syphilis go hand-in-hand, but Brazil would appear to have been syphilized before it was civilized. The first Europeans to come here were swallowed up in the aboriginal mass without leaving upon the latter any traces of their origin, other than those of syphilis and racial hybridism. They did not bring civilization, but there is evidence to show that they did bring the venereal plague to the population that absorbed them.

Brazil was a Portuguese colony from around 1500 to the early nineteenth century. The Dutch maintained Pernambuco as a colony between 1630 and 1654, as a ruling minority.

The first slaves were imported to Brazil in 1538 after Dom João III issued a royal decree permitting their importation from "Guinea," i.e., West and Central Africa.[3] The slaves who survived the "middle

---

1. Glenn A. Cheney, *Quilombo dos Palmares: Brazil's Lost Nation of Fugitive Slaves* (Hanover, CT: New London Librarium, 2014), 5-7.
2. Gilberto Freyre, *The Masters and the Slaves: A Study in the Development of Brazilian Civilization* (Berkeley: University of California Press, 1986), 71.
3. Cheney, *Quilombo dos Palmares*, 17.

passage" developed a camaraderie through shared misery. Thus, an informal bond of great importance made for an enduring nexus between enslaved Africans in Brazil, especially those from the same tribes. One can presume that the same quality of relationship arose between Africans transported to the Caribbean and North America.

Those who got to know each other were called *malungos,* a Bantu term that means "companions" or "shipmates." *Malunguinho* is a creolized derivation of the same. A quilombo in the Catucá forest near Pernambuco had a leader, João Batista, who was feared and wanted as a fugitive, dead or alive, between 1829 and 1835 and was personified as the Malunguinho.[4] The quilombolas there became known collectively as Malunguinhos. Historians have referred to the entire phenomenon of resistance through quilombos as the "Quilombo Malunguinho."

According to Reis and Gomes, Ganga Zumba was the leader or malunguinho of Palmares at least from about 1670 until 1687, but there is evidence that his rule began much earlier. He may have descended from African aristocracy. In choosing the leader of a quilombo the size and importance of Palmares, the rank and file would have gravitated toward a member who exuded the air of kingship or sprang from matrilineal dynastic politics.

An area worth discussing is how the names of key individuals in the Palmares saga were derived. Briefly, with regard to Ganga Zumba, Kent[5] asserts that the name derives from the Jaga/Imbangala religious title *ngana a nzumbi,* where "ngana" is a form of respectful address similar to sir, lord, or mister, and "nzumbi," from the Bantu language, means "ancestral spirit." Translations of Bantu by the Portuguese leave much to be desired. Suffice it to say that "Ganga

---

4. João José Reis and Flavio dos Santos Gomes, "Quilombo: Brazilian Maroons During Slavery." *Cultural Survival Quarterly Magazine,* April 28, 2010, www.culturalsurvival.org/publications/cultural-survival-quarterly/quilombo-brazilian-maroons-during-slavery/, 351.
5. R. K. Kent, "Palmares: An African State in Brazil," *Journal of African History* 6, no.2 (1965): 161-175, p. 169.

Zumba" has an exalted religious connotation and was "probably a title rather than a proper name."[6]

It is the opinion of some researchers[7] that Ganga Zumba was born in Palmares. He may have been one of its earliest inhabitants, and he had at least three children—Toculo, Acaiene, and Zambi—and ten grandchildren. Such a lineage is modest by some standards.

As noted above, members of the quilombo ascertained who was royalty and who was not. Diggs[8] notes, "Here was an independent state where the power was exercised by a king elected by reason of his greater valor and ability to organize; and perhaps he was selected from certain families considered royal in their native lands."

Ganga Zumba was recognized as leader by those born in Palmares and those who joined from the outside. He lived on a hill at the capital of Macaco—possibly founded in 1642, as noted by the Dutch in their documents[9]—in a palatial residence with his family and court officials. He was treated as a king, with all the rights, duties, and privileges accorded thereto. Subjects referred to him as "His Majesty" and obeyed him with reverence. Ganga Zumba was a strong and assertive leader. His boldness of action and incorporation of African culture into Palmares was intrinsic to its character.

"Macaco" comes from the Bantu *mokoko*, meaning "cock." Portuguese-speaking colonists translated the term to mean "monkeys." (Note: This is a similar, if not the same, term that was used by a White politician from Virginia years ago when addressing a heckler of color attending one of his rallies. He lost his election.) According to Diggs,[10] Ganga Zumba lived in the *casa del consejo* (council house), known as the "royal stockade" by the Portuguese

---

6. Robert Nelson Anderson, "The Quilombo of Palmares: A New Overview of a Maroon State in Seventeenth-Century Brazil," *Journal of Latin American Studies* 28, no. 3 (1996): 545-566.
7. Cheney, *Quilombo dos Palmares*, 80.
8. Irene Diggs, "Zumbi," 62-70, 69.
9. Reis and Gomes, "Quilombo," 27.
10. Diggs, "Zumbi," 65.

because it was the fortress town of the king. It and other villages in the settlement were surrounded by a palisade known as a *cerca real*, or royal fence. Citing Carneiro, Diggs estimates that over 5,000 Africans lived in this mocambo in 2,000 houses.

Based on the work of Kent and Diggs,[11] Ganga Zumba ruled with iron justice, permitting no disloyalty or infidelity among the inhabitants. If someone ran away, the king's African soldiers quickly apprehended and put them to death to instill fear among the Angolan Negroes. These scholars also note that neither medicine men nor witchcraft were permitted in the quilombo. Murder, robbery, theft, desertion, and adultery were dealt with harshly and in many cases resulted in death.

The king had three wives, a mulatta and two Africans. Polygamy is an African cultural practice of long standing. (However, it is worth noting that monogamy was widely practiced in pre-Islamic Africa.) It is understandable that African cultural practices would be preserved in a quilombo whose founders sought to recreate the culture lost after their capture and reestablish an African land in the Americas. In effect, this is what the quilombo represents in Brazil today: a preservation of African culture and resistance to the dominance of European culture.

Ganga Zumba, along with his many other duties, was the military chief of the quilombo. He and his brother, Ganga Zona, along with other principal deputies, fortified the encampment. They installed parapets and caltrops, built palisades, dug pits, erected ramparts, and fought using guerrilla strategies that the Portuguese labeled *guerra da floresta*, the "war of the woods": hit and run, deceive and confuse, wear down and frustrate, and live to fight again. This strategy worked on many occasions, causing the enemy soldiers to abandon their missions and return empty handed. Location was Palmares's ultimate defense, as was the case with so many other quilombos in the Americas.

Importantly, Aqualtune, also known as Arotirene or Aca Inene, the mother of Ganga Zumba and the grandmother of Zumbi—successor

---

11. Kent, "Palmares"; Diggs, "Zumbi."

to Ganga Zumba—was also a pivotal leader. She was possibly part of the founding leadership of Palmares and provided Ganga Zumba's supposed link to Kongo royalty. Without going into detail, for there is much history involving this subject and Kongo, during certain periods in precolonial times (1390 to 1665), Kongo was ruled by kinship clans known as *makanda* (singular *kanda*). According to historian John K. Thornton, "Kongo tradition remembered it as a struggle of three *makanda* known to later generations as the 'three stones on which Congo cooked,' the Kinlaza, Kimpanzu, and Kinkanga, the three familial lineage clans."[12]

I believe the genealogy of Ganga Zumba and therefore Zumbi can be traced to one of these kanda, or to another known as the Kilukeni. As discussed, the term "kilombo/quilombo" originates in Angola. Anderson asserts, "It is reasonable to assume that many, if not most, of the Palmaristas were the descendants of slaves from Angola, and many may have been recent arrivals from among the Imbangala."[13] The Imbangala, also known as the Jagas, a localized African population in Kongo, did not rule by lineage.

During the battle of Ulanga (or Mbwila) on October 29, 1665, the Portuguese defeated the kingdom of Kongo, decapitated their king, António I, and captured many subordinate rulers, their families, and next of kin. These nobles of elite clans were sold into slavery and wound up in northeast Brazil, more specifically Porto Calvo in Pernambuco, and other places in the Americas. The Europeans gave short shrift to African governance if they gave any shrift at all, treating them all as ignorant Africans. They made no attempt to elevate Africans of royal lineage or differentiate them from their subjects. They were thrown together in the bowels of slave ships destined for Brazil.[14]

To establish and maintain Palmares—"a rustic Republic, in its

---

12. John K. Thornton, "Elite Women in the Kingdom of Kongo: Historical Perspectives on Women's Political Power," *Journal of African History* 47, no. 3 (2006): 437-460.
13. Anderson, "Quilombo of Palmares," 559.
14. Thornton, "Elite Women."

way, well ordered"[15]—required leadership, vision, perseverance, courage, and the tradition of independence and resistance. The royalty of Kongo had all of these attributes. They had ruled Kongo for centuries, and they eschewed the indignity of slavery with determined resistance. Anderson says, "Of all of the historical examples of slave protests, Palmares is the most beautiful, the most heroic. It is a black Troy, and its story is an Iliad.... These rustic black republics revealed the dream of a social order founded on fraternal inequality."[16]

Yet the historian Richard Price mentions that establishing a quilombo was the more aggressive form of slave resistance on the spectrum. According to Price,[17] citing Edison Carneiro,

> There were three basic forms of active resistance; fugitive slave settlements called quilombos; attempts at seizure of power; and armed insurrections.... The quilombos constitute a pre-nineteenth-century phenomenon.... They came closest to the idea of re-creating African societies in a new environment and against consistently heavier odds. Once formed, the quilombos were regarded as a threat to the Portuguese plantation, an inducement for escape from the slave hut, senzala and, they were rarely, therefore, allowed to exist for a long time. Of the 10 major quilombos in colonial Brazil, seven were destroyed within two years of being formed. Four fell in the state of Bahia in 1632, 1636, 1646 and 1796. The other three met the same fate in Rio in 1650.

Laird W. Bergad[18] reports that "almost all conspiracies and

---

15. Anderson, "Quilombo of Palmares," 549-566.
16. Anderson, "Quilombo of Palmares."
17. Richard Price, ed., *Maroon Societies: Rebel Slave Communities in the Americas*, 3rd ed. (Baltimore: John Hopkins University Press, 1996).
18. Laird W. Bergad, *The Comparative Histories of Slavery in Brazil, Cuba, and the United States: New Approaches to the Americas* (New York: Cambridge University Press, 2007), 225, 228-249.

rebellions were led by African-origin slaves and nearly all participants in these uprisings were Africans as well." Moreover, "conspiracies and rebellions could not be stopped or curbed as slaves, especially the Africa-born, never lost sight of, or hope for, freedom," and it was "difficult for the security forces to penetrate the world of African-born slaves who spoke their own languages, kept their plans secret . . . and never lost sight of the possibilities for freedom, no matter how insurmountable the obstacles to success appeared." Ultimately, the constant importation of Africans, the majority of whom knew freedom and brought with them developed cultures, "reinforced general slave rebelliousness."

Slaves were tireless in their search for freedom; they never stopped running away, and in Brazil, they were remarkably successful at establishing maroon communities.

I embrace Anderson's point of view[19] that a mature Central African culture existed in the creole population of Palmares—in its titles and its political and public rituals and practices:

> The flexibility of the institution of the *Kilombo* as a mechanism for integrating a lineageless community engaged in warfare and self-defense, as was Palmares, explains why some adaptation of the Imbangala institution would thrive in Brazil, even if only a minority of Palmares's inhabitants were actually Imbangala.
>
> Certain African cultural forms and practices lent themselves to adaptation to the [problems] of the New World. In this instance, the Central African solution of the *quilombo* served the Brazilian maroons, uniting *malungos,* or comrades, from diverse ethnic backgrounds, not on the basis of lineage, but for the purposes of commodity production, raiding, and self-defense. The persistence and adaptation of African cultural elements such as the *quilombo* to the Afro-Brazilian creole context, in fact, demonstrates the continuity of African and African

---

19. Anderson, "Quilombo of Palmares," 565.

diasporic cultures in the process of New World transculturation.

In essence, he says the culture of Central Africa, specifically Kongo and Angola, was applied to the quilombo phenomenon. Even though the Imbangala were not a dominant population or overrepresented in Palmares, their mores were adopted as the mechanism for housing runaway slaves.

The predecessors of Ganga Zumba led the "red polity" effectively and kept it afloat until he capably took the helm in 1670. Based on available information, exactly how long Ganga Zumba ruled Palmares is difficult to ascertain; one or possibly two generations of rulers preceded him. Though he successfully defended Palmares against the Dutch and Portuguese for quite some time, the overall judgment of his leadership hung on the balance of his attempt to make a deal with the Portuguese in June 1678. The strategy to strike a deal was wise under the circumstances, but the negotiation and implementation of the accord were flawed. As is often true of significant leaders, a single issue can determine how history views their governance.

CHAPTER 5

ZUMBI: FROM KONGO TO PORTO CALVO

Lineage is, again, an essential cultural issue in certain African societies, often setting the stage for the assumption of leadership in the clan or society at large.

Research has shown[1] the probability that Zumbi's genealogical pathway proceeded through his grandmother Aqualtune, a princess and daughter of an unknown king of Kongo. She had three children: Sabina, Ganga Zumba, and Ganga Zona. Sabina was Zumbi's mother and Ganga Zumba and Ganga Zona his uncles. Thornton,[2] referring to a discussion regarding the mother of King Afonso of Kongo, advises that in the Kikongo language of Kongo, "there is no distinction between cousins and brothers (*mpanga*), but here it seems likely that the original genealogy did recognize this distinction." Though there is some speculation as to the authenticity of these relationships, Zumbi

---

1. Maria Suely da Costa, "Representações de Luta e Resistência Feminina na Poesia Popular," III Conedu, Congresso Nacional de Educação; André Nogueira, "De Princesa Africana a Escravizada em Solo Brasileiro: Aqualtune, a Avó de Zumbi," *Aventura na História*, https://aventurasnahistoria.uol.com.br/noticias/reportagem/de-princesa-africana-escravizada-em-solo-brasileiro-aqualtune-avo-de-zumbi.phtml/.
2. John K. Thornton, "The Kingdom of Kongo and the Thirty Years War," *Journal of World History* 27, no. 2 (2016): 189-213.

likely was closely related by blood to Kongo nobility.

Moreover, Thornton[3] reveals that "kinship played a role in succession and office holding" in Kongo during the seventeenth century—when Palmares was established. Zumbi's ancestors were probably part of a makanda, factions based on kinship and familial lineage known to exist in Kongo culture today.

Thus, according to Thornton, it can be surmised that the knowledge gained by the malungos during their passage to Brazil enabled them, notwithstanding the prohibitions placed upon them, to identify their natural-born leaders based on their African culture.

To summarize known history, Portugal and Kongo began as trading partners. After the Portuguese established a colony in Angola, formally part of Kongo, relations soured and fighting ensued, caused by the European scramble to control this part of Africa. A war between the Spanish and the Dutch—arch-competitors of the Portuguese—saw the Portuguese eventually forcing the Dutch out of portions of Kongo, as they did in Pernambuco in 1654.

From 1624 (or earlier) to 1648, Aqualtune, her relatives, and Queen Njinga Ndongo led a large infantry force that defeated the Portuguese in the battles at Ilamba and Kumbi, a province within the Kongo kingdom. Queen Njinga Ndongo was instrumental in thwarting the Portuguese and at times aligned herself with the Dutch to defend her kingdom. Both women fought valiantly, though at different times during the span of the war.[4]

The Battle of Mbwila concluded the war for the control of the Kongo kingdom that had lasted for over thirty years.

Anecdotal data reveals that some of Zumbi's family—Aqualtune and possibly Sabina—were among the captives and subsequently sold as slaves. This data also suggests that they were enslaved on the plantation of Santa Rita in Pernambuco. There, they led a rebellion, escaped, and later formed their own kingdom in the Quilombo dos

---

3. Thornton, "Kingdom of Kongo," 439.
4. Thornton, 189, 213.

Palmares. This maroon nation controlled large areas of northeast Brazil during the Dutch–Portuguese War.

There are few historiographical accounts of Zumbi's genealogy, early childhood, and adolescence other than what has already been discussed. The accounts described in this book represent consensus opinions from researchers and other interested parties. The school of thought adopted by Cheney[5] and detailed below is plausible on many levels, and it is reaffirmed, in part, by Anderson.[6]

The Dutch attacked Salvador in Bahia, located some 966 kilometers (600 miles) from Pernambuco, in May 1624. Subsequently, on March 1, 1630, Olinda, the capital of Pernambuco, was attacked as part of the Dutch strategy of Groot Desseyn. The objective was partially to remove the Portuguese from Angola, dominate the kingdom of Kongo, and eliminate funding by the Spanish to continue their war against the Dutch. The Dutch controlled the northeastern coast of Brazil for thirty years until 1654.[7]

In 1655, more than 121 years after the first Jesuits arrived in Brazil from Portugal and a year after the Dutch withdrew from Pernambuco, Sabina bore an infant son, Zumbi, who was captured during one of many military assaults against Palmares. As the story goes, Zumbi was then raised in a church.

According to Cheney,[8] an orphaned Black baby from Kongo, born free in Palmares—"born in the forest," as were so many other African babies whose mothers lived in quilombos—was gifted to the Portuguese Jesuit priest Friar António Melo. This account accords

---

5. Glenn A. Cheney, *Quilombo dos Palmares: Brazil's Lost Nation of Fugitive Slaves* (Hanover, CT: New London Librarium, 2014).
6. Robert Nelson Anderson, "The Quilombo of Palmares: A New Overview of a Maroon State in Seventeenth-Century Brazil," *Journal of Latin American Studies* 28, no. 3 (1996): 545-566.
7. Thornton, "Kingdom of Kongo."
8. Cheney, *Quilombo dos Palmares*.

with Stuart B. Schwartz[9] in *Rethinking Palmares*: "When children born in a quilombo were captured, they often became the property of the expedition's leader, and this may explain their absence from judicial records."

Friar Melo lived in Porto Calvo, a city in Alagoas, a region in Pernambuco that eventually became a separate state. Considered a commercial center by the warring colonial powers, Porto Calvo was the site of many conflicts, disputations, and battles between the Portuguese, Dutch, and Spanish during the colonial era. It was a strategic city because of its proximity to the coast. The city is, among other things, known for the desertion of Domingos Calabar, a prominent Portuguese official who fought in Pernambuco in 1632 under Mathias de Albuquerque. Calabar later betrayed the Portuguese and joined the Dutch, thereafter responsible for several Portuguese defeats. He was finally captured and hanged in a public execution in the city.[10]

This African baby, Zumbi, captured in battle and orphaned by events beyond his control, would grow up to inspire a nation of Afro-Brazilians. Through his story, he came to represent the resistance of African people to their enslavement and bondage by North American and European slavers.

It is ironic that a member of the Catholic Church—an institution that enabled slavery and the infliction of pain and suffering upon African people through its agents, priests, and theologians while preaching a soothing balm of moral rationality and rectitude to slave owners in Brazil and to the slaves—ended up raising an African child who would become one of the slave system's most ardent and feared opponents. Zumbi's steady resistance became a transcendent symbol for generations of African-descended people, a martyr for the cause

---

9. Stuart B. Schwartz, "Rethinking Palmares: Slave Resistance in Colonial Brazil," in *Critical Readings on Global Slavery*, eds. Damian Alan Pargas and Felicia Roşu (Leiden, Netherlands: Brill, 2005): 1294-1325, p. 1308.
10. Freyre, *Masters and the Slaves*, 269, note 195.

of slave resistance and racial equality.

As Cheney[11] describes, the friar baptized the infant and named him Francisco. To the friar, Francisco was possibly a novelty, a view shared by many European-descended slaveholders or slave enablers who took control of African infants or raised them. Black babies and children were the objects of speculation and investment. Some slaveholders traded horses for Black babies they then treated as pets, subject to temperamental affection, until they were old enough for productive labor. Historians John Hope Franklin and Loren Schweninger[12] quote a North American slaveholder who raised an enslaved baby as saying, "My favorite little Isaac, he is subject to a cough but seldom sick enough to lay up. The poor little fellow is laying at my feet and sound asleep. I wish I did not love him, as I do, but it is so, and I cannot help it."

Novelty or not, Friar Melo raised Francisco as the son he never had.

Francisco was not the name given to him by Sabina, who was probably cast into the abyss of anonymous slave labor. I have found no further information about her fate. In those days, Black mothers were treated as breeding stock, conduits to produce new slave labor. Nothing is known of Zumbi's biological father.

This type of naming was common practice in the slave world to erase any connection to the slave's ancestry. We cannot fault the friar because he knew nothing of this baby's ethnic or ancestral history and probably made no serious effort to ascertain them. Naming a child is serious business to Africans, where a name carries specific messages.

Francisco was Black in color only. He was raised in the culture of a Portuguese colony and could have passed for any middle-class, or *classe média*, Portuguese except for his skin. Melo tried to raise the boy as if his color did not matter—a worthwhile objective but not one grounded in reality. This practice was born of the Eurocentric

---

11. Cheney, *Quilombo dos Palmares*, 102.
12. John Hope Franklin and Loren Schweninger, *Runaway Slaves: Rebels on the Plantations* (New York: Oxford University Press, 1999), 49.

mentality, where everything in Friar Melo's world reflected European culture to the disdain of all others. Consequently, the boy reputedly was fluent in Portuguese and mastered Latin, the ancient language of the Catholic faith.

Because of his exposure to Latin, some authors have assumed that he was schooled in history, religion, the classics, and the humanities, a subject that embodied his later life. Much has been made of how he belied expectations related to his color and his race: a colonial state of mind that persists to this day. Francisco, or "Chico," was probably a precocious child. We know the Kongo elite sent their best to Portugal during the precolonial era to learn Portuguese and to write in Latin. Therefore, it would not be a stretch for Francisco to have the mental faculties that enabled him to master these subjects; the capability was in his genes.

Ultimately, the quality of Francisco's education is a matter of speculation. Was he exposed to the same quality of education given to a child of a *fidalgo*, a Portuguese nobleman or gentleman? Or did he receive an education more akin to that which a *preto, pardo, gente de cor, crioulo, ladino, mestiço, caboclo, cabra,* or *mulatto*—persons of a lower class in a color-based society—would receive?

The following is an excerpt taken from a discussion on Brazilian education during colonial times:

> The history of education in Brazil begins in the second half of the sixteenth century, when the Jesuits from the *Companhia de Jesus* (Company of Jesus) arrived in 1549. The Jesuits founded the first Brazilian elementary school in Salvador, in the state of Bahia. They followed the educational principles established in the *Ratio Studiorum* (a regulatory educational document written and promoted by Friar Inácio de Loyola). The Jesuits' work was driven not only by educational goals, but by a religious purpose as well: to spread the Christian faith among the indigenous population. For 210 years, the Jesuits

were responsible for the entire educational system in Brazil. Their primary and secondary schools were of good quality, and some of the secondary schools even offered higher-level studies. The Jesuits also created many missions in Brazil to educate and catechize the indigenous people. These missions would help the people escape from slavery.[13]

This educational system was primarily set up for the Indigenous peoples, who were classed slightly above slaves. For the best education during this time in Brazil, the slaveholding elites sent their children to Portugal. Francisco's education may have been somewhere in the middle.

As a side note, slave states in the United States chose no education whatsoever as their governance policy. In North Carolina, a statute was passed that made it illegal to educate slaves. It was thought that educating slaves would induce them to rebel and escape.

Because of his circumstances, Francisco was fortunate enough to have choices. He could have lived as a free Black and a member of the Portuguese middle class. Although the need to continually prove himself smart, capable, or equal in faculties because of his color was likely a perennial monkey on his back, many Africans in his position probably would have chosen this easier path to escape all that being Black and African entailed. And who could fault them for it? However, his life may have been less consequential. One must remember that the manifestations of racism always redound to the benefit of the dominant culture and extract a price from the subservient race.

Francisco was an unusual boy, an extraordinary talent living in unique circumstances. And he was called to do a remarkable thing: to be the standard-bearer for his people.

Francisco sat at the knee of his adopted father and imbibed the

---

13. State University.com Education Encyclopedia, "Brazil: History & Background," https://education.stateuniversity.com/pages/195/Brazil-HISTORY-BACKGROUND.html/.

lessons the friar preached and perhaps, to some extent, lived. He listened to sermons on the morality of a virtuous life built upon the sacraments of the Catholic faith, Christian values, and goodwill toward men. And Cheney[14] posits that Melo taught him about law, justice and injustice, and the horrors of racism and bigotry: a prejudicially applied societal norm in the colonial mind that applied only to Whites and left no space for the humanity of African people. Over time, the hypocrisy was not lost on the youth. His intelligence would not have allowed him to accept the inherent contradictions in the dogma his father preached and a society that tolerated and participated in the subjugation of people who looked like him.

As Francisco went about his daily activities, he would have witnessed the *pelourinho* administered to people of his color: hangings, cut Achilles tendons, castrations, and other mutilations. What separated him from these tortures was pure happenstance; as the English martyr John Bradford recited, "There but for the grace of God go I." The colonial state of mind was one of abject cruelty to people who were not European.

Cheney[15] asserts that at the age of fifteen, Francisco left the comfort of his home in Porto Calvo and ran off to Palmares, a coming-of-age decision in recognition of his plight and that of his people. Cheney notes that Francisco probably left a note telling his adopted father of his decision and perhaps where he intended to go. It is further indicated by Anderson[16] that "he later continued to pay the priest secret visits."

There is an interesting observation to make here. White parents often adopt children of African descent to give them "a better chance at life," perhaps out of misguided underestimation of the importance of ancestral culture, race, and ethnicity. On rare occasions, people of African descent have adopted White babies. But as can be seen by

---

14. Cheney, *Quilombo dos Palmares*, 103.
15. Cheney, 103.
16. Anderson, "Quilombo of Palmares."

Francisco's experience, color, heritage, and descent can augur more strongly than class and economics. Cultural heritage and ethnicity are pivotal and powerful forces in the development of an individual and determinants of future life direction.

Francisco left behind the trappings of middle-class colonial life to exist with his people in the forest—poor people whose lives were characterized by subsistence, but they were people who looked like him. In effect, he took an oath of poverty. He threw off the shackles of racial paternalism and the artificiality of his existence. He was the upside-down version of the prodigal son—one who did not squander his upbringing but used it in a valiant attempt to free his brethren. In the words of the Christian Bible he learned as a child and which assisted in the enslavement of his people, Francisco feared no evil, though "he walked in the valley of the shadow of death." He knew from his upbringing—not yet having learned about any other Western religion—that the God of heavenly hosts would protect him.

We can find analogies in Francisco's birth and adolescence to the plight of African-descended people in the Western world. We too were captured, orphaned, raised in a foreign land, deculturated, and left to survive the best we could in a hostile environment. Francisco's flight to Palmares in some ways mirrors the desire of some African-descended people to build Black towns and cities or to return to Africa, seeking refuge from the incessant injustices, depredations, and incivilities of life in the West.

By the time Francisco left Porto Calvo—presumably the place from which forty Guinean slaves had escaped to found Palmares[17]—the quilombo had existed for over sixty years. The settlement grew up in the forest around Pernambuco, a state on the northeast coast of Brazil. This frontier beyond the urban area of Pernambuco served several purposes: it was a barrier for those slaves who hid there,

---

17. Cheney, *Quilombo dos Palmares*, 34; Richard Price, ed., *Maroon Societies: Rebel Slave Communities in the Americas*, 3rd ed. (Baltimore: John Hopkins University Press, 1996), 178.

a deterrent to settlement by the colonizer, and a refuge for those seeking freedom from enslavement.

By dint of stark necessity, the maroons carried no bags. They traveled light with only their personages to salvage. They carried few possessions and harbored antipathy toward their pursuers. With a fervor to escape and the energy to persevere—accompanied by the powerful disincentive to be captured, knowing the severity of punishment upon default—they pushed themselves to exhaustion seeking refuge. Because of the consequences of capture, the fugitive slaves were able to lose themselves almost recklessly in the labyrinthine entanglements of the dense forest. Here, they were able to abscond with abandon, knowing that to survive meant accepting the forest as master and committing to a life provided by nature and their own ingenuity. In effect, the fugitive slave in the forest sought the color of indigeneity; they joined and cohabitated with the Indians. Why did Francisco choose Palmares? Was it because of its proximity to Porto Calvo? Did he know that Ganga Zumba was his uncle? Or could it have been because of the historical connection between Porto Calvo and Palmares? Perhaps Francisco became accustomed to an urban demographic. Habituated as he was to mingling with diverse peoples, maybe Palmares, with its variegated population—Africans, mainly from Kongo and other Bantu areas, as well as Indians, Jews, Muslims, and disaffected Whites—was attractive as well as inspirational to him.[18]

One of his first realizations upon arrival would have been that the settlement was under the control of a leader, a king: Ganga Zumba. Returning to the question of whether and when Francisco knew of his relation to Ganga Zumba, Francisco might have acquired knowledge of his uncle from existing slaves or from freed slaves who knew of his immediate family—perhaps even from Portuguese officials, considering his adopted father's connection to the ruling hierarchy. According to Freyre,[19]

---

18. Reis and Gomes, "Quilombo," 20-22.
19. Freyre, *Masters and the Slaves*, xxxix.

The friars also fulfilled the function of bankers in colonial times. Much money was given to them to keep in their monasteries, which were as strong and inaccessible as fortresses.... [T]he friars grew big-bellied and soft in fulfilling the functions of chaplains, ecclesiastical tutors, priestly uncles, and godfathers to the young ones, and they proceeded to accommodate themselves to the comfortable situation of members of the family or household, becoming allies and adherents of the patriarchal system.

There is no record of Francisco having known the identity of his mother or father, but one can imagine that this young man would want to find out who they were. Research suggests that his mother was Sabina, daughter of Aqualtune. Clearly, if Ganga Zumba was his uncle, he might extrapolate from there. One writer on the subject[20] has posited that Ganga Zumba was Aqualtune's son. In addition to this linkage, we are left to wonder about Francisco's brothers and sisters, nieces and nephews, aunts and uncles, if any others existed. We know that following the 1665 defeat of King António I of Kongo, many of his relatives were captured. Historians differ regarding these familial relationships. According to Cheney,[21] "King Ganga Zumba referred to young Francisco—Zumbi—as a nephew. In the African tradition that may have meant nothing more than a close political or social relationship, not a family relation."

Like many people of African descent in the diaspora, knowledge of ancestral heritage is an intricate puzzle that often defies resolution. The information is either absent or limited in availability. Because the record of this era is sparse at best, we are left to fill in the gaps. Many thanks to the modern historians who have written of the era in a light more favorable to Palmares. In telling this story, I have applied the principle of Occam's razor to arrive at a cogent scenario.

---

20. Da Costa, "Representações."
21. Cheney, *Quilombo dos Palmares*.

As noted earlier, Cheney says that Francisco left his adopted father a note explaining why he left. Francisco had become an exemplar of what a son should be, race notwithstanding. After all, left to its own devices, love does not limit itself to color but adheres to those things that matter to the individual. Surely Francisco valued the love and effort his adopted father put into his upbringing, saving him from a life of drudgery. And as a thoughtful, loving son would do, he spurned the notion of leaving his father without explaining his actions. The moral center embedded in the young man's person was a reflection of his father's religious training and his environment.

We can only speculate that among the things he said in his note, foremost was that he loved his adopted father and appreciated what the man had done for him but felt an irresistible compulsion to join his ancestral people and to contribute what talents he had to improve their plight—a clarion call that challenged him to rise above the factitiousness of his present life. And we must not ignore the possibility that his father may have urged him to go, to follow his inner voice. What father who truly loved his son would deny him his calling?

The other option available to Francisco was to live as a descendant of a Mouro, a Moor. Moors, defined as a dark-skinned people from North Africa, have a long history in Portugal, having at one time ruled portions of the Iberian Peninsula.[22] Historian Arwin Smallwood[23] states that "because of the influence of the North African Muslims on Portugal and Spain from 733 to 1492 and the West African slave trade, which the Portuguese had conducted since 1441, Africans had become a well-established part of Portuguese and Spanish society by 1492." This racial group had a long tradition in Portugal and because of that history was regarded as an exception in the ever-shifting goalposts of admixture in Portuguese racial hierarchy.

---

22. Freyre, *Masters and the Slaves*, 212.
23. Arwin D. Smallwood, "A History of Native American and African Relations from 1502 to 1900," *Negro History Bulletin* 62, no. 2/3 (April-September 1999), 18-31, 19.

Here we have the classic example of an African child who excelled in the learned world he was exposed to. Had he elected to stay in Porto Calvo, he would have fought without ever winning the Sisyphean task of proving his intelligence and worth to a race of people convinced of his inferiority. Francisco must have determined at a young age the futility of making such an effort. He would have understood the hypocrisy of it all. So, throwing caution to the wind, he chose a path redemptive of his capability to purge himself of a future filled with contempt in favor of a path of service to people who could benefit from his talents and would appreciate his contributions to their welfare. He could make a difference in their lives, and they in his—a calling not available among the European colonists, where he would be just another "lucky or exceptional African" or Negro at best, who could read, talk, and write like a White man.

Francisco did not fit the stereotype of the slave. There would be no bowing and scraping or being easily led. He was an educated, handsome young person with the will and fortitude to fight his oppressors. It is not surprising, then, that upon entering Palmares and at some point establishing his familial relationship with its king, he was elevated to a position of leadership in the quilombo because of his knowledge, exposure, and education. Leadership skills, I am sure, were a much sought-after trait in the ubiquitous war-footing environment.

CHAPTER 6

ZUMBI OF PALMARES

In 1670, at fifteen, Francisco shed his European moniker and took a name from African ideology: Zumbi. As mentioned previously, names in African culture tell us much about one's origins, social standing, heritage, politics, and presumed destiny. Most African cultures have a naming ceremony; I went through such an event in Ghana many years ago. Many notable African Americans have shed their slave names and taken on African names of significance to them.

The name Zumbi is used more often than Zambi, but both denote the same person formerly known as Francisco. Zambi is derived from an all-powerful creator god in the tradition of Candomblé, popular among Afro-Brazilians.[1] The historical record notes that there was "a

---

1. Richard Price, ed., *Maroon Societies: Rebel Slave Communities in the Americas*, 3rd ed. (Baltimore: John Hopkins University Press, 1996), 185; João José Reis and Flavio dos Santos Gomes, "Quilombo: Brazilian Maroons During Slavery," *Cultural Survival Quarterly Magazine*, April 28, 2010, www.culturalsurvival.org/publications/cultural-survival-quarterly/quilombo-brazilian-maroons-during-slavery/, 27; Robert Nelson Anderson, "The Quilombo of Palmares: A New Overview of a Maroon State in Seventeenth-Century Brazil," *Journal of Latin American Studies* 28, no. 3 (1996): 545-566, pp. 559-561.

*palmarista c*aptain named Zambi (whose uncle is Ganga Zona)."[2] As with the name Ganga Zumba, there is no certainty about the name Zumbi—whether it is the name of an individual or an honorific, as postulated by Reis and Gomes,[3] or even how it is spelled. Indeed, *nzumbi* is associated with priestly and military Bantu titles in Angola. The appellation Zumbi suggests he played an important spiritual role in the community.

Other historians, such as Anderson,[4] have rendered their opinions on the etymology of the name Zumbi. Essentially, it is "a matter of speculation how Zumbi came to receive his name, but there can be little doubt that his compatriots viewed the name within the paradigm of the cult of ancestors." Some thought that Francisco/Zumbi "had figuratively returned from the dead when he returned to Palmares." Furthermore, "it is uncertain whether 'Zumbi' was a proper name, title, epithet, or praise name." The historian Freitas advances the idea that it was not a title but a given name or even a nickname. Finally, historical documents have spelled the title variously as "Zumbi, Zambi, Zombi, as well as Zoomby. Ernesto Ennes the Portuguese historian refers to Zumbi as 'Zumby.'"

If we are to assume (as Cheney[5] suggests) that Francisco, hereinafter known as Zumbi, left Porto Calvo at age fifteen, perhaps having been born in Palmares—a school of thought propounded by Freitas and reiterated by Anderson and Cheney—a lot of planning

---

2. Richard Price, ed., *Maroon Societies: Rebel Slave Communities in the Americas*, 3rd ed. (Baltimore: John Hopkins University Press, 1996), 185; João José Reis and Flavio dos Santos Gomes, "Quilombo: Brazilian Maroons During Slavery," *Cultural Survival Quarterly Magazine*, April 28, 2010, www.culturalsurvival.org/publications/cultural-survival-quarterly/quilombo-brazilian-maroons-during-slavery/, 27; Robert Nelson Anderson, "The Quilombo of Palmares: A New Overview of a Maroon State in Seventeenth-Century Brazil," *Journal of Latin American Studies* 28, no. 3 (1996): 545-566, pp. 559-561.
3. Reis and Gomes, "Quilombo," 27.
4. Anderson, "Quilombo of Palmares."
5. Glenn A. Cheney, *Quilombo dos Palmares: Brazil's Lost Nation of Fugitive Slaves* (Hanover, CT: New London Librarium, 2014).

must have gone into the journey before he made that pivotal passage. First, he would have had to walk at least thirty leagues (anywhere from eighty to ninety miles) to get to the mocambo. He was likely accompanied by fellow Africans who knew the way. R. K. Kent[6] shares a story that in Palmares, "slaves had become less numerous than free commoners." Slaves that had been captured and brought to Palmares could earn their freedom "by going out on raids and returning with a substitute." The Angolas, Africans not born in Palmares, could redeem themselves by stealing another. It is doubtful that Zumbi was a "substitute," since we know of his background. Nevertheless, he had to traverse the forested trails to arrive at Palmares.

It was undoubtedly an exciting as well as a challenging time for Zumbi, who must have held the expectation that he would be reunited with members of his family and that he was embarking on a life that would be far more adventurous and meaningful than the one he left behind. He had no way of knowing that his presence and the application of his education and exposure would make a significant difference in the history and survival of the quilombo.

Zumbi's actions have been repeated throughout the ages: people have gone to foreign lands to study before returning home to apply that knowledge to help their native countries. African Americans, Asians, and Hispanics are doing the same today. When fate has ordained an individual a hero, that person usually self-actuates into the role. Possibility, ego, courage, intellect, education, purpose, and vision all converge to allow the person to seize their moment. That purpose grows within them, further enabling their capabilities. In this case, Zumbi grew into this role as he was captured by it. It was undoubtedly an exciting and challenging time for Zumbi as he embarked on a life that would be far more adventurous and meaningful than the one he left behind. He had no way of knowing that he would make a significant difference in the history and survival of the quilombo.

---

6. R. K. Kent, "Palmares: An African State in Brazil," *Journal of African History* 6, no.2 (1965): 161-175, p. 169.

From its inception in 1605 through 1670, this aborning Black republic successfully repelled its attackers, sustaining itself by the ingenuity of its leaders. Additional assaults followed in 1655 and then in 1660 and 1661. Early in 1669, an army of forces tried to conquer Palmares—unsuccessfully. Palmares was an encampment ready for war.[7] By the time Francisco arrived in 1670, the quilombo had been assaulted numerous times,[8] and the Portuguese initiated an unrelenting systematic campaign to destroy Palmares in 1671. Zumbi had the opportunity to distinguish himself in battle in 1674. Attacks followed in 1676 and 1678, and the most violent period for the quilombo stretched from 1679 to 1692, after Zumbi assumed leadership. The Portuguese were relentless, carrying out almost yearly assaults on Palmares's villages,[9] not including the "'little' *entradas* into Palmares . . . carried out by small private armies of plantation owners who sought to recapture lost [slaves] or to acquire new ones without paying for them."[10]

As mentioned earlier, the Palmaristas engaged in guerrilla warfare and other asymmetrical fighting strategies to defend themselves known as *guerra da floresta,* the "war of the woods." No doubt the Palmaristas learned much of their tactics from their ancestral traditions, as well as from the Indians and other *gente de cor* who resided with them. Disgruntled Whites, many ex-military, would also have contributed their expertise.

Not long after Zumbi gained familiarity with Palmares, he would have begun to help strengthen all the encampments' defenses. Ennes[11] says the following were encountered by the attackers:

> The final defense was very strong, of 2,470 fathoms [one

---

7. Cheney, *Quilombo dos Palmares,* 91-103.
8. Kent, "Palmares."
9. Reis and Gomes, "Quilombo," 27.
10. Kent, "Palmares," 170.
11. Ernesto Ennes, "The Palmares Republic of Pernambuco: Its Final Destruction, 1697," *Americas* 5, no. 2 (October 1948): 200-216, 209.

fathom is equal to six feet], with parapets of two fires at each fathom, complete with flanks, readouts, redans, faces, sentry-boxes . . . and the exterior terrain so full of caltrops and pits full of them at all levels—some at the feet, others at the groin, others at the throat—that it was absolutely impossible for anyone to come close to the said line of defense at all from any angle. . . . And, because the place was so declivous [downward sloping], hardly would a soldier reach the area of the caltrops to remove one of them.

According to Funari and de Carvalho,[12] "the political structure of Palmares . . . emphasized the existence of small settlements with some autonomy and local military leaders." These villages formed the Palmares Republic. There was a central military leader who had excellent decision-making power and influence—either Ganga Zumba, the other kings before him, or Zumbi, his successor and the last king.

After the controversial 1678 agreement that Ganga Zumba negotiated in Recife with the Portuguese (which is discussed later), the ensuing revolt against Ganga Zumba resulted in his murder. Zumbi, a leader in this rebellion, succeeded his uncle and became king. Before ascending to the leadership of Palmares, Zumbi married and had children.

In a capsule, Zumbi gave a good account of himself in battle, of which there were many. In one, Zumbi was wounded in his left leg. In another, he was captured but later escaped. He served as king until the *bandeirantes*, a group of bush fighters from São Paulo supported by an army assembled by the Portuguese, overran the kingdom and destroyed it in 1695. At this point, different versions of how he met his death emerge. His son Camuanga succeeded him in leadership.

---

12. Pedro Paulo A. Funari and Aline Vieira de Carvalho, "Palmares: A Rebel Polity through Archaeological Lenses," in João José Reis and Flávio dos Santos Gomes, eds., *Freedom by a Thread: The History of Quilombos in Brazil* (New York: Diasporic Africa Press, 2016).

It is unknown what happened to Camuanga or the rest of Zumbi's children. Zumbi today is considered a national hero in Brazil. More details will be provided in later chapters.

History will recall that Ganga Zumba was unable to achieve through the 1678 agreement what Price describes the Saamaka maroon community of Suriname as having achieved: a treaty (with the Dutch) that secured the survival of their people. Zumbi also failed, but not without a valiant effort. Zumbi's failure was occasioned by the lack of an offensive military operation beyond subsistence raids. Contrast that approach with the Haitian leader François-Dominique Toussaint Louverture of Haiti, who succeeded in his campaign to oust the French because he had both an offensive and defensive capability.

Still, citing the politician Astrojildo Pereira, Freyre[13] declares:

> For the fact of the matter, the Negroes in Brazil were not so passive. On the contrary, by reason of their more advanced stage of culture, they were able to put up a more effective resistance to exploitation by their white masters than were the Indians.... According to A. Pereira, we did have "an authentic class struggle that filled the centuries of our history and that had its culminating episode of heroism and greatness in the organization of the Republic of Palmares, headed by the epic figure of Zumbi, our Negro Spartacus."

---

13. Gilberto Freyre, *The Masters and the Slaves: A Study in the Development of Brazilian Civilization* (Berkeley: University of California Press, 1986), 250, note 148.

CHAPTER 7

QUILOMBOS IN NORTH AMERICA AND THE GENERAL OF THE SWAMPS

What follows is a brief discussion of how enslaved Africans in the United States sought to establish their maroon communities.

The Negro spiritual "Nobody Knows the Trouble I've Seen" epitomizes the plight of the enslaved African in America, not only during colonial times but through 1865 and beyond.

> Nobody knows the trouble I've seen
> Nobody knows but Jesus
> Nobody knows the trouble I've seen
> Glory hallelujah
> Sometimes I'm up, sometimes
> I'm down, oh, yes, Lord
> Sometimes I'm almost
> To the ground, oh yes, Lord.

The enslaved African in the Western world—especially in North

America, the Caribbean, and South America—faced many cruelties at the hands of the Whites. Surely no one knows the true torment they experienced, both physical and mental, except the god of their being.

Slaves have been running away since slavery began. Petit marronage, as described by Price and more fully researched by Historian Herbert Aptheker,[1] was "an everyday feature of southern plantation life." Escape was the most direct path to freedom but also the most consequential, challenging, and perilous. Some would simply say that running away was a fool's errand. With no way to sustain themselves or their families except through pillage, robbery, benign cooperation from well-meaning Whites, or the clandestine cooperation of like-minded enslaved and sympathetic free Black people, runaway slaves lived a precarious existence.

Often, the fugitive slave was betrayed by their own people; other times, they were betrayed by Indians, who though dissimilar in some respects were not spared the brutality of White supremacy and the harsh avarice of capitalism. The African was surrounded by enemies. Only a few brethren, militantly determined to free themselves at any cost, could be trusted to do what was necessary. In addition, subsistence was limited to self-sustaining agriculture when the length of their tenuous freedom permitted it. At best, whether in Brazil, the Caribbean, or North America, the predicament of the maroon at inception was the same: no resources, limited sustainability, no reinforcement, and little enrichment, except for bartering and periodic trade with nearby towns that accepted the risk.

Historians have determined that the first Africans arrived on North American shores in the summer of 1526, 250 years before the American Revolution and ninety-three years before the first enslaved Africans arrived in Virginia in 1619. They were brought by

---

1. Richard Price, ed., *Maroon Societies: Rebel Slave Communities in the Americas*, 3rd ed. (Baltimore: John Hopkins University Press, 1996); Herbert Aptheker, "Maroons Within the Present Limits of the United States," *Journal of Negro History* 24, no. 2 (1939): 167-184.

Spanish colonizers led by Lucas Vazquez de Ayllon from Haiti, who established a community near the mouth of what is known today as the Pee Dee River near Myrtle Beach, South Carolina, named for the Indian tribe that still occupies some of the surrounding lands.

Price explains, "The settlement consisted of about five hundred Spaniards and one hundred Negro slaves"[2] before Ayllon died from an illness that caused the deaths of many other inhabitants. The Indian tribes became suspicious of the Spaniards' intent, and conflict arose; "in November, several of the slaves rebelled and fled to the Indians. The next month what was left of the adventurers, some one hundred and fifty souls, returned to Haiti, leaving the rebel Negroes with their Indian friends—as the first permanent inhabitants, other than the Indians, in what was to be the United States."[3]

Were Africans enslaved in seventeenth-century North America doing similar things? Were they running away and trying to establish North American versions of the quilombos in nearby swamps and forested areas? Clearly, there was a basis for absconding. The depth of the hostility felt by the slaves toward their owners and overseers extended far beyond what was promoted and written by the Whites during that time.

Slaves in North America rebelled against owners in several ways: they refused to work at times, enacted violence, ran away, vandalized equipment, and staged work slowdowns, not to mention slave rebellions. Over 250 slave rebellions occurred before the end of the Civil War in 1865. Some notable uprisings include the New York Slave Revolt in 1712; the Stono Rebellion in 1739 near Charleston, South Carolina; the *Hope* slave ship revolt in 1764; the German Coast uprising in Mississippi in 1811; Nat Turner's Rebellion of 1831; and the *Amistad* slave ship revolt of 1839.

Let's turn to the question of why some slaves ran away. First and obviously, though they could do nothing about the overall predicament

---

2. Price, *Maroon Societies*, 149.
3. Aptheker.

of their people, they did not want to be enslaved and vehemently resented it. Second, they were aggrieved on many occasions by numerous cruelties and inhumanities, "some [fleeing] to protect themselves from the unwanted advances of white men."[4] Third, they resented the care they received: inadequate food, clothing, and shelter. And fourth, they resented the work they were required to perform and the methods of operation, such as working from sunup to sundown, six days a week, yet being characterized as lazy and shiftless and with no "get up" or initiative of their own. Franklin and Schweninger additionally cite housing and the selling of family and relatives, and they say that such a list fails to address the "complexities of the human experience" that formed the life of the slave.

The enslaved Africans in North America, like those in Brazil, were ingenious, crafty, and keenly aware of their location relative to border states, free territories, and Mexico and Canada. Franklin and Schweninger go on to say,

> Slaves who live in close proximity to free territory—near the Pennsylvania line along the Ohio River and the west or near the Indian nations on the border with Florida, or in southern Texas—frequently tempted fate by striking out for freedom.... [T]he Mexican border was not far away, and there were "always Mexicans who are ready and willing to help the slaves.... Such slaves always succeeded in escaping.[5]

Professor of history Ronnie C. Tyler notes, "Mexico, in fact, sheltered thousands of Negro fugitives by 1851."[6] The Mexican government even allowed them to occupy some of its frontier territory, and Indians as well. Moreover, Mexico had a steadfast

---

4. Franklin and Schweninger, *Runaway Slaves*.
5. Franklin and Schweninger, 26.
6. Ronnie C. Tyler, "Fugitive Slaves in Mexico," *Journal of Negro History* 57, no. 1 (1972): 1-12.

policy of resistance to the recapture of fleeing slaves. Tyler[7] writes, "No foreign government would be allowed to touch a slave who had sought refuge in Mexico."

One might ask, How would the slaves know about these avenues of escape? How would they know to flee to Mexico? The answer is simple: they listened carefully to the Whites, absorbed information like sponges, talked among themselves, engaged in logical reasoning, sought information from any sources attainable, and a few could read and write.

Aptheker estimates that over fifty maroon communities existed in various locations in the United States between 1672 and 1864. Franklin and Schweninger[8] agree with other sources that these communities lived in the swampy, forested, and mountainous areas of South Carolina, North Carolina, Virginia, Louisiana, Florida, Georgia, Mississippi, and Alabama.

As in Brazil, many inhabitants of these fugitive settlements sought to make a home for themselves where none existed. They raised cattle, grew and harvested crops, built houses, and traded with the Whites in nearby communities as well as raiding nearby plantations for food (and to liberate slaves). A sometimes parasitic, sometimes symbiotic relationship developed between the maroons and neighboring communities. If the maroons were not considered a threat to the safety of White inhabitants, they were tolerated.

The most prominent of these maroon encampments were located in the Great Dismal Swamp between the southeastern coastal plain of Virginia and the northeastern region of North Carolina. Aptheker[9] estimates that over 2,000 Negroes populated communities here. Franklin and Schweninger[10] report that it was a refuge for Black slaves who sought safety, liberty, and relief from

---

7. Tyler, "Fugitive Slaves."
8. Franklin and Schweninger, *Runaway Slaves*; Aptheker, "Maroons."
9. Aptheker, "Maroons."
10. Aptheker, 27; Franklin and Schweninger, *Runaway Slaves*, 86.

the unbridled cruelties exacted upon them. Whole families lived in the Dismal Swamp, some of whom had never seen a White person.

The most credible information about maroons in North America indicates that these settlements mostly appeared in the eighteenth and nineteenth centuries along the Middle Atlantic region, the Southeast, and in Georgia and Florida.

> If proximity to free territory prompted slaves to run away, so, too, did living in areas where runaways congregated. While the number of such locations declined as Southerners moved to the west, cleared new lands during the 1820s and 1830s, or sent militia units into areas to destroy "outlaw" camps, runaways continued to congregate deep in the woods or swamps. These included remote areas of the backcountry such as the Great Dismal Swamp; Elliott's Cut, between the Ashpoo and Pon Pon Rivers; Goose Creek; St. James Parish; South Carolina; and the Florida Everglades. To the west were the Indian nations in Alabama and Mississippi at least until the late 1830s, and swampy areas and forest of the lower Mississippi River Valley in Louisiana. Slave owners and residents of King William County, Virginia, noted in 1843, there were sections of their county used as "the general resort of free Negroes from all parts of the country" and a harbor for runaway slaves.[11]

In these areas, free women of color exerted a great deal of influence and stubbornly refused to be deported to West Africa, where Whites wished to send free Blacks. They not only were willing to harbor runaways but, by rejecting emigration, also assisted slaves by maintaining stable free Black communities where runaways could find refuge.[12]

Historians make the point that in many instances, the slaves in

---

11. Franklin and Schweninger, 27–28.
12. Franklin and Schweninger, 110.

North America were unable to establish long-term settlements or communities like the Afro-Brazilian quilombos—though not for lack of trying. They often failed to sustain themselves due to harsh wilderness conditions and their lack of supplies. Additionally, because slave owners suffered economic losses when slaves ran away or absconded even for short periods, they hunted runaways relentlessly and passed fugitive slave laws to make it a crime to harbor runaway slaves. Even if those slaves successfully made it into free territory, there was no guarantee they wouldn't be shipped back off.

It has been postulated that the geographical and topographical characteristics of Brazil, with so much frontier land available, made it easier for African slaves in Brazil to hide—not to mention the technology of the colonial slave bureaucracy in Brazil, which lagged far behind its North American counterpart. Conversely, in America, not as much uncleared frontier existed along the slaveholding coastal regions of the South. During the eighteenth and nineteenth centuries, technological and industrial innovations, albeit primitive, enabled greater efficiency in hunting slaves.

During the seventeenth century, some notable events occurred in the swamps and mountainous areas of the Middle Atlantic and Southeast of the United States. Between 1672 and 1691, maroons in Virginia established themselves sufficiently to draw notice. Aptheker[13] mentions a notable slave named Mingoe from Middlesex County, Virginia. Mingoe and his followers stole cattle and hogs and obtained firearms for protection. Their base of operations was somewhere in the Dismal Swamp. Aptheker also mentions a slave named Sebastian, who was "tracked down and killed by an Indian hunter" in June 1711. The fugitive slaves led by Sebastian, based in the mountains, allegedly provoked great fear in the inhabitants surrounding the colony of South Carolina.

Much is made of the fact that these maroons committed the crimes of robbery and theft, but what they stole were the necessities

---

13. Aptheker, "Maroons."

of life—typically food for themselves and their children. Having absconded with nothing but the clothes on their backs in most cases, they did what they needed to do to survive. This activity played into the hands of the slave bureaucracy because committing crimes, however justified by circumstances, made them outlaws and subject to the maximum penalty for violations of the law.

It is also worth noting that in June and July 1795, several runaway slaves fled to the swamps and the woods surrounding the city of Wilmington, North Carolina. The leader of this band, whose name is unknown, was branded the "General of the Swamps" and a "swamp fox."[14] His cunning and guile enabled him and his fellow maroons to lead a life of Robin Hood–style banditry. They were at times referred to as "a nest of miscreants" and were known to have killed "at least one white man, an overseer, and severely wounded another."[15] In August 1822, a reward of $200 was posted for the capture of another band of maroons numbering about twenty, located around Jacksonboro, South Carolina. It was thought at the time that these Negroes were part of the Denmark Vesey rebellion. Fighting for survival and their lives, maroons also allied with Indians who supported their cause. Many maroons were "good soldiers."

Whites in the early nineteenth century demonized runaways, describing them as outliers, "lurking assassins," "desperados," thieves, and killers, all to rationalize the killing, maiming, or other severe punishments exacted upon them. I find the punishments described by Franklin and Schweninger[16] unbearable to read. I was taken aback by the brutality and the hatred manifested in the capricious imposition of malicious and severe injury—the taking of a limb or life from defenseless people undeserving of their predicament. These maroons were only looking to survive on their journey to free territory or otherwise elude the grasp of their relentless pursuers.

---

14. Aptheker, 154.
15. Aptheker, 158.
16. Franklin and Schweninger, *Runaway Slaves*.

A maroon named Isam, also known as "General Jackson," died from a public flogging administered at Cape Fear, North Carolina, a place where I have spent a considerable amount of time. General Jackson is reputed to have been a maroon leader in Onslow, Carteret, and Bladen Counties in North Carolina. The authorities mustered a militia of some 300 men, who hunted the maroons down for twenty-five days before dispersing the band, apprehending many, and destroying their camps.

Aptheker[17] also mentions a community of maroons classified as outlaws near Mobile, Alabama, consisting of men, women, and children. Apparently, they persisted for several years by "plundering neighboring plantations." These maroons were in the process of building a stockade fort before they were attacked and disbanded. The slaveholders who led the attack noted that "the maroons made a desperate resistance, fighting like Spartans." Some were wounded and killed, while others escaped. Aptheker discusses another maroon colony, of some 100 men, women, and children in Surry County, Virginia, who were sought by three armed Whites, all of whom lost their lives in pursuit.

In another instance, a slave named Squire who roamed the backlands of New Orleans, Louisiana, starting around 1834, had a career that lasted three years and was considered an outlaw, having reportedly killed several White men. When he was killed in 1837, "a guard of soldiers was sent to the swamp for his body, which was exhibited for several days in the public square of the city."[18]

The counties of Sampson, Bladen, Onslow, Jones, New Hanover, and Dublin in North Carolina, as well as areas near New Bern and Elizabeth City, formed a region rife with runaways and maroons. The threat was such that the Whites there solicited military aid to eradicate the threat. Aptheker quotes a newspaper article from 1831 that reads, "There has been much shooting of Negroes in this neighborhood recently, in consequence of 'symptoms of liberty'

---

17. Aptheker, "Maroons."
18. Aptheker, 161.

having been discovered among them."[19]

"The symptoms of liberty" were caused by the disease of slavery. One wonders whether the purveyors of this language ever considered why the symptoms became manifest. On my frequent travels through southeastern North Carolina, I often pass road signs designating exits to the above-mentioned counties. I live not far from some of them. But before embarking on this research, I had no idea that my African ancestors sought refuge in these swamps and forests so close to home.

A contemporaneous Richmond newspaper openly pondered whether the runaway slaves and maroons gathered somewhere between New Bern and Wilmington were part of Nat Turner's Rebellion of August 1831. Paranoia was high among the nearby slave plantations and farms. Some slave owners, out of a sense of exasperation, exclaimed that "[slaves] go and come and when and where they please, and if an attempt is made to correct them, they immediately fly to the woods and there continue for months and years committing grievous depredations on our cattle, hogs and sheep."[20]

The language used by newspapers and reporters[21] at that time to describe the acts of maroons included such terms and phrases as "depredations," "a numerous collection of outcast mulattos, mustees and free Negroes," "blot out the menace," "a few deluded followers," "the murdering aim of these monsters in human shape," "vicious slaves," and "Negro fighters." The latter were "the most formidable foe, more bloodthirsty, active, and revengeful, than the Indian." Reports declared, "There are several runaways of bad and daring character—destructive of all kinds of Stock and dangerous to all persons living by or near said swamp." This phrasing was intended to whip up a groundswell of hysteria and portray the runaway slaves as evil and worthy of contempt.

The enumerated personalities and incidents reflect only a few of the assorted maroon communities and runaway slave camps that existed

---

19. Aptheker.
20. Aptheker, 160
21. As detailed in Aptheker, 153; Franklin and Schweninger, *Runaway Slaves*.

throughout the slave states of the South and along the coast. Aptheker's notes on some 300 former Florida maroons who left their homes in Oklahoma to flee to Mexico also bear mentioning. Citing Joshua R. Giddings from 1858, Aptheker says that "some 1,500 former American slaves aided the Comanche Indians of Mexico in their fighting. Five hundred of these Negroes were from Texas."[22] The slaveholders of Texas unsuccessfully sought to recover these slaves. Tyler[23] tells us that they were thwarted not only by the Mexican government but also by tribes of Indians who aided the slaves in their defense.

Aptheker's concluding thoughts can be summarized as follows: the often recited notion that Africans and African American slaves were somehow docile and compliant in their servitude is fallacious. The evidence is overwhelmingly to the contrary. Slaves during the eighteenth and nineteenth centuries rebelled with great zeal, ever mindful of their unwinnable position. They sought, using the limited means at their disposal, to free themselves from the tyranny of White slave owners. Though they were often unsuccessful, they continued to flee, causing much chagrin, aggravation, cost, and dislocation to the slave system—perhaps, unbeknownst to them, hastening the end of this system.

• • •

COMPARING NORTH AND SOUTH AMERICAN FUGITIVE-SLAVE COMMUNITIES

Before leaving this subject, I want to share additional observations from Franklin and Schweninger[24] regarding runaway slaves. There were many similarities between American runaway slaves and Brazilian slaves who "hid out in the woods" for months, sometimes years. Certainly, the immediate objectives were the same: to shed the shackles of a brutal

---

22. Aptheker 161.
23. Tyler, "Fugitive Slaves."
24. Franklin and Schweninger, *Runaway Slaves*.

and onerous system and establish an alternative society. These were major accomplishments regardless of their longevity.

There were also many parallels between the behavior of maroons in Brazil and North America regarding times of war and upheaval. As Weik[25] describes, "the disorder caused by European rivalries probably facilitated escape for many enslaved people." During the War of Independence in North America, slaves sought refuge under the British flag, which promised them safety and freedom in Canada.[26] Like their fellow bondsmen in Brazil, the maroons in North America were informed about national, regional, and local conflicts that existed between the slaveholding community and outside political powers, such as those between European rivals in North America in the eighteenth and nineteenth centuries.

The maroons in Brazil likewise took advantage of the Cisplatine War—the war for the independence of Uruguay—and the Inconfidência Mineira conflict for Brazilian independence to advance their goal of freedom. Slaves in Brazil also used the chaos of wars against various Indigenous tribes, including against the Aimoré and Tupinambá, to escape and form maroon communities. So, the political savvy of the maroons on both continents is not to be understated or underestimated. Both groups were aware of European conflicts, potential allies, Indigenous peoples' revolts, and the imperial aspirations of their host countries. They chose to flee wherever cracks developed. Any break in the wall was an avenue to freedom. Furthermore, the maroons took advantage of these conflicts to enhance their status and to strike treaties and agreements with the enslaving powers. Neither the slaves nor the Indians took their enslavement without resistance.

Franklin and Schweninger[27] write:

---

25. Terry Weik, "The Archaeology of Maroon Societies in the Americas: Resistance, Cultural Continuity, and Transformation in the African Diaspora," *Historical Archaeology* 31, no. 2 (1997): 81-92.
26. Michael A. Gomez, *Reversing Sail: A History of the African Diaspora, New Approaches to African History* (New York: Cambridge University Press, 2005).
27. Franklin and Schweninger, *Runaway Slaves*, 87.

In a fourteen-page memorial to the Territorial Governor William P. Duval, the new Legislative Council warned of the "existing evils" following the acquisition of [Central Florida] from Spain of "great numbers of Negroes belonging to the planters, availing themselves of existing disorders" and running away only to take "refuge among the Indians." They were beyond the reach of their owners, and some of them were escaping to the island of Cuba, "from whence in all probability they will never be recovered."

Not surprisingly, as in Brazil, many escaped slaves allied themselves with Indians for their own protection and to aid the Indians in their fight against the Whites. Franklin and Schweninger offer several contemporaneous quotes to that effect:

"I have ascertained beyond any doubt, not only that a connection exists between a portion of the slave population and the Seminoles," an Army officer wrote in 1837, "but that there was an understanding that a considerable force should join on the first blow being struck." . . .

In 1836, residents along the Chattahoochee River in Alabama feared that a band of hostile Creek Indians were "collecting all the force they can among themselves, and from the negroes," to attack people in Georgia. In the same year . . . Major General William Irwin wrote Governor Clement C. Clay of Alabama. "I cannot withhold from your Excellency that my fears on account of the Negroes—there are large bodies of them in this place and neighborhood who have had uninterrupted intercourse with the Indians for a great length of time and may have matured some plan of cooperation.

Franklin and Schweninger confirm the general's fears:

A group of fifty or sixty white families complained that sections along the Cuba Hatchee River were "remarkable for the extent and impervious nature of their swamps and the morasses," and were excellent hideouts for groups of Indians and camps of "armed Negroes."[28] . . .

Despite such activities [establishing runaway slave hideouts], however, it was extremely difficult for gangs of runaways to sustain themselves over long periods of time. Their dilemma was how to steal from farmers and planters without evoking a response from local militia or patrols. The more they pillaged, the more likely they were to arouse groups of white men to search out their encampments. Those who did sustain themselves for any length of time hid out in densely forested, swampy areas that were virtually inaccessible to anyone unfamiliar with the terrain. Even whites who knew these areas feared entering them. Even when few in number, gangs of outliers struck fear in the hearts of white inhabitants.[29]

Contrast the timeworn problem of intermediate and long-term sustainability for the maroons in North America to the quilombos of Brazil, where runaway slaves hid and established villages and encampments for years at a time, although most were destroyed within two years of their establishment. The durability of the quilombolas enabled them to intermingle with the Indigenous population, sell goods to free Blacks in local markets, trade with the local farmers and planters, and raise crops. However, Sundiata Keita Cha-Jua[30] does mention "that in Illinois the maroons gained the chance to determine their own destiny." Just as the Palmaristas did.

---

28. Franklin and Schweninger, 88.
29. Franklin and Schweninger, 89.
30. Sundiata Keita Cha-Jua, *America's First Black Town: Brooklyn, Illinois, 1830-1915* (Chicago: University of Illinois Press, 2002), 5.

CHAPTER 8

THE ADVENT OF BLACK TOWNS IN NORTH AMERICA

Maroon societies and organized Black communities, the main manifestations of territorial nationalism during the antebellum era, have proven almost impossible to reconstruct using traditional historical sources and methods. Hence the academic fracas about the significance of Palmares. Nonetheless, historians[1] have described maroon societies that were precursors to Black towns and settlements, such as Culpeper Island, North Carolina, which had hundreds of maroons; Indian Woods in North Carolina; Pilaklakaha, which had from five to as many as one hundred inhabitants at any given time; and Fort Mose in Florida. There was also the establishment of Black Seminole sites such as "Abraham's old town," which lasted several decades in Florida's central swamps.[2]

Sundiata Keita Cha-Jua[3] explores this subject and observes:

---

1. Franklin and Schweninger, *Runaway Slaves*; Weik, "Archaeology of Maroon Societies"; Arwin D. Smallwood, "A History of Native American and African Relations from 1502 to 1900," *Negro History Bulletin* 62, no. 2/3 (1999): 18-31.
2. Weik, "Archaeology of Maroon Societies."
3. Sundiata Keita Cha-Jua, *America's First Black Town: Brooklyn, Illinois, 1830-1915* (Chicago: University of Illinois Press, 2002), 5.

> The historical significance of Brooklyn, Illinois, lies mainly in its being the oldest Black town in the United States. Nonetheless, outside the St. Louis metropolitan area, Brooklyn is largely unknown. Very few Americans, Black or White, have heard of it.... Many more African Americans know this town by its popular name, Lovejoy, than by its official designation.... Few Black towns have become part of the nation's consciousness. Mound Bayou, Mississippi, and Nicodemus, Kansas, are better known in Black America.... This is amazing considering that African Americans have built Black towns in every period of their existence in the United States.

The urgency was unrelenting to reestablish African culture, or better yet, to forge an African American culture:

> Black town construction was a component of a more comprehensive nationalist element in African American ideology and praxis. The creation of maroon societies and the establishment of freedom villages and organized Black communities on free soil were the initial expressions of the territorial nationalist undercurrent. This wave of Black nationalism crested during what the historian Rayford Logan termed "the nadir," 1890–1915, a time of extraordinary physical and political repression. During this era, African Americans built more than sixty Black towns.[4]

On the subject of Brooklyn, Illinois, Cha-Jua[5] makes the following additional points:

> [The founding group of families were] far above the average

---

4. Cha-Jua, *America's First Black Town*, 5.
5. Cha-Jua, 5, 32, 45.

of their race in intelligence and manhood.... By establishing a home on free soil, some sought to free themselves from slavery's exploitation and oppressive grip, while others sought the opportunity to capitalize on their intelligence and hard work. In Illinois, the maroons gained the chance to determine their own destiny. They squatted near the river, in the American bottoms, the most fertile section of the county. This area had an abundance of natural wealth: fertile soil, timber, wildlife, and fish. Part of America's racial paradox is the contrast between a beautiful and inviting landscape and an ugly and hostile social geography.... The beginnings of Brooklyn represented something new in the African American experience. The colony of fugitive and free Blacks who escaped slavery on the Missouri side of the Mississippi River transcended the contemporary expression of territorial nationalism-maroon settlements, freedom villages, and organized Black communities—by starting the first Black town.

I argue that the spirit of Palmares left an indelible imprint on the Black diaspora, instilling the indomitable will to resist and be independent and self-sufficient. Palmares, among its other legacies, was thus the precursor of Black towns such as Fort Mose and Rosewood in Florida; Greenwood in Tulsa, Oklahoma; Seneca Village, Weeksville, and Five Points District in New York; Allensworth in California; Freedmen's Town in Texas; Davis Bend in Mississippi; the Iowa Black towns of Muchakinock and Buxton; Black towns in Illinois such as New Philadelphia and Pin Oak Colony; Blackdom in New Mexico; and Freedman's Village in Virginia—not to mention enclaves of African-descended people in districts and cities that were massacred, such as in Atlanta in 1906; Wilmington, North Carolina, in 1898; Colfax, Louisiana, in 1873; the Springfield, Illinois, massacre in 1908; the Elaine massacre in Arkansas in 1919; and the East St. Louis, Illinois, massacre of 1917—just to mention a few.

Many of these Black settlements shared a fate of destruction, dissolution by White people, or the natural evolution of society that resulted in their transformation. White people felt threatened or endangered by Black independence, economic sufficiency, and cultural preservation. This common thread binds these towns and districts to Palmares and the Brazilian quilombos.

Beginning in 1672—twenty years before the end of Palmares—North American African maroons started to establish their redoubts.[6] A century and a half later, in 1791, the Haitian Revolution took place, and in 1861, less than 100 years later, the Civil War began in the United States of America. Why did it take the repeated occurrence of these events—disjointed as they may seem, spread over centuries yet woven in a tapestry of struggle—to reach the holy grail of freedom from bondage? Because the oppressor in each case was of the same vintage, and the colonizer's vehemence to maintain that oppression was and remains relentless.

One ponders how the messages, the animating principle, and the soul essence of a people can be communicated to descendants spread across centuries and thousands of miles. This energizing force must be an innate characteristic of a people related by genealogy, spirit, and circumstance. The extent to which the maroon communities in North America and Brazil differed in longevity and independence might be traced in part to how closely the populations identified with this heritage.

Weik,[7] citing other historians, reiterates that "Latin American maroons were more likely to exhibit African cultural continuities than North American maroons, based on larger population ratios of Africans to Europeans in the Caribbean and Latin America and plantation systems." Weik further hypothesizes,

---

6. Herbert Aptheker, "Maroons Within the Present Limits of the United States," *Journal of Negro History* 24, no. 2 (1939): 167-184.
7. Terry Weik, "The Archaeology of Maroon Societies in the Americas: Resistance, Cultural Continuity, and Transformation in the African Diaspora," *Historical Archaeology* 31, no. 2 (1997): 81-92.

Marronage in the sixteenth and seventeenth century was more "restorationist" in character—Maroons attempted to recreate African institutions—compared to eighteenth and nineteenth century types of *marronage* which were more "assimilationist" in nature, i.e., religion. That is, Maroons were more likely to be creolized or assimilated into the slave society surrounding them in the last centuries of slavery than in the former.

This point is made more clearly by historians Robert Fogel and Stanley Engerman,[8] who observe:

> Blacks in the US colonies were typically a minority of the population and lived on small units which brought them into continuous contact with their white masters. US slaves were not only in closer contact with European culture, they were also more removed from their African origins than were slaves in the Caribbean.... [N]ative-born blacks made up the majority of the slave population in the US colonies as early as 1680. By the end of the American revolution, the African-born component of the black population had shrunk to 20 percent.... By 1860 all but one percent of US slaves were native-born, and most of them were second, third, fourth, or fifth generation Americans. These Americans not only had no personal experience with Africa but were generally cut off from contact with persons who had such direct experience. To a considerable extent, the word that reached them about the African origins was filtered through minds and emotions of parents, grandparents, and great-grandparents who had always walked on the North American continent. This is not to deny the contribution of an African heritage in shaping the culture of blacks, but rather to stress

---

8. Robert William Fogel and Stanley L. Engerman, *Time on the Cross: The Economics of American Negro Slavery* (Boston: Little, Brown and Company, 1974), 22-24.

the extent to which black culture had, by 1860, been exposed to indigenous American influences.

People subjected daily to an environment, no matter how heinous, consciously and subconsciously incorporate elements of it into their daily lives—such as in the use of the word "nigger" and other derogatory terms. Hence, the incorporation of negative pathologies into the inchoate culture of African Americans. W. E. B. Du Bois opines on this phenomenon in his study *The Philadelphia Negro*. People get used to a good thing just like they get used to a bad thing, and it is hard to wean oneself of either, especially when ignorant of one's history.

Clearly, the maroons in the seventeenth century in Brazil had a closer nexus to Africa, in time and space, and carried with them a stronger natural anti-assimilationist resistance to their enslavement. The Africans enslaved in North America, on the other hand, had a more attenuated relationship with Africa and incorporated, over generations, many negative as well as positive aspects of the Anglo-American culture they were steeped in.

CHAPTER 9

INDIANS AND MAROONS: AN ALLIANCE OF CONVENIENCE

Stewart B. Schwartz[1] quotes colonist Duarte Gomes de Silveira, from Paraiba, about 161 miles north of Pernambuco, as having written the following in 1633:

> There is no doubt that without Indians in Brazil there can be no Negroes of Guinea, or better said, there can be no Brazil, for without them nothing can be done and they are 10 times more numerous than the whites; and if today it is costly to dominate them with the Indians whom they greatly fear . . . what will happen without the Indians? The next day they will revolt and it is a great risk to resist domestic enemies.

This quote sums up the importance of Indians in the scheme of control exercised by the colonial slave bureaucracy in Brazil.

There were more than 2,000 Indigenous tribes in Brazil prior to colonization in the 1500s. According to Weik, "the Brazilian

---

1. Stuart B. Schwartz, "Rethinking Palmares: Slave Resistance in Colonial Brazil," in *Critical Readings on Global Slavery*, eds. Damian Alan Pargas and Felicia Roşu (Leiden, Netherlands: Brill, 2005): 1294-1325, p. 1304.

Amerindians such as the *Aimoré* and the *Cabixes* both allied themselves with the quilombos,"² as did others.

It should come as no surprise to keen observers or students of history that the goal of the Portuguese and the Dutch in Brazil was to pacify the Indigenous population as much as it was to enslave the Africans taken from Kongo. Some notable Indian tribes associated with quilombos were the Botocudos, Kayapó, Xavante, Krahô, Canoeiro, Tupi, Apinajé, Karajá, Bororo, Akroá, and the Cariris/Kiriri.

To acquire the labor required to plant, grow, harvest, and export sugar, the Portuguese first used the Amerindians. These Indians were called *gentio da terra*, or gentiles—meaning non-Jews—of the land. It is noteworthy that during this time, Portugal was Catholic. But the Portuguese used terminology that defined non-Jews as non-Christians, which, in fact, they were.

For the most part, the use of Indians sufficed for the purpose of clearing the land in the early years. But as time passed, the Portuguese grew to see the Indians as insufficiently eager to work, and their productivity was less than encouraging. Essentially, the Portuguese viewed the Indians as heathens in need of civilizing and Christianizing, which were one and the same.

The pacification process involved either persuasion or destruction. The Indians' receptivity to the colonializing process, slavery, and Christian indoctrination were the operative denominators. If they rejected any of these practices, the Indian was doomed.

To Christianize the Indians, the Portuguese brought in missionaries, the Jesuits. The Society of Jesus, a religious order of the Catholic Church, was established in 1540 with the pope's blessing. The Jesuits arrived in Brazil in 1549. It was their job to turn the Indians into an army of capitalist workers—all to make money for the Portuguese

---

2. Terry Weik, "The Archaeology of Maroon Societies in the Americas: Resistance, Cultural Continuity, and Transformation in the African Diaspora," *Historical Archaeology* 31, no. 2 (1997): 81-92.

by working their farms and sugar plantations.³ The Jesuits would be instrumental in achieving the same goal with Africans.

The fates of the Indigenous and Africans were again interwoven in the struggle for freedom. History professor and scholar Bruce Dain,[4] in his review of Matthew Restall's *Beyond Black and Red*, emphasizes Restall's point that "debunks the hallowed idea of an unremitting hostility between Indians and Africans in colonial Latin America. The idea becomes largely a myth promoted by colonial administrators and other Europeans intent on a strategy of divide-and-conquer." It was essential to Palmares's survival for Ganga Zumba and later Zumbi to establish and maintain relations with the Indians who lived nearby, no less important than trading with the settler Whites. Any leader worth his salt would enlist the aid of the Indians when possible.

That is not to say that differences between the populations did not exist or that conflicts or hostilities did not arise, but self-interest and self-preservation influenced the politics and strategies for coexistence and forced them to seek ways of accommodation for their mutual survival. Permanent interests rather than friendship were the controlling element. Restall asserts that "racial formalism" (i.e., scientific racism based upon biology) was of no real concern to the Indians or Africans, much to the chagrin of the Europeans, for whom such a rejection undermined the process of White domination as they envisioned it.

However, despite the Indians and former slaves coming together to form a bulwark against Eurocentrism, Freyre,[5] pulling from the work of Edgar Roquette Pinto (the noted Brazilian writer, ethnologist,

---

3. Glenn A. Cheney, *Quilombo dos Palmares: Brazil's Lost Nation of Fugitive Slaves* (Hanover, CT: New London Librarium, 2014), 14.
4. Bruce Dain, "Beyond Black and Red: African Native Relations in Colonial America, and: To Intermix with Out White Brothers: Indian Mixed Bloods in the United States from Earliest Times to the Indian Removals (review)," *Journal of the Early Republic* 27, no. 1 (2007): 180-184.
5. Gilberto Freyre, *The Masters and the Slaves: A Study in the Development of Brazilian Civilization* (Berkeley: University of California Press, 1986), 285.

and anthropologist), writes that the Indians of central Brazil were Europeanized through the effect of the "Negro *quilombos*":

> Runaway slaves had spread among the Indians a knowledge of the Portuguese language and the Catholic religion before any white missionary had done so. Having set up their quilombos in the highland where the Parecí Indians dwelt, the fugitive Negroes had interbred with women whom they had taken from the Indians. A *bandeira* that was sent out to disperse them, in the eighteenth century, found these former slaves ruling over the *cafuzo* populations in their quilombos. They found large plantations, poultry-raising, cotton under cultivation, and the manufacture of heavy cloth. And the *bandeirantes* further discovered that the Negro-Indian mestizos of mature age "knew something of Christian doctrine which they had learned from the Negroes . . . they all spoke Portuguese with the same skill as the black who had taught them."

The Indians and Africans were not quite equal in the eyes of the colonizer, despite their similar circumstances. According to author Laura de Mello e Souza, "under the Ancien Regime . . . the indigenous population were people, equal to the white man; they could not be enslaved. Yet once they proved bellicose and resistant to conversion to Christianity, they lost their human status, joining the ranks of animals, untamed beasts liable to the law of irons and guns."[6] Essentially, resistance to Christianity was what made these two populations irredeemable in the minds of the Portuguese.

North American colonists took a similar approach and quickly ran into a paradox that afflicted the institution of slavery in all purportedly Christian nations:

---

6. Laura de Mello e Souza, "Violence in Frontier Lands," in João José Reis and Flávio dos Santos Gomes, eds., *Freedom by a Thread: The History of Quilombos in Brazil* (New York: Diasporic Africa Press, 2016).

> Conversion to Christianity shielded many of the first Africans because Christians were forbidden from enslaving a fellow or sister Christian. However, as greed and avarice overtook religion, that protection came into question.... To ensure perpetual labor, the act of baptism could not preclude Africans from slavery. Africans were baptized as a pretense of Christianity.[7]

◆ ◆ ◆

FRIENDS OR ENEMIES?

Smallwood[8] relates an example of Indian and African integration in a small rural community in northeastern North Carolina known as Indian Woods: a community of African, Indian, and European mixtures who have lived together for over 400 years. These "mixed-blooded people" could pass for either Indian or White, and those who could not pass became part of the African American community.

Smallwood also explains that many African slaves were taken in by friendly and cooperative Native Americans who intermarried and absorbed them culturally, forged alliances, and accepted the slaves as members of their nations. Some Africans were used as slaves in Indian nations, and some Africans and their descendants rose to become warriors, chiefs, and great shamans. The enslavement of Africans by Native Americans was obviously vastly different from the slavery practiced by Europeans.

Another example of African and Indian integration was found in Brazil with the Indigenous people known as the Santidade, a branch of the Tupinambá Indians. They rejected Christianity and refused to accept slavery. In fact, it is reported that these natives devoured the Portuguese as well as the *mamelucos* (first-generation children of a European and Amerindian who served as slave catchers)

---

7. Gloria J. Browne-Marshall, "1619 to 1819: Tell Them We Fought Back, A Socio-Legal Perspective," *Phylon* 57, no. 1 (2020): 37-55, p. 57.
8. Smallwood, "A History," 18.

in cannibalistic fashion in an attempt to replace, spiritually, the members of their tribe lost to the Portuguese through enslavement or war. These were a courageous group of Amerindians, and the Africans gladly joined the Santidade "in ceremonies and wars that were markedly anti-colonialist," not to mention anti-Christian. After all, many of the Africans brought to Brazil from Angola were Muslim.

Vainfas elaborates,

> The *santidade* of Bahia was quite rebellious . . . setting fire to the sugar mills and Jesuit villages, and promising to its adepts legal freedom in a "land bereft of evil," a *Tupi* paradise, as well as the future death and enslavement of the Portuguese by the very indigenous people they had attempted to colonize.[9]

While many Africans joined Indian communities, Indians also joined quilombos, "ethnically mixing themselves and living with them. . . . In some cases, if both indigenous peoples and *caboclos* [people of mixed Indigenous and European heritage] were taken into account, 'Indians' even reached leadership and majority in the quilombos."[10] The colonial authorities "complained about the great number of indigenous people who had fled their [villages] and formed quilombos."[11] As mentioned previously, the Indigenous people often became allies of fugitive slaves, giving them techniques to survive the forest, the *cerrado*, and the wetland.

Meanwhile, Price[12] describes relationships between the Indians and Africans as "reluctant neighbors." He writes,

> In a number of cases, groups of Indians and maroons "fused," both culturally and genetically, but their relative positions

---

9. Vainfas, "God Against Palmares," 51-71.
10. Reis and Gomes, Introduction to *Freedom by a Thread*, 13.
11. Karasch, "Quilombos of Gold," 186.
12. Richard Price, ed., *Maroon Societies: Rebel Slave Communities in the Americas*, 3rd ed. (Baltimore: John Hopkins University Press, 1996), 15-16.

varied. . . . And throughout Brazil, groups of maroons and Indians merged in a wide variety of political and cultural arrangements. . . . Hostile relations were common, often encouraged by the local whites. . . . It was probably the mere presence of hostile Indians in large numbers that prevented the establishment of viable maroon communities, and, as mentioned earlier, Indians were commonly employed by the whites both to hunt down individual runaways and to serve as troops in major battles against maroon communities.

In Brazil, the slaves had to fight off Indians, *bandeira*, bush men from São Paulo, *mameluco* expeditions sent to destroy them, slave catchers, and relentless attacks from colonial authorities. They could not win; they had too many enemies.

Fighting for existence was a way of life for these communities. This continuous state of warfare "strongly influenced many aspects of their political and social organization." The Tupi insurrection in Jaguaribe in the sixteenth century was perhaps the most significant Indigenous insurrection and served as the Indigenous precursor to Palmares. According to Vainfas, "it was mainly constituted by indigenous people, particularly from the Tupinambid ethnic group, some of which were Christians, others pagans." Black people "were attracted by the 'promise of freedom' announced during the rebellious indigenous ritual."[13] Male and female "blacks from Guinea" (as slaves from Africa were called then) participated in "the great indigenous insurrection of sixteenth century Brazil."

In 1608, a colonial governor proposed the radical idea of substituting Indigenous people for the Black slaves. It was his thinking that the "blacks were always rebelling and that no one could defeat them. They may grow in a manner that in order to defeat them,

---

13. Ronaldo Vainfas, "God Against Palmares: Lordly Representations and Jesuitical Ideas," in Reis and Gomes, *Freedom by a Thread*.

we will have to pay a high price."[14] But just as there were runaway African slaves, there were also runaway natives. Every population that was enslaved, subjugated, or bastardized by the Europeans was running away, marooning, or fighting.

Smallwood[15] asserts the precedent of Indian enslavement in North America when he mentions that "slavery had been practiced by the English in Virginia as early as 1610":

> After raiding the Spanish Caribbean with the help of African and Indian maroons and slaves in 1586, thirty-two years before the purchase of 19 Africans from the Dutch in Jamestown, Virginia, Sir Francis Drake rewarded more than 300 of the victors with their freedom. . . . Many of these early slaves were Native Americans, mostly Algonquins of coastal Virginia and North Carolina. . . . So many Indian slaves were traded to Pennsylvania that a law was passed in 1705 forbidding the importation of Carolina Indian slaves. . . . From 1680 to 1715, the English sold thousands of Indians into slavery. . . . Indian slavery, however, had many problems, not the least of which were Indian attacks, and by 1720, most colonies in North America had abandoned it for African slavery.

Returning to the theme of friendly relations, Smallwood writes that Africans forged a relationship with the Tuscarora of North Carolina and the Seminoles of Florida. The Tuscarora were Iroquois and were part of the "Five Nations" Iroquois Confederacy, which included the Mohawks, Cayugas, Oneidas, Senecas, and Onondagas. These nations grew to abhor frontier plantations of Whites and "allowed Africans to go free or join their nations."[16] In fact, "the Seminoles of Florida became so mixed that like the Tuscarora and

---

14. Vainfas, "God Against Palmares," 55.
15. Smallwood, 20–22.
16. Smallwood, 22.

other Iroquois, many of their people were as much African as Indian."

As the mixture of Africans and Indians intensified on both continents, colonial authorities and elites became more frustrated by their inability to neatly categorize the populations. These "mixed-bloods" further complicated racial classifications and subsequently were alienated from both the Indian community and the White community.[17]

The French and Indian War between 1755 and 1763 led to more mixing of Africans and Native Americans, who fought on both sides based upon a promise of freedom. Smallwood[18] mentions that this "could be seen in Crispus Attucks, who in 1770, became the first American to die in the American Revolution in the Boston Massacre. Attucks was also part Native American and was known among them as 'little deer.'"

We can compare the actions by and toward the slaves in South America to the British position regarding North American slaves during the American Revolutionary War. After 1775 in North America, slaves sought opportunities for freedom. In the North, the slaves fled to safe havens to join the British as well as American forces. In Virginia, Lord Dunmore, the colonial governor, offered freedom to slaves if they would join the British Army and created what became known as the "Ethiopian Regiment," and "at the end of the Revolutionary War, the British and their Indian allies freed thousands of slaves. The British alone took more than 14,000 Africans when they withdrew from America.[19]

In the Southern states, the same process unfolded during the Civil War: slaves joined the Union as well as Confederate armies in return for freedom.[20]

---

17. Dain, "Beyond Black and Red."
18. Smallwood, 4.
19. Smallwood, "A History," 24.
20. Reis and Gomes, *Freedom by a Thread*, 184; Laird W. Bergad, *The Comparative Histories of Slavery in Brazil, Cuba, and the United States: New Approaches to the Americas* (New York: Cambridge University Press, 2007), 241.

AMERINDIANS OF BRAZIL

Antagonistic relationships between Africans and Indians developed in many cases. Narrowing the focus here to Brazil, the Xavante and the Kayapó, two autonomous Indigenous people of Goiás, currently a state in the center-west of Brazil, were involved in the destruction of quilombos. Eighteenth-century sources suggest that Indigenous people destroyed more quilombos than Portuguese *bandeira* expeditions: "They routinely raided local fazendas, killing settlers and their black slaves,"[21] who were identified as enemies and were attacked and killed "whether enslaved or free." A state of war existed between the Xavante and Black people until the 1760s, after which time the Xavante encouraged fugitive Blacks to take refuge with them and to marry their women. Thereafter, "a racially mixed peasant community that was Afro-Xavante in origin continued to farm lands well into the 1880s."

In some instances, antipathy was engendered because Indians indiscriminately associated African slaves with their captors. Indigenous people captured during wartime were enslaved and escaped at the first opportunity. A major group of such fugitives was found in certain mining areas of Goiás. The Tupi fled the bandeiras "and became the implacable enemies of the settlers and their slaves. . . . They refused to be pacified and settled in villages because of their fear of re-enslavement. Other nations who appear as war captives included the Kayapó, Xavante, and Krahô."[22] Scholar Mary Karasch goes on to mention that when the Kayapó discovered "a great city of fugitive blacks on an island in the Grande River," they "killed and decapitated them." The African slaves had their hands full of trouble.

In contrast to Indian hatred of the colonizers as the motiving

---

21. Mary Karasch, "The Quilombos of Gold in the Captaincy of Goiás," in Reis and Gomes, *Freedom by a Thread*, 203-222, pp. 218-219.
22. Karasch, "Quilombos of Gold," 207.

force, the Karajá, a tribe with the same political objectives as the Kayapó—that is, to capture African slaves—"expected to receive typical gifts and rewards for their services . . . tools, textiles, and food. . . . The Portuguese were more than willing to pay the gifts in order to secure the return of fugitive slaves and for the destruction of the quilombos."[23]

The scarcity of women was another major incentive for these tribes to attack quilombos, whose residents had been known in the past to abduct Indian women. This was more of an issue in Brazil than in North America because of the lopsided difference between the number of African males imported into slavery compared to females in Portuguese America. In North America, the ratio of African male slaves to female slaves also disproportionately favored males, but not to the same extent.

An interesting example of this can be found in the Carlota quilombo. These quilombolas lived in a state of constant war with the Indigenous. Karasch claims, "The quilombolas had survived by raising foodstuffs and raiding the local indigenous groups for women."[24] They were obviously successful, because this quilombo lasted from 1770 to 1795.

Over the years, some Indian nations became assimilated into the colonizer's society. They lived in missions run by Jesuits or other religious groups. They formed what became known as the *pedestres*, "a barefoot frontier force who engaged in anti-quilombo activity," explains Reis. These skilled frontiersmen carried out a variety of anti-quilombo assignments for the government. Clearly, "the ability to use indigenous people against the quilombolas was very common in several regions in Brazilian slavery in different periods."[25]

Slaveholders in both Americas leveraged their force through

---

23. Karasch, 219.
24. Karasch, 215.
25. João José Reis, "Slaves and the Coiteiros in the Quilombo of Oitzeiro, Bahia, 1806," in Reis and Gomes, *Freedom by a Thread*, 298.

Indians and disaffected Blacks. Smallwood[26] mentions the process of "conscripting Indians and blacks—called 'Rangers'":

> These Rangers were used against the maroons in Brazil . . . and the United States. . . . The Rangers proved more adroit than their European counterparts, as they were better trackers than whites and were superb guerrilla fighters. There were more than fifty maroon communities in the United States and hundreds in South America. . . . Although many maroon communities were eventually destroyed, some existed into the twentieth century.

Similarly, the Apinajé, Indigenous people who at one time were located near the modern city of Marabá in the Tocantins region, destroyed the quilombo Pederneiras. At one time, this quilombo distinguished itself as a noticeably large settlement of fugitive slaves ruled by a woman. When the Indians captured the quilombolas, they "cut off their heads, impaling them on sticks and displaying them along the riverbanks."[27]

However, Indians also cooperated with the *calhambolas* in repelling militia attacks from the colonial authorities. In one case, when a *capitão do mato*, a bushman, and his team attacked a quilombo near Villa Rica, the capital of Minas Gerais, a mining region of Brazil, the attack was met by a "great portion of Indians, *gentio*, who instantaneously repulsed them with a great shower of arrows resulting in the wounding of three *Capitãos do mato*."[28]

Finally, in a discussion of the pottery discovered at Palmares, Orser and Funari[29] see "a convergence of African and native

---

26. Smallwood, "A History," 20.
27. Karasch, "Quilombos of Gold," 210.
28. Donald Ramos, "The Quilombo and the Slave System in Eighteenth Century Minas Gerais," in Reis and Gomes, *Freedom by a Thread*, 167.
29. Charles E. Orser, Jr., and Pedro P. A. Funari, "Archaeology and Slave Resistance and Rebellion," *World Archaeology* 33, no. 1 (2001): 61-72.

traditions." They continue, "There is no doubt that the pottery is of native South American style, probably because it was made by female native Brazilians who were married to maroon residents."

> The escaped Africans may have felt comfortable with the Tupinamba pottery specifically because it did resemble that made in their native homeland. . . . The pottery used thus attests both to the integration of the runaway polity into a much wider world of exchanges—from the Brazilian coast to Africa and to Europe—and to the polity's unique character. The material world of Palmares was not native, European, or African; it was specific, forged in their fight for freedom.

So, we can discern that from the founding of Palmares, its leaders had quite a challenge before them as they navigated diplomacy with the Indians. They had to distinguish the unfriendly from those who would cooperate with them—no easy task as the ever-shifting sands of politics swayed these alliances. The colonialists fought hard to drive wedges wherever an opening existed to separate the two populations.

Likewise, the slaves took advantage when the colonists fought for and against each other, as with the Dutch and the Portuguese. This same political strategy entered America's politics from Jim Crow times through modernity. The strategy of setting poor Whites against the beleaguered African American community is nothing new. John Hope Franklin discusses this phenomenon quite vividly in *From Slavery to Freedom* (2007). If these cohorts ever forged a "faithful alliance"—not merely through unionization but in "realpolitik"—the efficacy of divide and conquer would be greatly diminished as a political stratagem, and the politics of race would lose its potency and much of its currency.

In summary, the Indian–fugitive slave relationship was conflicted, to say the least, but in the best of times, there was an integration of strategies and culture for their common survival. As Vainfas[30] reminds us, "the communities of runaway natives that had escaped slavery and religious conversion . . . could be seen as the true ancestors of the *quilombo*s on Brazilian soil." The commonalities of their struggles far outweighed their differences.

---

30. Vainfas, "God Against Palmares," 52.

CHAPTER 10

THE ROLE OF WOMEN IN THE QUILOMBO

"Every black woman is a maroon."

Jarid Arraes

"Every time a black woman or man learns about the lives of these women, the fight against racism is strengthened."

Odete Assis and Jennifer Tristan[1]

The story of Palmares begins in precolonial Kongo in the fifteenth century. The founders, those persons responsible for the initial idea as well as the establishment and maintenance of the Palmares quilombo, were inheritors of the culture and traditions of this noble kingdom. The notable female players in Kongo's precolonial culture—in the struggle against the Dutch policy of Groot Desseyn in Kongo, the colonization of Angola, and the Spanish conquest of this region—brought with them a background of independence, the dignity of freedom, and a predisposition toward self-determination and self-reliance.

---

1. Odete Assis and Jennifer Tristan, "Dandara, Aqualtune e Luiza Mahin: Mulheres Negras na Luta Contra a Escravidão no Brasil," *Esquerda Diário*, July 25, 2018, https://www.esquerdadiario.com.br/Dandara-Aqualtune-e-Luiza-Mahin-Mulheres-negras-na-luta-contra-a-escravidao-no-Brasil/.

According to Franz van der Puye,[2] though European culture and influence invaded African countries and was impactful, it was not ultimately dispositive of their fate: "Elements of African culture survived in its various languages, performing and other arts, religions, oration, and literature and depicts the strength of African culture. These elements also underscore African resistance to annihilation and cultural destruction."

Certain noble female leaders and their successors distinguished themselves in quilombos and in subsequent resistance movements against slavery in Brazil, playing a fundamental role in escapes, the formation of maroon societies, and resistance to slave owners using various devices, including poisonings, sabotage, abortion, and guile. In my observation of the quilombo phenomenon, African and African-descended women were intrinsically involved in, responsible for, and essential to the leadership, maintenance, and preservation of these settlements. Here is a brief synopsis of some heroic African women of the quilombo movement.

• • •

QUEEN NJINGA

Thornton[3] makes note of several women who were instrumental in fighting the Portuguese in the seventeenth century in Kongo. One such woman was Queen Njinga of Ndongo, mentioned earlier, who sent armies to attack the Portuguese when she came to power in 1624. She even "established her own capital, which was an armed

---

2. Franz van der Puye, "Media and the Preservation of Culture in Africa," *Cultural Survival Quarterly* 22, no. 2 (1998), https://www.culturalsurvival.org/publications/cultural-survival-quarterly/media-and-preservation-culture-africa/.
3. John K. Thornton, "The Kingdom of Kongo and the Thirty Years' War," *Journal of World History* 27, no. 2 (June 2016): 189-213, pp. 209-212.

and protected camp that she always called *quilombo* (*kilombo*)."⁴ She reached a treaty with Portugal in 1639 that left her uneasy following the series of hard-fought wars against the Portuguese since she came to power in 1624, so she advanced her army into territory near the capital of Ndongo and from there attacked other Portuguese positions, often personally leading her forces.

At a military review in 1662, when a Capuchin priest praised her martial prowess, "noting her agility despite her age (nearly 80) and sex, she replied, 'Excuse me, father, for I am old, but when I was young I yielded nothing in agility or ability to wound to any Jaga [Imbangala], and I was not afraid to face twenty-five armed men.'"⁵ She added that she "might have faced twenty-five armed men alone but not if they had muskets, for against a musket there is no remedy."

Queen Njinga allied with Garcia II, the king of Kongo (at the time, Ndongo and Kongo were adjoining provinces), to continue the war against the Portuguese attempting to form a colony in Matamba and Angola. But, according to Thornton, the politics in Kongo changed in such a way that disenabled Garcia to continue the fight. Queen Njinga's armies, alongside the Dutch, fought against Portugal in major battles in 1644 and 1646. In 1646, because of halfhearted support from the Dutch, she suffered a significant defeat; however, with renewed support from the Dutch and Garcia II at the Battle of Kumbi in July 1647, Queen Njinga defeated the Portuguese decisively. This victory was followed by a subsequent defeat of the Portuguese at Ilamba on August 1, 1648, "which left the Portuguese in a desperate situation as Queen Njinga's forces besieged all the Portuguese forts."⁶

Queen Njinga played an integral role in the Angolan War, which involved an intricate web of treaties and alliances: between the Dutch

---

4. John K. Thornton and Linda Heywood, *Central Africans, Atlantic Creoles, and the Foundation of the Americas, 1585-1660* (University of Cambridge Press, 2007), 134.
5. Thornton, "Kingdom of Kongo."
6. Thornton.

and the Portuguese, the Dutch and Queen Njinga, and Queen Njinga and Garcia II. In addition, the 1640 Portuguese revolt from Spain resulted in subsequent Spanish alliances with the Dutch, but perhaps most important were the politics of the ruling class in Kongo. It was the battle of Mbumbi in 1622 between the Portuguese and Kongo "which left the flower of Kongo's nobility dead on the field."[7]

Queen Njinga was, in many respects, a woman without scruples. She would do anything to rule or to defeat her adversaries in battle, be they the Dutch or the Portuguese. Thornton discloses that "she decided to become an Imbangala herself"[8] to support her rule over Ndongo. She used slaves to enhance her revenues and power. She converted to Christianity to gain the favor of the Portuguese, even though Portuguese officials "formed the opinion that Njinga had a long-standing hatred of the Portuguese and Christianity and could never negotiate." Moreover, "she had her nephew killed in order to assume power herself" and "married dependent men, who ruled nominally as kings, while she exercised the real power." In a bid to secure her power against her adversaries who felt she could not rule because of her sex, "at some point in the 1640s, Njinga decided to 'become a man,' Njinga's husbands became her 'concubines,' and she took several at the same time."

Amid the welter of Kongo hierarchical entanglements, Queen Njinga's efflorescence was a pedestal upon which later African women would build their contributions to the quilombo movement. Some of Queen Njinga's legacy emerges in the other women who played key roles in the quilombos that followed. Her actions set a standard of tenacity for her female successors.

I mentioned earlier the importance of lineages and their role in the identification of the leaders of Kongo and the quilombos.

---

7. John K. Thornton, "The Art of War in Angola, 1575-1680," *Comparative Studies in Society and History* 30, no. 2 (1988): 360-378, p. 374.
8. John K. Thornton, "Legitimacy and Political Power: Queen Njinga, 1624-1663," *Journal of African History* 32, no. 1 (1991): 25-40.

Interestingly, Thornton[9] identifies a category of women called "elite women," also known as "queen mothers" in West Africa. Many of these women exercised their power through their male relatives or ideologically and symbolically. In matrilineal cultures, women were the heads of lineages and "as mothers of important male political figures . . . had a degree of independent power."[10] Queen Njinga exercised her power openly and notoriously and "believed that descent ought to play a role in determining who should be elected, for her own claim rested firmly on the fact that she was the sister of her predecessor who was himself of royal line." Moreover, Njinga "used genealogy to support her claim to the throne of Ndongo against aristocratic rivals who might claim it by descent."[11]

It is important to note that Thornton also relays, "Kongo did not accept the possibility of a woman as head of state even though some females operated at the regional level." This point is reiterated in the genealogies of Ganga Zumba, Ganga Zona, and Zumbi, all posited to have descended from "Queen Mother" Aqualtune.

• • •

AQUALTUNE

The history of Aqualtune, also known, as Arotirene and Aca Inene, as mentioned earlier, is based on a synthesis of putative fact and opinion. Her story is one of myth, legend, rumor, and debate—a mixture of possible reality and fiction, not all of which is ahistorical.

Aqualtune was a prominent African warrior and princess of Angola. It is thought that she was born sometime during the late sixteenth century and was a member of the house of Kinlaza through her father, a king, perhaps the brother of António I, which would

---

9. John K. Thornton, "Elite Women in the Kingdom of Kongo: Historical Perspectives on Women's Political Power," *Journal of African History* 47, no. 3 (2006): 437-460, p. 438.
10. Thornton, "Elite Women."
11. Thornton, "Legitimacy and Political Power."

make her father Garcia II. During this time, "the king of Spain (or Portugal) shipped 'more than twenty-four thousand blacks annually from there [Kongo] to Brazil, the West-Indies and other places.'"[12]

Aqualtune was instrumental in combat, leading and fighting alongside a sizable army of men in consequential battles against the Portuguese in the early seventeenth century. Before she was captured, these actions were crucial in deciding the postcolonial fate of Kongo.

Vinicius Martins[13] relates that following her capture after one of these battles, she was transported to the state of Pernambuco in Brazil and sold to a farmer in Recife. She may have been held for a time in Ghana at Elmina Castle, a fort that detained many slaves awaiting transport to the Americas. It would have been there that she was branded with a hot iron on her left breast, marking her for the rest of her life as a slave. Debased and repeatedly raped, she was kept as a breeding slave. Aqualtune is credited with having jumped from the slave ship that carried her and her countrymen to Brazil in a vain attempt to swim back to her beloved Angola.

Discontented and aggrieved, she tenaciously pursued her freedom, organizing more than 200 of her fellow Africans to make their way to Palmares without the benefit of proper matériel. In the Quilombo of Palmares, for a long while she found a modicum of peace, dignity, and contentment, interspersed by attacks on the quilombo by the Dutch, the Portuguese, and hostile plantation owners.

While living in Palmares, she had three children: Ganga Zumba, the future leader of Palmares; a daughter, Sabina, the mother of Zumbi; and Ganga Zona. Ganga Zona led one of the mocambos that formed Palmares. Aqualtune ably assisted her fellow quilombolas in

---

12. Thornton, "Kingdom of Kongo," 199.
13. Vinicius Martins, "Aqualtune, a Luz de Palmares," *Alma Preta* (July 21, 2017), https://almapreta.com.br/sessao/cotidiano/aqualtune-a-luz-de-palmares/.

repelling many attacks, as she had done in Kongo before her capture.

The decline of Aqualtune's legacy began in 1678 when Ganga Zumba was killed. One can only postulate as to when, how, or where she died, whether by natural causes or during an attack. But it is the conclusion of many that from the early founding of the quilombo, she was the queen mother of Palmares in African matrilineal tradition.

• • •

DANDARA

According to blogger Broderick Russell Jr.,[14] the name Dandara has among its meanings *"a mais bela"*—"the most beautiful." As with Aqualtune, the usual confounding issue of authentication persists, but that is not to say that sinews of a credible story do not exist.

As the story is told, Dandara was the wife of Zumbi. Among her myriad other functions, she was a hardworking, ardent supporter of Palmares in every respect. It is unclear from the record whether she was born in Palmares or escaped and made her way there. What is known, however, is that she worked to produce food. She was the leader of a female army adjunct to the main fighting force of Palmares that fought alongside the men to repel attacks against the quilombo. By all accounts, Dandara was a de facto aide-de-camp to Ganga Zumba and subsequently occupied the same position for her husband.

Perhaps one of her most notable achievements was bearing Zumbi three children. Dandara's genealogy traces back to the Nagó, a Yoruba subgroup in Benin, a West African country bounded by Togo, Nigeria, Burkina Faso, and Niger. The Portuguese raided all these countries for slaves; she or her immediate ancestors were in all likelihood swept up in this slave-raiding and trading process.

---

14. Broderick Russell, Jr., "Zumbi & Dandara," *Honest Media Blog* (December 7, 2019), https://honestmediablog.com/2019/12/07/zumbi-dandara/.

Russell[15] postulates that Dandara urged her husband to reject the treaty negotiated by Ganga Zumba with the Portuguese in 1678, thereby bearing complicity in Ganga Zumba's usurpation and death. In her view, the treaty was a pretext to return the Palmaristas to slavery—and she was correct. Dandara also participated in attacks on slave plantations to free slaves and to acquire foodstuffs, ammunition, and agricultural implements.

After her capture during the battle that ultimately destroyed Palmares in 1694, she chose suicide rather than a return to slavery. Dandara hurled herself off a cliff abutting her compound, in a manner befitting the lyrics of the post–Civil War African American song "Oh Freedom!":

> Oh freedom, Oh freedom, Oh freedom over me,
> And before I'd be a slave, I'd be buried in my grave,
> And go home to my Lord and be free, Oh, freedom.

•••

TEREZA DE BENQUELA

Tereza de Benquela was also known as Rainha Teresa or Queen Tereza. Her surname was derived from Benguela, the pivotal Portuguese land base in Angola, where she was born in the early seventeenth century. Transported to Brazil after her capture by the Portuguese, she was sold and sent to Mato Grosso—the "great forest," now known as the Amazon. During her enslavement to Captain Timóteo Pereira Gomes, she married and, with the help of her husband, José Piolho, established the maroon community of Quaritere, further inland from where she had been enslaved. The dense forest made the quilombo impregnable for many years.

"Inhabited by over 100 people, 79 Blacks (between men and

---

15. Russell, "Zumbi & Dandara."

women) and about 30 indigenous persons,"[16] Quaritere was typical in the way it survived: on subsistence agriculture, trade with neighboring communities, and a defense sufficient to fend off attacks from the slave bureaucracy. Fugitive slaves flocked to the quilombo; some took refuge on the Spanish side of the border, which is now Bolivia.

Around 1750, José Piolho died, and Tereza assumed leadership of the Quaritere quilombo—the "widowed queen." Her rule resembled a parliamentary system, with a council of warrior elders over whom she presided that convened weekly to help her govern the mocambo. Scholar Luiza Rios Ricci Volpato reports that she ruled harshly, using severe punishments (as her predecessors did) to prevent escapes and betrayal. These practices were not unusual and were also used by Ganga Zumba in Palmares. She led by example, participating in raids on plantations to acquire weapons, food, and other useful products. She also participated in trade missions to exchange quilombo-grown and manufactured products for weapons and spices. The quilombo managed to grow cotton, tobacco, and manioc. The residents used the cotton to make fabrics. In addition, they had a blacksmithing operation. The quilombo existed in that state for over twenty years; at one time, over 300 people called it their home.

The Quaritere quilombo was initially destroyed in 1770, according to available records and oral histories.[17] The widowed queen was captured, returned to slavery, imprisoned, and reportedly went mad. She was later executed and her head put on a pike to be displayed in the quilombo she had led. This was a common practice of the Portuguese, but this attempt to undermine the martyrdom and heroism of the beheaded leader did not work. Her history transcended her tortured demise. The records reveal that although many inhabitants were captured and killed, enough residents escaped

---

16. Luiza Rios Ricci Volpato, "Quilombos in Mato Grosso: Black Resistance in a Border Area," in Reis and Gomes, *Freedom by a Thread*, 188.
17. Volpato, "Mato Grosso," 188; Manu Escrita, "Tereza de Benguela," *illustrated Women in History* (January 3, 2018), https://illustratedwomeninhistory.com/this-weeks-illustrated-women-in-history-was-7/.

to reestablish the settlement, which was ultimately destroyed in 1795—100 years after Palmares. Thus ended the existence of the Quaritere quilombo, which survived for over three decades.

• • •

FEMALE LEADERS IN QUILOMBOS

There are several instances of women leading quilombos either by succession following the death of a male leader or husband, as aforementioned, or because they were a founder of the quilombo. Regardless of their station, women played an essential role in maintaining and preserving the quilombos. They expanded the population and provided the necessary labor to produce food products, fabrics, and pottery for sale or exchange with the neighboring communities.

As previously mentioned, the ratio of men to women was heavily slanted in favor of males. In certain regions, especially in south Brazil, the ratio of males to females was three to one. Therefore, young Black men were highly motivated to capture young women. The recruitment of slaves by force, in particular female slaves, was widespread in Brazilian quilombos, and Palmares was no exception. Interestingly, this was often welcomed by the enslaved women, who "considered their abduction to be a liberation from oppression,"[18] and was necessary, as noted earlier, for the long-term survival of the population.

The Preta Vitória quilombo—possibly founded by a Black woman named Vitória, who escaped from her enslavement in 1831 and lived in the mountains for sixteen years or more—in the Couto District near the city of Taguatinga represented the general standard in the mid-nineteenth and early twentieth centuries for quilombos located on the southern plateau, far from the main concentration

---

18. Pedro Paulo A. Funari and Aline Vieira de Carvalho, "Palmares: A Rebel Polity through Archaeological Lenses," in Reis and Gomes, *Freedom by a Thread*, 33.

of slave runaways. It had about twenty members and existed for around twenty years, frequented by runaway captives sometimes accompanied by spouses. They lived on two large ranches and survived by hunting, fishing, and agriculture. Vitória was in her senior years when the quilombo was attacked and destroyed.

The scholar Mary Karasch[19] notes that "a quilombo in Mato Grosso whose location is uncertain, is the quilombo of Carlota, perhaps ruled by a woman, which lasted at least from 1770 to 1795. The quilombolas survived by raising foodstuffs and raiding local indigenous groups for women." In Carlota, the quilombolas lived at constant war with the Indigenous nations to steal their women; natural reproduction aided their longevity.

Karasch notes that the Goiás captaincy was a perfect location for quilombos. It was miles away from any Portuguese administrative centers on the coast, and it was distant from the colonial forces that were obligated to destroy mocambos. The quilombos of Quaritere and Carlota were in the gold-mining region of Brazil, in the latter part of the eighteenth century, and led by women.

Karasch[20] also notes another quilombo in the region of the Tocantins River near Goiás, an area where quilombos were mostly populated by Black people. This quilombo, known as Pederneiras, was once the site of a large mocambo headed by a woman—before its destruction by the Indigenous Apinaje.

Incidentally, in Brazil, there is a general lack of reference to children and newborns in reports of attacks on quilombos. The attackers divided the children born in the quilombos among themselves, or they killed them whenever they disturbed the returning march. The children were considered of little commercial value.[21]

In addition to the regular functions of Black women in quilombos,

---

19. Mary Karasch, "The Quilombos of Gold in the Captaincy of Goiás," in Reis and Gomes, *Freedom by a Thread*, 203-222.
20. Karasch, "Quilombos of Gold."
21. Maestri, "Black Plains."

in some the women formed an honor guard for the quilombo leaders. For example, Pataca, who led a group of rebels, "traveled with an honor guard of black women conducting batuques [drumming rituals] in the wilderness, on certain area plantations."[22]

The status of women, be they colonial, enslaved, or Indigenous, fluctuated among the besieged peoples, who at any time could be allies or combatants. We return to the example of the Indigenous Xavante tribe, which, though initially hostile, after the 1760s encouraged fugitive Blacks to take refuge with them and to marry their women. The Xavante intermarried with Black slaves.

The Brazilian author, journalist, and historian Clóvis Moura[23] has suggested a reversal of social roles at times in quilombos, enabling women to mate with several males due to the gender imbalance. He characterizes it as "an empowerment of chattel slaves" that engendered other empowerment mechanisms in the quilombos. Polyandry, where a woman has more than one husband, existed alongside polygamy, where a man has more than one wife, the latter being orthodox in some African traditions. Polyandry was not considered "as a regression to matriarchy . . . but as a new, maroon-born social relation, empowering women and thus showing the innovative political organization of runaway settlements."[24] The circumstances seemed to dictate sexual mores in the quilombos.

I close this section with the work of Roger Bastide,[25] who reports the following:

> Traces of *mocambos* of Negro fugitives have been discovered as far away as Amazonia . . . where one was headed by a

---

22. Marcus Joaquim M. Carvalho, "The Quilombo of Malunguinho, the King of the Forest of Pernambuco," in Reis and Gomes, *Freedom by a Thread*, 357.
23. As cited in Funari and Carvalho, "Rebel Polity," 32.
24. Funari and Carvalho, "Rebel Polity."
25. Roger Bastide, "The Other Quilombos," in Richard Price, ed., *Maroon Societies: Rebel Slave Communities in the Americas*, 3rd ed. (Baltimore: John Hopkins University Press, 1996), 191-201.

Negress, Filippa Maria Aranha, who was so powerful that the Portuguese had to form an alliance with her instead of fighting her. . . . When the Portuguese arrived at Passanha (state of Minas), the land was settled by Malali Indians, among whom were living some Negro fugitives, and these Indians had accepted as their chief another Negress. . . . Saint-Hilaire found that they [Malali Indians] looked more like mulattos than Indians, and the captain of the Malalis claimed his grandmother had been a Negress.

ILLUSTRATIONS

Picture at Quilombo do Campinho da Independência outside of Paraty: from left, residents of the quilombo; Otis Lee in center with wife, Michelle Lee, to his right and tour guide Rege Galvão. February 23, 2012.

A depiction of Aqualtune, also known as Arotirene

Dandara of Palmares: wife of Zumbi

A depiction of Ganga Zumba

A typical village in Palmares surrounded by palisades

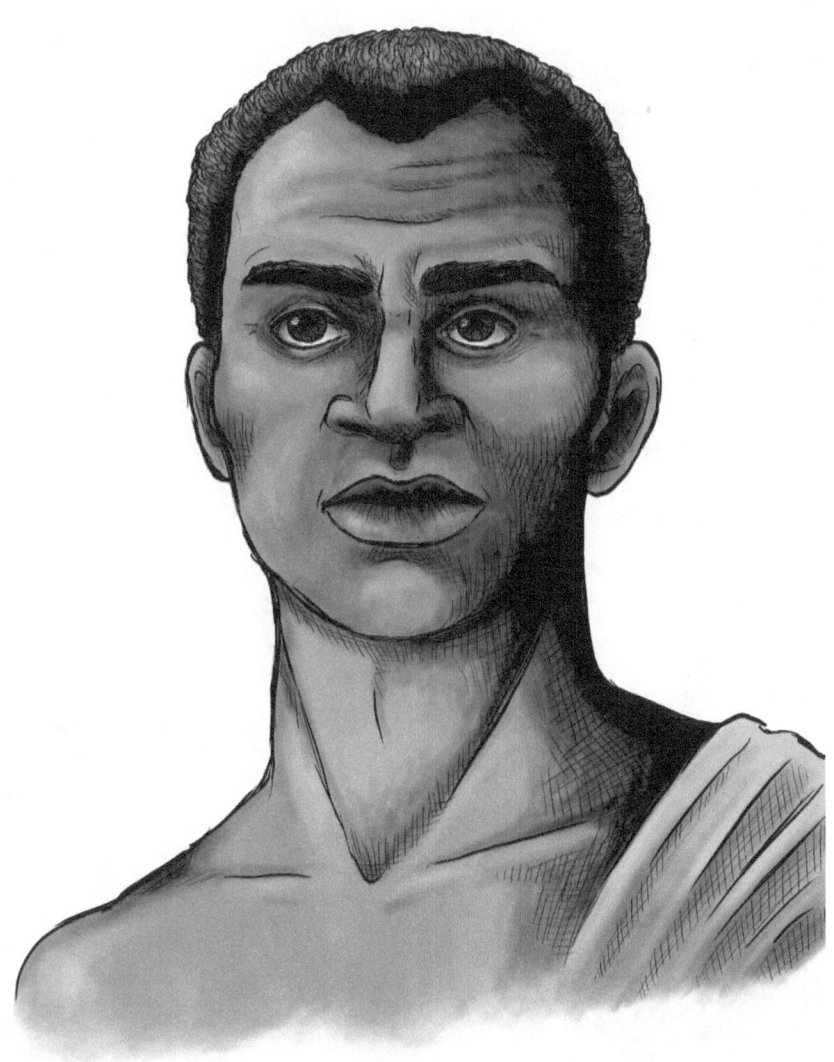

Zumbi of Palmares, an illustration

Locations of Villages in Palmares

CHAPTER 11

THE CHILDREN OF GOD'S FIRE AND THE ROLE OF CHRISTIANITY IN THE QUILOMBOS

In Brazil, the agents of Catholicism set God against Palmares.

This chapter discusses several important strands of religious indoctrination that the Catholic Church imposed upon the slaves in Brazil. Its doctrine and dogma formed the philosophical framework for the Jesuit Order, its prime agents for implementation.

Two principal personalities of the Catholic Church most associated with the quilombo era were (1) António Vieira, a Jesuit and a Catholic nationalist, and (2) the Franciscan friar Divinus Antonius, known as St. Anthony of Lisbon, the "heavenly Negro-catcher"[1] and a holy warrior of Christianity in the capture of runaway slaves.

António Vieira was physically present during prominent segments of the Palmares quilombo era between 1605 and 1694. Divinus Antonius, or St. Anthony, lived in a different era, from 1195 to 1231; however, the name, image, likeness, and hagiography of St. Anthony was used by various proponents of slavery during the Palmares era. These symbols were used to catch slaves and return

---

1. Mott, 116.

them to their owners, discourage slaves from running away to form quilombos, and destroy the quilombos.

Divinus Antonius came of age during the Fifth Crusade (1217–1221) pioneered by Pope Innocent III, overseen by Honorius III, and fought by King Andrew of Hungary. His fellow Franciscans were martyred in Morocco during this time. He then served as a missionary in North Africa, where he became imbued with an aversion to Africans, infidels, and all Muslims.

Between the two of them, St. Anthony and Vieira literally and figuratively—through religious persuasion individually or through the figment of others' imaginations—enabled the enslavement of Africans in a manner similar to an American cattle drive. Christianity was an expediter and enabler of colonization and deculturation of the African. According to Funari,[2] "Iberians, Portuguese, and Spanish were keen to Christianize the souls of new subjects and enforce compliance with the Roman Catholic philosophy." In addition, Funari (quoting Glassman) opines that "enslaved people were trained to be apathetic, while the elite stayed in otiose consumption. However, slaves were not 'socially dead'; they did not necessarily internalize their master's opinion that they were 'brute beasts.'"

The colonizing powers of Brazil had little or no appreciation for the preexisting religious practices and beliefs of the Africans they enslaved. Academic Gauri Viswanathan[3] quotes the anthropologist Johannes Fabian as saying that "terms like 'primitive' and 'savage' have temporal resonances that reflect their origins in world-historical models developed during European colonialism." Christianity was an expediter and enabler of colonization. Christianity followed the gun, the ultimate pacifier, faute de mieux. Missionaries sought to persuade the Africans to abandon their venerable traditions, to

---

2. Pedro Paulo A. Funari, "Conflict and the Interpretation of Palmares, a Brazilian Runaway Polity," *Historical Archaeology* 37, no. 3 (2003): 81-92.
3. Gauri Viswanathan, *Outside the Fold: Conversion, Modernity, and Belief* (Princeton: Princeton University Press, 1998), xii.

despise themselves and their color, and to embrace White European culture as the exemplar of beauty, value, and all things good.

The Jesuits were the prime movers of Christian indoctrination and conversion in colonial Brazil during the Palmares quilombo epoch. Because of their impact, I shall focus on these "God's Marines." The Jesuits put forward a moral rationale enshrouded in religious dogma for the subjugation of Indians and the enslavement of Africans. Thornton[4] points out that they were "the elite of European intellectuals, created out of the Counter-Reformation with the goal of facing the theological challenges raised by the Protestant Reformation and bringing the new concepts of Christianity to the rest of the world as missionaries."

Interestingly enough, "Kongo was one of the first countries outside of Europe to receive Jesuits, even before Brazil."[5] The Kongo elite were first introduced to Christianity in 1483; at that time, King Nzinga, a Nkuwu, professed his desire to become a Christian, a decision possibly based on political machinations. His son and successor, Alfonso I, would be the principal vector through which Kongo developed a syncretized version of Christianity. Therefore, some of the Africans brought to Brazil from Kongo as slaves had already been exposed to Christianity in their homeland, although many other slaves had their own religious beliefs, including Islam and a blend of native belief systems. For example, the names Zambi/Nzambi and Ganga/Nganga in the Bantu language of Kikongo mean "divinity" and "lord." "Nzambi a Mpungu," a term widely used in Central Africa, referred to God as understood in Christianity.

According to Thornton, "one of their [the Jesuits'] first tasks was to create a catechism, a new tool for teaching all Christians the Counter-Reformation conception of Christianity."[6] The Catholics

---

4. John K. Thornton, "Afro-Christian Syncretism in the Kingdom of Kongo," *Journal of African History* 54, no. 1 (2013): 53-77, pp. 57-67.
5. Thornton, "Afro-Christian Syncretism."
6. Thornton.

warned the slave masters in Brazil that if they mistreated their slaves, they would be banned from paradise—meaning heaven—and subject to eternal damnation. Such damnation began in this life, with the establishment of Palmares and other seditions and rebellions.[7] These admonitions fell on deaf ears. Cruelty persisted—cutting Achilles tendons as punishment for escaping, severing limbs, and savage whippings, to name a few—and there was little Catholic indignation in response.

By 1645, according to Kent,[8] "there was a greater degree of religious acculturation." Christianity taught Africans to forsake their traditions, both religious and nonreligious, and to be unwitting accomplices and docile facilitators of colonialism. The missionary was just as lethal to the African as the master and his whip, the soldier and his gun, and the rampant miscegenation in the engenhos and the *senzalas*, or slave quarters.

Anthropologist Luiz Mott[9] writes:

> The Catholic Church at this time, in the seventeenth century, was ruled by the philosophy of Thomas Aquinas. Thomas Aquinas is noted for his sensitization of Aristotelian philosophy. A high-sounding phrase which basically saw slavery as operating under the auspices of the church and operating within its doctrinal "four corners." Under this philosophy the Catholic Church saw slavery as a lawful and ethical institution, according to which the slaves should be submissive, and the slave owner should be generous.

---

7. Ronaldo Vainfas, "God Against Palmares: Lordly Representations and Jesuitical Ideas," in Reis and Gomes, *Freedom by a Thread*, 51-71, p. 63.
8. R. K. Kent, "Palmares: An African State in Brazil," *Journal of African History* 6, no.2 (1965): 161-175, p. 169.
9. Luiz Mott, "St. Anthony, the Divine Capitão-Do-Mato," in João José Reis and Flávio dos Santos Gomes (eds.), *Freedom by a Thread: The History of Quilombos in Brazil* (New York: Diasporic Africa Press, 2016), 94-120, p. 107.

The seventeenth-century Catholic Church encouraged slavery and viewed it as the execution of its religious doctrine in Portuguese America. The religious officers who plied their trade in Brazil during this time operated under this guiding Aristotelian-Thomistic philosophy.

Ronaldo Vainfas[10] states, "Christianization versus enslavement was the dilemma" for the Jesuits. They believed that being a slave and a Christian were mutually exclusive conditions for Africans—a hypocrisy not easily explained. The Jesuits were Ignatians, "the flower of the flock among the Portuguese intelligentsia, the drivers of education, the apologists of Christian humanism in Trent, heirs of St. Thomas's scholasticism, masters of Baroque preaching, doctors in the art of transfiguration made of allegories and metaphors designed to edify their moral example. . . . Few Jesuits spoke about Palmares explicitly, but they spoke a lot about African slavery."[11]

It was difficult for the Jesuits to reconcile the requirement of the Council of Trent to Christianize everyone while enabling the enslavement of Black people. Jesuits in the seventeenth and eighteenth centuries also "managed to gather valuable assets, including sugar mills and slaves," even as they preached to the slaves against the accumulation of material things.

As Vainfas explains, "Jesuits dreamed of reconciling slavery and Catholicism of blacks." They sought to give colonial slavery Christian features to prevent Black people from rising up and ruining the whole colony—"avoiding another Palmares." Irony and hypocrisy flourished unabated. In fact, it was only in October 1866 that the Brazilian state freed slaves owned by the church and religious orders.

Meanwhile, Bergad[12] explains, slaves created religious institutions that were unique to them. These African religious

---

10. Vainfas, "God Against Palmares," 60.
11. Vainfas, 60.
12. Laird W. Bergad, *The Comparative Histories of Slavery in Brazil, Cuba, and the United States: New Approaches to the Americas* (New York: Cambridge University Press, 2007), 180-183.

institutions ran parallel with the Catholicism imposed upon them, and "African deities continued to be worshiped through the epoch of slavery, often in forms that incorporated Catholic saints, and that legacy remained strong after abolition and even down to the present." John Thornton and Roger Bastide[13] champion the view that African religion played a role in the cultural resistance to slavery in Brazil. Paganism and the elevation of African women to leadership roles in quilombos because of their religiosity both influenced the fact that Catholicism typically melded with rather than replacing African beliefs. In precolonial Kongo, women were "renowned for their devotion to the church, arranging for the rapid construction of church buildings, as well as personally attending many church functions."[14] Kongo women saw religion as a way to exercise influence and obtain leadership positions. Hence, it is not surprising that while "the dominant influence [came] from African civilization, which supplied both the liturgy and the mythology for the Negro priest and the procedures for the magical cures of the Negro doctor[,] . . . this syncretism encompassed elements of white culture as well, and the Negro became an instrument for the diffusion of Portuguese Catholicism[,] albeit in a modified and corrupt form, among the Indians."[15]

In another example of this syncretism, Kent[16] discusses the observations of Jurgens Reijmbach, a Dutch Army lieutenant, upon his 1645 arrival in Palmares: "And although these barbarians have all but forgotten their subjugation, they have not completely lost allegiance to the church. There is a *capela*, to which they flock whenever time allows, and *imagens* to which they direct their worship."

---

13. Thornton, "Afro-Christian Syncretism"; and Roger Bastide, "The Other Quilombos," in Richard Price (ed.), *Maroon Societies: Rebel Slave Communities in the Americas* (Baltimore: John Hopkins University Press, 1996), 191-201.
14. Thornton, "Afro-Christian Syncretism."
15. Thornton.
16. Kent, "Palmares," 168

• • •

AFRICAN DEITIES

The Africans had their own conception of deities that they called orishas. According to Bergad, "there are seven principal orishas, known as the 'seven powers,' and they were organized hierarchically, although there were additional minor orishas as well. Each of these orishas came to be identified with Catholic saints in Brazil."[17] In blending their religious conceptions with Catholicism, Africans formed a ritual unique to their heritage: Candomblé, "a nineteenth-century term bestowed upon multifaceted West African religious forms that were practiced among distinct ethnic groups during the epoch of slavery, and after, in slave and free communities alike."[18]

Candomblé was a significant derivation of Catholic dogma practiced by free Black and mixed-race people, a uniquely Brazilian slave religious practice that is still widespread. And because diverse West African ethnic populations were enslaved in Brazil, further variations on the theme emerged.

Moreover, Candomblé gave rise to the establishment of African religious "brotherhoods," which we will discuss later in this chapter. Through these brotherhoods (also known as *irmandades*), enslaved Africans experienced more freedom and were able to exercise their leadership abilities. The Catholic religious hierarchy viewed the brotherhoods as a means to control the enslaved Africans as well as free Blacks in their promotion of social control and acculturation. The Catholic Church and slave masters presumed the brotherhoods to be essentially benign—because the Africans were adept at cloaking their religious practices in a veneer of Catholicism—and even forced Brazilian slaves to join them.

Bergad cites three strands of Candomblé: Ketu, Bantu, and Jeje. Ketu is the most impactful of the three. The Bantu version is the

---

17. Bergad, *Comparative Histories*, 183.
18. Bergad, 183.

second-largest faction and offers the concept of an all-powerful creator god called Zambi. You will recall that Zambi was one of the names associated with Zumbi. The Jeje faction has similarities to the Bantu group. Bergad informs us that there is a "blended *espiritismo*, or worship of spirits" in all these variations that, when taken as a whole, make up a significant portion of Candomblé.

The variation of Candomblé associated with my African genealogy is Jeje, which originated among the Ewe people, my people, drawn from the Togo and Dahomey region of Africa known as Togoland. A detailed discussion of each version of Candomblé is beyond the scope of this chapter.

Voodoo (also known as Vodun) and Jurema are two other Afro-Brazilian religions practiced during the slaveholding era in Brazil that remain active today.

Regarding the former, Voodoo is the English translation, and Vodun is the Spanish translation. Voodoo, a polytheistic religion, is practiced by a number of Bantu populations, including the Ewe and Fon. Voodoo is chiefly associated with the Haitian leader Makandal, known as the Black Messiah. Makandal survived the middle passage from Loango, Angola, to St. Dominique. He escaped to a maroon colony in St. Dominique and led insurrections and rebellions in what is now Haiti.

Makandal's personage has ascended to the level of divinity in the Voodoo religion, but he is a crossover religious personality also celebrated in Jurema. Because of his many exploits and talents, he is credited with having inspired the Haitian revolution and is a venerated hero of the Haitian people. He is characterized as a Malunguinho, a creole derivation of the word "malungo," as mentioned earlier in relation to João Baptista. Malunguinho entered into popular culture as a part of the cult of sacred Jurema and is worshipped in northeast Brazil. Often referred to as the "King of Pernambuco's wilderness,"[19] he is perhaps not limited to one individual but to the king of any quilombo.

---

19. Carvalho, "Quilombo of Malunguinho," 366.

In Carvalho's[20] opinion, Jurema generally deified the malungos, those captive Africans who survived the passage from Kongo to Brazil. This religion was practiced in Brazil as early as the sixteenth century, first among Indigenous people before generating an eclectic following of other Brazilians, both African and European. Jurema is symbolized by an evergreen plant, a spirit, a spiritual tradition, and a wine. Two principal spirits are celebrated in Jurema: Caboclos, an Indigenous spirit evoking paradise, and Master, a healing spirit composite of African and European derivations.

On the question of converting African slaves to Western religion, some agree with academic Gauri Viswanathan,[21] who compares cultural anthropologist Talal Asad's *Genealogies of Religions* with Lord Herbert's *De Veritate*. (Lord Herbert was the first Baron of Cherbury, between 1583 and 1648.) Viswanathan recites Asad's position that "the only legitimate space allowed to Christianity by post-Enlightenment society [is] the right to individual belief." It is in *De Veritate*, Viswanathan avers, that Herbert's "search for a common denominator for all religions in an era of early colonial expansion led him to represent religion as a set of propositions to which believers give their assent—propositions that would hence be known as beliefs." She also notes that "conversion is typically regarded as an assimilative act—a form of incorporation into the dominant culture of belief. Clearly the goal of colonial Portuguese authorities and their Catholic compatriots was not to allow space for individual beliefs but rather to proselytize by force Catholic theology to the Africans they enslaved."

It is often suggested that education and religion are intended to conform those outside the primary political system—the subaltern— to that system; in effect, they are acculturation mechanisms. In the case of slaves, however, religion was used to make Africans

---

20. Marcus Joaquim M. Carvalho, "The Quilombo of Malunguinho, the King of the Forest of Pernambuco," in Reis and Gomes, *Freedom by a Thread*.
21. Viswanathan, *Outside the Fold*.

compliant, not would-be citizens of Portugal or Brazil. Religion was simply a tool for subjugation condoned by the religious hierarchy. Moreover, Viswanathan[22] quotes Edward Said as positing that culture and religion are "systems of authority" and that religion is "clearly central to the state's functioning." Religion is undeniably a useful adjunct to state power.

•••

ANTÓNIO VIEIRA

Because of his eloquence and proximity to the Crown, the Jesuit António Vieira worked as the "point man" leading the slaves to slaughter (literally and figuratively) by preaching the succor of a better life after death, urging them to accept their plight of servitude and mistreatment as a form of martyrdom. Mott[23] quotes Vieira, who describes the missionary character of the saint who returns lost sheep: "Taking them from the realm of idolatry, subjecting them to Christ, converting mosques and pagodas in temples; Gentile in Christians, barbarians in men, beasts in sheep." Vieira asks: "Could there be a better destination for a fugitive from Christianity?"

Cheney[24] describes what Vieira preached to the slaves at a sugar production facility: "You are imitators of Christ crucified... because you suffer in much the same fashion that the Lord himself suffered on his cross, and in his whole passion." In the same sermon, he declares:

> Christ was naked and you are naked; Christ ate nothing and you are hungry; Christ was mistreated in all things and you are mistreated in everything. Irons, prisons, whippings, wounds, offensive names, all of these is your imitation made up, and if

---

22. Viswanathan, *Outside the Fold*, pp. 45, 109.
23. Mott, "St. Anthony," 108.
24. Glenn A. Cheney, "Thus They Go Without Punishment," in *Quilombo dos Palmares: Brazil's Lost Nation of Fugitive Slaves* (Hanover, CT: New London Librarium, 2014), 51.

accompanied by patience, it will also achieve the worthiness of martyrdom.

To slave masters, the tone was usually a threatening one of punishment in heaven and on earth if they did not take care of Black people's spiritual and human salvation.

Vainfas[25] affirms that Vieira urged the "Ethiopians" (as a general reference to all Black people) to be patient and wait on the Lord, a view that the slave owners greatly appreciated. (Is 500 years long enough?) He also urged them to believe they "were God's elected ones and created in Christ's image to save humankind through sacrifice." In other words, in the view of the Portuguese, the Dutch, and the Spanish during these times, Africans and Black people everywhere were born to be slaves to the White race. It was ordained by God, he said. This was the Christian view likewise adopted by North American slavers to rationalize their enslavement of Africans. The more things change, the more they stay the same.

Various writers have expressed their opinions on the use of religion in slavery in colonial and postcolonial times. Viswanathan[26] calls our attention to Thomas Carlyle's *Occasional Discourse on the Nigger Question*, written in the nineteenth century, as an example of some portion of the European view of Black labor in the service of Whites carried over from the colonial period. Carlyle asserted that Negroes were "servants to those that are born lords of you—servants to the whites." John Stuart Mill, a contemporary, rebutted Carlyle's principal view that White people were the lords of Black people in "The Negro Question," but it remains striking that the Catholic view espoused in the sixteenth century would still find traction 300 years later in quarters occupied by Britain's elites and political leaders and in its leading academies of letters, universities, and think tanks. Anglicans, Catholics, and Presbyterians dominated the religious

---

25. Vainfas, "God Against Palmares," 62-63.
26. Viswanathan, *Outside the Fold*.

scene in England throughout the nineteenth century.

You have no doubt noticed that even in modern times, the mantra from the governing White authority has always been that Black people should wait patiently and feel no urgency for their freedom. Recall the words of Dr. Martin Luther King regarding the "fierce urgency of now!" These philosophies of delay have historical roots, having been preached for centuries.

Vieira was a defender of Indigenous peoples but not of Africans. He[27] used the following to justify slavery on both logical and biblical grounds when addressing the Black Brothers of the Rosary in a sermon entitled "Children of God's Fire."

> You are the brothers of God's preparation and the children of God's fire, the children of God's fire of the present transmigration of slavery, because in this condition God's fire impressed the mark of slavery upon you; and, granted that this is the mark of oppression, it has also, like fire, illuminated you, because it has brought you the light of the faith in the knowledge of Christ's mysteries, which are those which you solidly profess on the Rosary. But in this same condition of the first transmigration, which is that of temporal slavery, God and his most holy mother are preparing you for the second transmigration, that of eternal freedom. . . . Your brotherhood of our Lady of the Rosary [the Saint of Blacks and slaves] promises all of you a certificate of freedom with which you will not only enjoy eternal liberation in the second transmigration of the other life, but with which you will also free yourselves in this life from the most terrible captivity of the first transmigration.

Vieira even advocated the use of native-born Angolan priests to intercede with the rebels and quilombolas, hoping they would ease

---

27. As quoted in Cheney, *Quilombo dos Palmares*, 51.

the antipathy the slaves had toward White people and dissuade others from escaping, rebelling, and establishing quilombo communities.

The sentiments expressed by the Jesuits remind me of the Nina Simone song "Ain't Got No, I Got Life." Some of the lyrics are:

> Ain't got no home, ain't got no shoes, ain't got no money, ain't got no class, ain't got no friends, ain't got no schooling, ain't got no wear, ain't got no job, ain't got no money, no place to stay . . . ain't got no clothes, no country . . . no food, no home . . . ain't got long to live, ain't got no love, but what have I got? Let me tell ya what I've got that nobody going to take away. . . . I got my life.

This was the predicament of the native Kongo slave in colonial Brazil, as well as crioulos, African slaves born in Brazil, as viewed by many influential Catholics of this era. The slaves had nothing but the labor from their backs.

After the Recife agreement of 1678, the followers of Ganga Zumba were guaranteed their freedom in the territory of Cacaú, an area in the southwest of Brazil's Goiás state. This was the new homeland for those who went into exile with Ganga Zumba. There, "they became Christians, were baptized, and confirmed, and instructed in the holy Catholic faith."[28] They were prevented, because of their status as political prisoners operating outside of the state, from falling "into religious bondage because that was against the law of the state." They could only be re-enslaved by way of a legal sentence "because slavery equals death, and death does not take place without hearing the defendant."

The slave system was an integrated religious and governmental endeavor, just as important to the state as it was to the church—both benefited from it, and both got rich because of it. Religion was an artifice used by the state to achieve its goal of securing trade and

---

28. Vainfas, 58-59.

wealth, and it allowed its coconspirator the church to get wealthy in the process.

Vieira believed that the Palmaristas could not receive the "grace of God" if they remained rebellious.[29] It was because of his doctrines as espoused in a letter of July 2, 1691, that we know he knew about the refuge of Cacaú, of the assassination of Ganga Zumba, and of the internecine conflict that followed. The Jesuits wanted the Palmaristas to promise that they would no longer attack Portuguese villages and sugar mills, nor permit new runaways into their mocambos. The Jesuits wanted to turn "Palmares into something similar to Jesuit settlements: mocambos comparable to missions." To do that, the Jesuits theoretically would have to grant the Palmaristas their manumission and then submit them to indoctrination. Converting Palmares into a Jesuit settlement would be a monumental victory of the Christian slavery project promoted by the Jesuits arising out of the Council of Trent; it would epitomize "the triumph of colonialism, sugar mills, and slavery." Vieira would have none of it because he felt that the rebelling Palmaristas "were in mortal sin and, hence, did not deserve the grace of God." They could not be educated in the theology of Catholicism because "they owned no more than their own body—a body enslaved to the masters—since the soul was enslaved to the devil. When it comes to Blacks, catechesis would only make sense if they were slaves."[30]

Vainfas recites that Vieira preached sermons amid Palmarian battles as well as shortly after the quilombo's destruction, "sermons committed to give colonial slavery Christian features so that Blacks would be instructed in the 'true faith.'" Cheney[31] reproduces a poignant sermon from 1633:

> There is no labor or way of life more similar to the cross and

---

29. Vainfas.
30. Vainfas, 70.
31. Cheney, *Quilombo dos Palmares*.

passion of Christ than yours at these mills.... Most fortunate are you if you recognize the fortune of your state and your conformity to an imitation of such a high and divine similarity by using and sanctifying labor! At a sugar mill you are the imitators of Christ crucified because you suffered in much the same way that our Lord suffered and in his passion.... Here, too, you have no shortage of cane, and cane is mentioned twice in the passion. ... The passion of Christ went through a night of no sleep and through a day of no rest, and such are your nights and your days.

All you lack is a cross for your mill to be completely and perfectly similar.... Slaves, obey your earthly masters with respect and fear, and with sincerity of heart, just as you would obey Christ. Obey them not only to win their favor when their eye is on you, but as slaves of Christ, doing the will of God from your heart. Serve wholeheartedly, as if you were serving the Lord, not people, because you know that the Lord will reward each one for whatever good they do, whether they are slave or free. And Masters, treat your slaves in the same way.

The Jesuits' intent for this sermon was to comfort his Black flock by comparing them and their plight to that of Christ. This comparison is not unfamiliar to churchgoers today and is often incorporated into the vision and practice of their worship. Parishioners like to see themselves laboring as Christ did, and suffering as he did, saved by redemption, crucifixion, and ultimately resurrection.

Not long after Vieira's position became known by King Pedro II, the Crown ceased all efforts toward compromise. Palmares was soon destroyed, and Zumbi died. The Jesuits remained consistent in not educating the seditious Blacks in Catholic catechism and in maintaining the ideas of bondage and Christianization of Black slaves, but the Jesuits did not achieve their "holy purpose" of establishing Christian slavery in Brazil. The clash between God and Palmares would have no winner.

Vieira wrote a book, published in 1705 in Rome, that became the manual for the Christianization of masters and slaves—the "new bible" for the slave class in Brazil. Among other issues, the book sought to "strengthen slave hierarchy and slave order."[32] It also promoted the sacrament of matrimony among Africans and discouraged the masters from allowing miscegenation, for the slaves were seen as licentious. Vieira sought to forge what he called a God-fearing captive community, totally adapted to a Christian style of bondage (the best type): "A moderate, just, rational, profitable, and balanced bondage. A bondage that is perfectly compliant with the Council of Trent's rules and dogmas and completely immune to rebellions, and to another Palmares." Masters were instructed how "to treat slaves: . . . bread, discipline, or punishment, and work, a formula extracted from Ecclesiastes combined with Aristotle." Religion and philosophy were the tenets of rationalization.

• • •

ST. ANTHONY

Divinus Antonius—St. Anthony—was a Franciscan of the mendicant order of the Catholic Church who served as the "drag rider," in the language of the Western cattle drive, using his charisma to ensure the capture of any wayward, wandering, or nonconforming slaves that may stray from the herd to establish quilombos. Mott[33] portrays him as a patron saint of all Portuguese society. His image and reputation are invoked to capture slaves, heal the sick, and raise the dead. To St. Anthony, according to Mott,

> Insubordination or escape from captivity would be a grievance and would deeply disturb the natural order of life in society. Thus, to recover the escaped slave, St. Anthony reconciled the

---
32. Vainfas, 65.
33. Mott, "St. Anthony."

black prodigal son to the bosom of his holy mother, the church, because, as taught by the dogmatic theology . . . outside the church there is no salvation.

Of course, the African slave was doomed whether inside or outside the church. Between Vieira the Jesuit and St. Anthony the Franciscan, both ends of the spectrum were covered. The strategy was triangular in its configuration and application. The institution of the Catholic Church occupied the top vertex, while Vieira and St. Anthony filled the two adjoining angles. At any one time, the relative weights of these powers could shift depending on how the slavery strategy was applied. Each player drew strength from the others.

Mott[34] writes, "Since one of the Christian justifications for the slave traffic was that Africans transported to the Christian kingdoms were thus rescued from the empire of the Devil, allowing them to flee or to live in quilombos was the equivalent of sending them back to the power of darkness." Their world—their African homelands, the communities that they would settle in the forest—were the empires of the devil and darkness. In contrast, the Christian world of slavery in which they suffered and died was the world of salvation and light, and yes, resurrection into a better life. Mott continues, "That is why returning them to the authority of their legitimate and Catholic owners was perceived as a missionary and charitable action." The recovery of runaway slaves was such a crucial element of the slave system that the Catholic Church all but deified St. Anthony as the quintessential slave catcher and promoted a hagiography that embodied, among other things, this skill.

St. Anthony was characterized as the savior of the Portuguese in Brazil, "the main holy warrior of Christianity," and as the "divine *capitão-do-mato*," the divine slave capturer. He was the precursor to (and a talisman in the Christian imagination) the much-feared slave catcher. He performed magic and miracles when it came to the

---

34. Mott, 100-108.

enterprise of slavery: "Wonders were attributed to his mediation."[35] St. Anthony's legacy worked against "the throbbing menace of the indomitable slaves ... in the recovery of blacks who had fled or who were living in quilombos." Followers preached in his name against the evil of the quilombos. He was more renowned than Vasco da Gama, the famous Portuguese explorer, and he was also said to be a "thaumaturge," a worker of miracles and magic, a second coming of Jesus Christ.[36]

Vieira, more than any other Catholic figure, heralded St. Anthony through speeches and sermons, saying that he "was so great that Christ before him seems small," equating St. Anthony to the sun and the son of God to a simple lamp. Vieira anointed him the "universal saint."[37]

Mott informs us that among his many imaginative attributes, St. Anthony was "a defender of Portuguese America from the menace of mobs, especially the slaves, always motivated to rebellions; and second, the separator of fugitive slaves, he restituted the owners of their property and the flock of Christ with the lost sheep." In essence, the aura, image, and reputation of St. Anthony were used to defend the Portuguese enslavement of Black people. He wanted to separate good slaves from fugitive slaves, as if the two were different, and to return owners' "property."

These Catholics in effect engaged in idolatry of St. Anthony even though they eschewed the practice outside their religion. Among his many titles, St. Anthony was the Son of Seraph, or the son of angels, with the power not only to recover certain runaway slaves but, in his glory and mythology, to cause the surrender of Ganga Zumba and Palmares in the year 1678, after which Ganga Zumba and his entourage prayed in the Cathedral of Recife for their blessings.[38] Among Black people, St. Anthony was a bogeyman.

---

35. Mott, 100.
36. Mott, 94.
37. Mott, 99.
38. Mott, 109.

OUR LADY OF THE ROSARY

Returning to the subject of Black brotherhoods, these communities provided a physical space for people of color to congregate, talk, debate, and evaluate their conditions and the qualities of slave owners. They prayed and reminisced, and this interchange allowed them to reinforce their values. Just like modern-day churches, these brotherhoods provided opportunities for leaders and leadership skills to develop. This in turn allowed those who partook a sense of identity that had otherwise been denied to the slaves.

Donald Ramos[39] identifies one common brotherhood, Our Lady of the Rosary of the African Blacks, and asserts: "The blacks conduct their festivals with much grandness: because in no way do they want to show themselves inferior to the others, especially to the whites." There was even competition between the various Black brotherhoods that manifested in the construction of altars and in their regalia.

We have of course established that, as Stuart B. Schwartz[40] writes, "although [the church] mitigated the rigors of slavery in Brazil, [it] also reinforced the institution. Christianization was often imposed, and at one point in the eighteenth century, the Crown had to command the Bishop of Bahia to halt his practice of fining slaves for not attending Mass and forcing them to join religious brotherhoods." However, the irony of this Catholic indoctrination of slaves is that it helped slave leaders to achieve importance beyond the slave/master relationship. Some slave leaders in these brotherhoods became godfathers to other slaves and replaced slave masters as authority figures. Often, slave leaders in the brotherhoods encouraged other slaves to escape.

---

39. Ramos, "The Quilombo."
40. Stuart B. Schwartz, "The Mocambo: Slave Resistance in Colonial Bahia," *Journal of Social History* 3, no. 4 (1970): 313-333.

Black members of the Catholic Church resisted control by the Whites, but to some extent, they accepted this religion. Whether native and traditional or acculturated, religion created a moral alcove within which the slaves could rest and reflect, however fleetingly, on the ultimate disposition of their souls. The cost to acquire this space was incorporating a Western religion as a vehicle for transmitting Portuguese Brazilian culture. Under the circumstances of slavery, the tradeoff was worth it.

The Black church today continues to serve this palliative purpose. But this blissful interlude exists within a premise that heaven or hell exists and that life after death will be better than life on earth—that the Christian God will save his followers. The use of religion by the Portuguese in this manner was a cruel hoax, the equivalent of a medicinal placebo. Indeed, Karl Marx's view of religion as an opiate when real peace and satisfaction cannot be obtained is apt.

The problem with the Portuguese strategy of heavy religious indoctrination is that any education trains the mind and changes the person, regardless of the educator's intent. Zumbi is a classic example. You have read that Zumbi was educated by his adopted father, Friar Melo. That education changed his disposition, allowing him to see the hypocrisy of the Portuguese slave system and vocalize and act on his disgruntlement. He thus became a leader at Palmares when his time arose. And even before he ascended to that position, his education propelled him to leadership as a military commander in the quilombo.

The Portuguese unwittingly expanded the horizons of the Africans by providing access to religious education. Ramos[41] avers that the Portuguese king saw it as his responsibility to religiously educate the slaves so they would obey the state according to Catholic values. The baptism of slaves was very important, and so was catechization—so much so that officials notified those slave owners whose slaves refused the baptism rite so that punitive action could be taken against them.

---

41. Ramos, 148-150.

Africans as enslaved people were *always* treated differently, in all aspects of their humanity, whether they were in Brazil or North America, but crucially in regard to their education and Christianization and the concomitant impact upon their enslavement. Vainfas explains,[42] "In the case of Africans, the more that blacks became Christians, the better slaves they would be—so thought Ignatians in Brazil, especially Vieira in the seventeenth century." By contrast, Indigenous people were at different times enslaved, but their Christianization exempted them from some of the harshest aspects of slavery and even in certain cases forbade their enslavement. Vainfas[43] calls out "a historical inconsistency" in that "Jesuits had always justified and defended slavery of blacks, even when they were Christians, although they fought against captivity of indigenous people," a position not grounded on any logic except color, ethnogeography, and ethnocentricity.

Likewise, according to civil rights attorney Gloria J. Browne-Marshall, baptism[44] in North America didn't mean anything substantive. It was all a rationalization, a pretext, a lie. Marshall asserts that "with heavy dependence on a labor-intensive tobacco crop, the Virginia colonists sold their souls and created legalized slave labor in their world based in religion." She expounds that "supporters of human bondage quoted scripture to alleviate their guilt," such as the stories of Ham and Cain in the Book of Genesis.

Quilombos were anathema to the Jesuits and their cohorts, the antithesis of what Catholicism sought to maintain, perpetuate, profit from, and accomplish. Consequently, the Jesuits rarely talked about Palmares; at most, they talked about the dangers of mocambos, riots, escapes, and vengeance. Astonishingly, Palmarian resistance to slavery revealed itself to be just as tenacious and famous as their

---

42. Vainfas, "God Against Palmares," 59.
43. Vainfas, 59.
44. Gloria J. Browne-Marshall, "1619 to 1819: Tell Them We Fought Back, A Socio-Legal Perspective," *Phylon* 57, no. 1 (Summer 2020): 37-55.

detractors' efforts were to reenslave them. Palmarian resistance was the motif of Jesuit discourse.

In summary, Luiz Mott[45] concludes that the Catholic Church in the seventeenth century promoted slavery as the execution of its religious doctrine in Portuguese America.

Thus, we see the use of the Bible to justify slavery both in the North American Baptist construction and in colonial Brazilian Christianity. To those in power, it was the "best of all possible worlds," as described by Gottfried Leibniz in 1710.[46] The world that God created—the one in which slavery existed—was a deliberate, divine choice, so it must be the best. The church used this and similar theories to support its position as the putative spiritual savior of humankind and enrich itself and its cobeneficiaries.

It is a shame that the Enlightenment, a European philosophical movement of the seventeenth century that centered around the ideas of liberty, fraternity, tolerance, and progress, did not make its way to Brazil or to the Portuguese who administered the colony in time to save the African.

Much irony exists. To the chagrin of the Jesuits, in 1758, the Order was dispossessed of its holdings in Portugal and the Portuguese colonies and expelled from Portugal by its king. There is much to this story, but the long and short of it is that the Jesuits received their comeuppance in good measure because of their deceit, avarice, arrogance, and backroom shenanigans involving the "Távor affair," an attempted assassination of the Portuguese king. For a period, that failure brought low the Jesuitical house of Catholicism in Portugal.

---

45. Mott, "St. Anthony."
46. Maria Rosa Antognazza, *Leibniz: A Very Short Introduction* (Oxford, 2016).

CHAPTER 12

THE BOULEVERSEMENT

"The lion's story is often told by the hunter."
—African Proverb

In accordance with many Central and West African traditions of matrilineal inheritance, Ganga Zumba in all probability came to power in Palmares after the death of his mother, Aqualtune. This scenario is accounted for not by historiography but by legend. However, this view coincides with that of historians such as Anderson,[1] who states that "the Ganga Zumba known to history may have been a native Palmarino of the Ardra nation, identifiable with the Ewe-speaking Allada state on the Slave Coast." Ardra today is known as southern Benin. Toussaint L'Ouverture, the founding father of Haiti, was the son of an Alladan prince.

Central Africa is a significant concomitant element in Ganga Zumba's heritage. This adds a degree of credulity to the Aqualtune genealogy enumerated earlier, even though the countries of origin may differ. As I mentioned, Ganga Zumba was the leader of Palmares until 1678 or shortly thereafter, when an insurrection—a "palace

---

1. Robert Nelson Anderson, "The Quilombo of Palmares: A New Overview of a Maroon State in Seventeenth-Century Brazil," *Journal of Latin American Studies* 28, no. 3 (October 1996): 545-566.

revolt"—led by Zumbi and two other lieutenants resulted in Zumba's death and his nephew's ascension to power.

Anderson[2] recites that *"nganga a nzumbi* was a religious title among the Imbangala, one whose responsibilities included relieving sufferings caused by an unhappy spirit of a lineage ancestor.... Schwartz speculates that Ganga-Zumba of Palmares held such an office." Again, we can see the Kongo connection through the influence of the Imbangala culture.

Perhaps you are wondering what such a major player in the history of Palmares looked like. I can find no historical mention of his physical features, but by drawing upon his Kongolese heritage, I imagine Ganga Zumba as being less than six feet tall (the Kongolese people are known for their short stature), regal in nature and bearing, sub-Saharan in color with hair textured and formed in an Afrocentric style, meaning braided ornamentally to denote his cultural heritage or worn closely cropped. According to Chidera Anushiem,[3] a contributing writer to the website *African Vibes*:

> One symbol of Africa's rich cultural heritage is the traditional African hairstyles. It distinguishes one culture from one another. In the culture of ancient African societies, the hairstyle was a significant element. It symbolizes status—economic, marital, and social. It was also used as an instrument of spiritual divination.... While some are almost extinct, many remain peculiar to their origins.... [T]hey even help to identify individuals belonging to certain ethnic groups.

Ganga Zumba was a wily figure, having learned many strategies

---

2. Anderson, "Quilombo of Palmares," citing heavily from Stuart B. Schwartz, *Slaves, Peasants, and Rebels: Reconsidering Brazilian Slavery* (University of Illinois Press, 1995).
3. Chidera Anushiem, "10 Traditional African Hairstyles and Their Origin," *African Vibes Magazine*, July 26, 2022, https://hair.africanvibes.com/10-traditional-african-hairstyles-and-their-origins/.

from his mother before he took power. He outmaneuvered the Dutch and Portuguese on numerous occasions as they sought to dislodge his settlement. These two colonial powers were unable to defeat him during a twenty-four-year period, 1654 to 1678, just as they had failed to defeat Palmares before his ascension to the throne.

However, some attacks hurt and caused much trepidation among the Palmaristas; one notable campaign was led against the Amaro mocambo by Fernão de Carrilho in 1677. Ganga Zumba and Aqualtune barely escaped with their lives, and not without injury. Ganga Zumba was growing old and likely tired of fighting and constantly rebuilding. As we shall see, these elements sowed the seeds for a midcourse correction, a rethinking of his leadership strategy and future prospects.

Regarding his governance, he allegedly ruled with an "iron fist" and, as previously mentioned, he was accorded the honor and salutations of a king. Under him was a council of advisors drawn from the nine to eleven "population centers" of the federated mocambos, including the capital of Macaco, which included chiefs, potentates, and lineage-based officeholders. His mother, Aqualtune, reportedly lived in a mocambo that at one time bore her name.[4]

According to Anderson,[5] perhaps one of the most important contributions Palmares made to African history was proof that an African political system could be transferred to a different continent; that it could come to govern not only individuals from a variety of ethnic groups from Africa but also those born in Brazil, pitch Black or almost White, Latinized or close to Amerindian roots; and that it could endure for almost a full century against two European powers, Holland and Portugal.

I am sure you will recall the stereotype leveled against Black people of African descent that they were incapable of ruling

---

4. Pedro Paulo A. Funari, "Conflict and the Interpretation of Palmares, a Brazilian Runaway Polity," *Historical Archaeology* 37, no. 3 (2003): 81-92, p. 84.
5. Anderson, "Quilombo of Palmares," 547-548.

themselves. Clearly, history contradicts such a disparagement. The fact that Ganga Zumba and his leadership team survived constant onslaughts can be attributed to the Kongolese clans from which they sprang. The Kongolese had a rich history of fighting the Dutch and the Portuguese in Kongo in the fifteenth and sixteenth centuries. For people of African descent, the notion of being on a "war footing" is a literal as well as figurative psychology to be maintained in the Western world, where acculturation has yet to be fully achieved and where creolization—the process by which different cultures blend to become a new culture—for African-descended people is modular and dynamic based upon the dominant culture's resilience. In Palmares, they made good use of their quiet time by rebuilding and refortifying their defenses and renewing their resolve, an essential daily act of survival. At times, these intervals, according to historians, were "few and far between."

The success of the Palmaristas in thwarting attacks from the Dutch and Portuguese had a lot to do with their fortifications. Palmares's defenses were similar to those of another well-known quilombo named Buraco de Tatú ("Armadillo's Hole"), located on the outskirts of Salvador in Bahia.

Ennes and Cheney[6] describe Palmares's defenses as being in essence a palisaded encampment with elevated, concentric circles interwoven with terraced obstructions designed to kill or severely injure anyone unfamiliar with the settlement. Schwartz[7] notes that "covered traps and sharpened stakes were used for village protection in Africa from Nigeria southward to the old Kingdom of Kongo and were also used at Palmares and other fugitive communities."

Who was responsible for designing and building such a formidable defense, and where did the ingenuity come from? The

---

6. Ernesto Ennes, "The Palmares Republic of Pernambuco: Its Final Destruction, 1697," *Americas* 5, no. 2 (October 1948): 200-216; Glenn A. Cheney, *Quilombo dos Palmares: Brazil's Lost Nation of Fugitive Slaves* (Hanover, CT: New London Librarium, 2014).

7. Schwartz, "Rethinking Palmares," 1310.

answer lies with the progeny of Aqualtune and her successors and assigns. Again, they used their cultural heritage from Kongo.

• • •

GANGA ZUMBA, ZUMBI, AND THE 1678 PAPER

Ganga Zumba's predicament was like that of a rowboat captain in the middle of the sea, facing waves of storm and gale and with only a few oars. His challenge, as it was for his predecessors and would be for his successor, was to get that rowboat with its precious cargo safely to the nearest shore and avoid oblivion. And what was his shore? A secure African state in Brazil?

As the sun rose each morning over the Serra da Barriga mountains, its warm, invigorating, and illuminating hues reflecting upon his dark-complected skin, Ganga Zumba might have surveyed all that had been accomplished and felt assured that he had done the best he could do for his people. Did he have all the answers? No. His navigation tools were inadequate and obsolete, unable to unravel the chicanery of "a tricky dog," as the Africans from his home country would say of his opponents. Were the odds of his success good? No. But at least thus far, the people who had relied upon his leadership were free, and his captainship had sustained them.

The declaration "Give me liberty or give me death!" from Patrick Henry, the American colonial patriot, at the advent of the Revolutionary War was a hypocritical statement made by a free White man of privilege who owned slaves. But less than 200 years earlier, high in the obscurity of the Brazilian mountains, the meaning of such a statement was manifest. Those who occupied the villages of Palmares had chosen liberty over slavery at the cost of death.

I am sure Ganga Zumba was aware that in the long run, he could not win—depending on how one defines "long run" or "winning." In the history of states, societies, and civilizations, one century is a short term. For African people operating against a torrent of hostility and deprivation in a foreign land, however, existing for almost 100 years could be considered a success. There was no pipeline for food, munitions, and other necessities of long-term survival. They had no mother country to save them, no allies, nor a rearguard or chow line on the battlefield; all they had were themselves and their ingenuity.

So, what to do? For Ganga Zumba, knowing that he and his people were inevitably doomed, victory must have had a narrow definition. What would a prudent leader do under these circumstances? He sued for peace.

Ganga Zumba was a man of great prestige and bearing among his people. He was charismatic and revered by slaves who heard only rumors of his exploits, but he was not unapproachable. The chiefs and potentates who ruled alongside him had no qualms about airing their grievances on matters that threatened their lives; the 1678 agreement was one of those issues.

The Portuguese thought well of him and reluctantly accepted him as the leader of this polity. They respected what had been achieved by a band of erstwhile slaves under his leadership, who to them were no more than "barbarians at the gate," but he was also their nemesis, a saboteur and a rival for the hearts and minds of African slaves.

At each conducive opportunity, after consulting with his chiefs and carefully considering his prospects, Ganga Zumba would sue for peace. Whenever the governorship turned over in Pernambuco, as it did periodically, Zumba attempted diplomacy. There is some controversy in the record as to whether Ganga Zumba took the initiative or the Portuguese broached the subject first. Zumba sought to achieve ownership over the lands of Palmares and freedom for those born in the mocambos. He was not successful at each offering, but gradually, a treaty and manumission for the Palmaristas were discussed as plausible alternatives for an enemy weary of the constant antagonism. This view toward acceptance emerged between 1661 and 1664.

Vainfas[8] reports that the then governor of Pernambuco, though fretful and disbelieving in the benefit of a treaty, "suggested the agreement with the Palmarians, although he did not hide an extreme distrust he felt with regard to those barbarian people." No agreement was reached, and hostilities resumed. It was not until the mid-1670s that new life was breathed into the armistice project. It fell to Pedro de Almeida, the resident head of government, to sanction this détente, but it was Aires de Souza e Castro in 1678 who implemented the treaty.

Nevertheless, as in all treaty negotiations between the subjugated and the powerful, hidden clauses shrouded in obtuse phrasing embedded an exit strategy for the oppressors. Kent[9] recounts, "Zumba's peace proposal contained two clauses that could not be fulfilled," both having to do with autonomy, freedom from coerced servitude, and the right of self-determination for the Palmaristas. Foremost in the minds of the colonial authorities was that any agreement that guaranteed those rights and legal commitments would conflict with "a 150-year-old policy of exclusive Portuguese claim to Brazil." The Palmaristas proceeded naively apace, not knowing that their fate had been preordained.

The Portuguese authorities kicked that bucket down the road—an issue to be resolved later. The 1678 agreement between the Palmares of Ganga Zumba and the Portuguese was made faute de mieux. Though the question of Palmares's territorial limits was not settled in any precise way, Kent asserts, translating a quote from Nina Rodrigues's *Os Africanus no Brazil*: "The solemnity which surrounded all these acts ... gave real importance to the Negro State which now the colony treated as one nation to another [for] this was no mere pact of a strong party concluded with disorganized bands of fugitive Negroes." At least, that's how the Palmaristas likely saw the proceedings.

---

8. Vainfas, "God Against Palmares," 57.
9. R. K. Kent, "Palmares: An African State in Brazil," *Journal of African History* 6, no.2 (1965): 173.

Vainfas[10] proclaims that at the time of settlement, the Black king brought forward a "grandiose entourage," with his lieutenants dressed in the most African of regalia at their disposal, harkening back to the glory days of the Kongo kingdom. Ganga Zumba was represented by his sons and other potentates of the various mocambos. Scholars such as Price, Kent, and Vainfas have all asserted that Aires de Souza took precautions with Ganga Zumba's wife and sons, who remained in de Souza's company during the negotiations. The Portuguese had an assortment of soldiers, lieutenants, and officers at their disposal. Both sides had a retinue; even former governor Pedro de Almeida was present at the closing.

At least three letters were exchanged between the principals to delineate, define, and explicate the minutiae of the agreement; the parties exchanged gifts as well. The officiousness of the proceedings adhered to the protocols used by the Portuguese in their political negotiations and usurpations of kingdoms in Central Africa where vassalage was the objective.

The negotiations reflected the Portuguese recognition of Ganga Zumba as king and lord of his people and lands. Furthermore, the pact acknowledged that Ganga Zumba was the leader of the ruling kinship clan, an investiture of heredity, a line of heirship reflected in the governance and military administration of Palmares and which was firmly rooted in the kinship clans of Central Africa and Kongo, as Thornton[11] explains. Though Ganga Zumba may have been elected according to the ethnic politics existing in Palmares, the lineageless Imbangala influence competing with the Kongo kinship clan hierarchy, the electoral process was a hybrid form of democracy as we know it today.

In essence, the Portuguese government accepted the military and

---

10. Vainfas, "God Against Palmares," 58.
11. John K. Thornton, "Elite Women in the Kingdom of Kongo: Historical Perspectives on Women's Political Power," *Journal of African History* 47, no. 3 (2006): 437-460.

political organization of Palmares and recognized it as a viable political entity coexisting within the sovereignty of their colony—a predicate, ostensibly, for the elevation of negotiations between the parties.

Palmares straddled the states of Alagoas and Pernambuco in Northeast Brazil. Palmares was thought to contain two large mocambos. The larger mocambo had streets that were six feet wide and contained 220 buildings: it had a church that stood in the middle of the street, four blacksmithing buildings, a government house, and a minister of justice. Palmares had the essential elements for a republic, the sine qua non to be called a civilization (according to the Portuguese) with its capital being Macaco. Moreover, it had a religious orthodoxy, a syncretic form of African beliefs and Catholicism. It had a system of administering justice and a wise man who served as the arbiter of fact (perhaps a Ladino—mestizo or Hispanicized people), more schooled in the mores of European culture and the tenets of Catholicism and fluent in Portuguese, to settle disputes. What's more, Palmares had a king. Historians say that this system of government and society distinguished Palmares and its inhabitants from other lesser quilombos and from the Indigenous people of Brazil.

The people living in the federation of mocambos that formed Palmares numbered anywhere from 11,000 to 30,000, though Schwartz[12] maintains the view that 20,000 residents is an overestimation and a miscalculation. The numbers vary depending upon who relates the information. But there is broad agreement that at any one time, there were at least 10,000 inhabitants spread out over several villages. It was an eclectic mix of people to say the least—mixed race, Angolans, Kongolese, crioulos (those born in Brazil of African or mixed parentage), disaffected Whites on the

---

12 Stuart B. Schwartz, "Rethinking Palmares: Slave Resistance in Colonial Brazil," in *Critical Readings on Global Slavery*, eds. Damian Alan Pargas and Felicia Roşu (Leiden, Netherlands: Brill, 2005): 1294-1325.

run from the law, Amerindians, and other castaways. Guimarães[13] notes that "there were slaves designed as leaders and performed a fundamental task: convincing other slaves to flee; acting as guides for new quilombolas; and in making connections between various quilombos"—a precursor to Harriet Tubman's legacy.

The Palmares economy was primarily parasitic, but reciprocity did exist. Their economy operated by trading with nearby townspeople and in the towns themselves, as well as by raiding nearby farms and plantations for slaves both male and female along with foodstuffs, arms, and anything else that would make their lives easier and safer. Consequently, the more they raided, the more hatred they engendered.

Ganga Zumba accepted the peace that offered manumission for himself and those born in Palmares. It offered his people land in the Cucaú Valley, an unsettled area twenty miles from Serinhaém, one of the existing mocambos in the settlement. The area had plenty of palm trees for their sustenance, an abundance of forest, and fertile soil. Jesuits, as was the custom of the Portuguese and their vassal territories, would be assigned to Christianize the unchristian.

In Ganga Zumba's mind, this moment was the belle epoque of his people's existence, the *Zeitenwende*, a changing of an era—but this vision, however well intentioned, sealed his fate. The provision to relocate to the Cucaú Valley was a contrivance equivalent to asking an armed enemy to lay down their weapons. Relocating to the Cucaú Valley brought them closer to the colonial authorities in Pernambuco and to the coast, making them more accessible to the military forces of the colonial authorities and thereby forfeiting a pivotal element of their natural defense: the forest. And it lulled them into thinking they would be safe, live in peace, raise their crops, trade with and

---

13 Carlos Magno Guimarães, "Mining, Quilombos, and Palmares: Minas Gerais in the Eighteenth Century," in João José Reis and Flávio dos Santos Gomes, eds., *Freedom by a Thread: The History of Quilombos in Brazil* (New York: Diasporic Africa Press, 2016), 137.

in the local markets, and be allowed to live without the threat of reenslavement. It was indeed a ruse.

The agreement also required the Palmaristas to return to the colonists those community members who were not born in Palmares; this "poison pill" sowed a seed of discontent. The native-to-newcomer or African-to-crioulos ratio was unevenly distributed among the mocambos, and this provision could break up families, friendships, and personal allegiances. Zumbi's mocambo, located fifty-six miles from Porto Calvo, probably had more newcomers as occupants than Macaco, the capital where Ganga Zumba resided, an unknown number of miles from the Serra da Barriga and 155 miles from Porto Calvo.

Price[14] tells us that such a provision was common in treaties between colonists and maroon societies. The Portuguese were well aware of the logistical problems of returning thousands of nonnative Palmaristas to Pernambuco; this was an added incentive to allow the community to live in the Cucaú Valley. But the very thought of this concession caused much unrest in Palmares.

Historian Silvia Hunold Lara opines[15] that the terms of the agreement were restated in an exchange of documents between officers of the Pernambuco government and the leaders of Palmares; this took place between June and November 1678. Translators—known as "tongues"—were dispatched from the governmental authority to Ganga Zumba to ensure an understanding of the terms.

The Portuguese even recruited a member of the Henriques Dias Regiment, a military force named in honor of a former slave, to facilitate the signing of the agreement. Henriques Dias distinguished himself

---

14. Richard Price, ed., *Maroon Societies: Rebel Slave Communities in the Americas*, 3rd ed. (Baltimore: John Hopkins University Press, 1996), 46.
15. Silvia Hunold Lara, "Palmares and Cucaú: Political Dimensions of a Maroon Community in Late Seventeenth-Century Brazil" (paper presented at the 12th Annual Gilder Lehrman Center International Conference at Yale University: "American Counterpoint: New Approaches to Slavery and Abolition in Brazil," October 29-30, 2010).

during the Luso–Pernambucan uprising, the Portuguese campaign against the Dutch for control of Pernambuco. Because of that valiant service, he was elevated from Black regiment captain to the head of all "colored people" in Pernambuco. Military service, then as now, offered a pathway to freedom in the king's service. However, a number of Black people in that service became disillusioned when the Portuguese failed to uphold their part of the bargain. Many left the regiment; some joined the fight to save Palmares. There is a parallel here to those African-descended soldiers who fought in the US Revolutionary and Civil Wars—and later, two World Wars—on behalf of their country, only to receive similar mistreatment when they returned home.

The Portuguese knew what they wanted out of the deal from the inception of talks: a vassal state—a formula that had worked for centuries in their colonized world. A vassal state is subject to a dominating state, given varying degrees of autonomy over its internal affairs but no foreign policy powers.

The formula used to create the 1678 agreement was modeled on the same program used against the native Brazilians. The Portuguese wanted the Indians to leave their villages in the mountains and settle in designated areas managed by a Portuguese official or "captain" with a priest or religious official to do the proselytization. This pattern, as you will recall, was used by North Americans against the Indigenous people of that continent in the form of Indian reservations comparable to *aldeias* in Portuguese America. The parallels are striking: the same people (or their descendants), the same objectives, and the same strategy.

The Portuguese never intended to share their sovereignty in Brazil with Africans. Their ethnocentrism and disdain for Black people would never allow it. In the world of realpolitik, all the Portuguese wanted was to arrest the threat. And Zumbi, being astute, was aware of that. Law is politics shrouded in black robes and ornate courtrooms. But when the accoutrements of justice are taken away, it comes down to "permanent interests" and control of society. The

Portuguese intended to attain both. As an old friend often reminds me, "There is no such thing as permanent friends, only permanent interests." The Portuguese befriended Ganga Zumba to achieve their own ends. To them, he was king for a day, not a monarch threatening Lusitanian existence in Brazil.

In addition to the above, the "great lord" had to pledge on behalf of his people obedience to the ruling authority—in this case, the government of Portugal and its king—as well as acceptance and adoption of the Christian church, its doctrines, edicts, ecclesiastical hierarchy, and mandates thereof; military assistance in time of war; and an obligation to refrain from whipping fugitives.

In exchange, the Palmaristas received a pledge not to be attacked and qualified autonomy over their internal affairs if they followed the dictates of the agreement and obeyed the laws of the Crown. This was an unequal bargain. In the law, we would say a "contract of adhesion," where there is unequal bargaining power in favor of one party over the other.

Perhaps Ganga Zumba was trying to save his lineage and his subjects from the "quagmire of oblivion" after the attacks of Fernão de Carrilho, or even to defend and stabilize the "kingdom of Palmares," the recreated Kingdom of Kongo in Brazil, that he reimagined from the stories his mother and older relatives had shared in their inner family councils and in his bedtime stories. But there was a disconnect between himself and his opposition in that Ganga Zumba, having been born in Palmares, had not witnessed nor personally experienced the brutality of slavery. Hearing about the atrocities—the severing of limbs, cutting of Achilles tendons, rape of mothers, daughters, and wives, unbridled miscegenation, hangings, and floggings—and experiencing them are poles apart.

The requirement in the 1678 agreement that the Palmaristas return nonnative residents to the colonial authorities for reenslavement was an explicit dealbreaker within the councils of

Palmares. Some historians[16] consider this acquiescence "to be the measure of Ganga-Zumba's weakness and the cause of his ultimate downfall." Opposition festered and engendered resentment. Palmares would thereafter split into two factions, and no similar societies or states were in proximity to aid in diplomacy to close the schism.

Kent[17] proposes several what-if questions about whether Ganga Zumba's objectives for Palmares could have been realized had Palmares and its leaders withstood the machinations of the Portuguese. For example, what if the Palmaristas had observed the duty to return those residents not born in Palmares? What if Palmares had been a homogeneous society with hereditary rulers? What if Palmares had been contiguous to other similar states? Price[18] uses the Saamaka, an African maroon community in Suriname under the oppression of the Dutch, as an example of what could be achieved and withstood by a maroon slave community. In my view, Palmares could only have survived if another comparable maroon community were located a reasonable distance away and if an alliance between the two communities existed relating to their mutual defense. Absent that, from whence would come the help?

As one might expect, the Palmaristas did not comply with the requirement to send nonnative *moradores* ("residents") back to the colonial authorities. Palmares was too heterogeneous at this point to comply with such an onerous requirement.

Zumbi and his comrades, angered by the agreement, spearheaded an insurrection that continued the resistance against the colonial authorities. Kent[19] relates that "by 1679, ... Zambi ... was in revolt with João Mulato, Canhonga, Gaspar [and] Amaro, having done the person of Ganga-Zumba to death." Zumbi kept his own counsel and shared his unrest only with a trusted group of loyalists. He saw the fallacies in

---

16. Reis and Gomes, *Freedom by a Thread*; specifically Richard Price, "Refiguring Palmares," 46.
17. Kent, "Palmares," 173.
18. Price, "Refiguring Palmares," 44-49.
19. Kent, "Palmares," 173.

Ganga Zumba's reasoning and, having lost the battle of persuasion, took matters into his own hands. Zumbi chose his compatriots wisely. They were his malungos in arms. All those who joined him were committed to paying with their lives for their chosen path.

Because of the peace accord, some moradores descended to the Cucaú Valley; others remained in the mountains. In the valley, the "New" Palmaristas were allowed the rights of vassals: to live without being attacked, to raise and grow their crops, and to be exempt from providing slave labor except "for that of the said master," interpreted to mean the king of Portugal. Until his overthrow, Ganga Zumba was considered the leader of both "Old" Palmares in the mountains and those Palmaristas who moved to Cucaú Valley.

The schism between those who trusted the colonial authorities and those who did not was now the new reality. Vainfas[20] notes that "many inhabitants of Cucaú were children of a young age, others were ill, and many neither had conspired against Ganga Zumba nor were allied to the Palmarian faction." The young bucks in the mountains, meanwhile, would rather fight to the death than risk their fate to an intractable enemy who over the centuries had shown no regard for the humanity of African people.

The 1678 agreement granted freedom to the moradores of Palmares who abided by its terms. In the minds of the colonial authorities—and it was their interpretation that mattered—any breach would provide a pretext for rescinding the agreement and a legal rationale to attack the aldeias of the Cucaú Valley and reenslave the people therein. The death of Ganga Zumba, coupled with the failure of the Palmaristas to return nonnatives to the colonial authorities, resulted in the Portuguese annulment of the 1678 agreement. In other words, the "escape hatch" of noncompliance, whether minor or of more consequence, constituted "noncompliance" as defined in the document and gave the colonial authorities the pretext to rescind the much hated agreement the "paper," as the Portuguese

---

20. Vainfas, "God Against Palmares," 59.

derisively referred to the treaty. Cumulatively, the death of Ganga Zumba and the "refusal of return" stoked the preexisting anxiety of the Portuguese authorities such that it warranted, in their view, the destruction of the aldeias in the Cucaú Valley.

Zumbi emerges as a "general das armas of Palmares"[21]—general at arms—in the writings of Pedro de Almeida, the governor of Pernambuco. The governor describes him as a "black man of singular valour, great spirit, and rare constancy. He is the overseer of the rest, because of his industry, judgment and strength to our people serve as an obstacle; to his, as an example."[22] Anderson,[23] citing Décio Freitas, refers to a document received by the Conselho Ultramarino (Portugal's "Overseas Council") that "attributes Palmares's resistance to 'military practice made warlike in the discipline of their captain and general, Zumbi, who made them very handy in the use of all arms, of which they have many and in great quantity—firearms, as well as swords, lances, and arrows.'"

Zumbi symbolized the warrior spirit among his people. There is much discussion about the derivation of Zumbi's name, but I prefer Anderson's conclusion, mentioned earlier, that "his compatriots viewed the name within the paradigm of the cult of ancestors." He was viewed as either a religious leader, a spiritual icon, or an ancestor who rose from the dead. During an attack led by Manuel Lopes Galvão between 1675 and 1676, Zumbi suffered a leg wound that left him with a discernible limp, a badge of courage. There was no medicine for his injury beyond those remedies drawn from traditional practices and what nature could apply.

This proud and majestic individual, sub-Saharan in color, tall and erect, proud of his heritage, knowledgeable and astute in the ways of his enemy, was not easily swayed by the vague, double-tongued promises of the Portuguese. After all, he had known them intimately

---

21. Anderson, "Quilombo of Palmares," 560-562.
22. Cheney, *Quilombo dos Palmares*, 113.
23. Anderson, "Quilombo of Palmares," 560.

from infancy to early adolescence. As Francisco, he had operated in the theater of racism. He saw the stage and all its actors. But here in the forest, what he saw was not an act; it was physical brutality, and it was real life. Moreover, he had seen how greed, avarice, and bigotry digested into the hard stool of slavery. He had heard the Portuguese say, "Beneath the equator, there is no sin."

From 1678 to 1687, Zumbi managed to keep Old Palmares together. But he had enemies on two fronts: the residents of Cucaú and the authorities in Pernambuco. The Portuguese made numerous attempts to subdue Zumbi and his fellow Palmaristas between 1679 and 1692, as one general after another attacked Palmares, all to no avail. Meanwhile, the warfare between the residents of Cucaú and Old Palmares caused Governor Aires de Souza de Castro to call upon his trusted general—Manuel Lopes Galvão, the leader of the attack in which Zumbi had been wounded—to quell the uprising. Ganga Zumba's brother was also actively engaged in warfare against Zumbi.

Because of constant conflict, there was no lasting peace as envisioned by the treaty supporters in Cucaú. This, combined with the vulnerability of the valley, disheartened the people. Many regretted their decision and fled back to Old Palmares. Traitors among the residents of Cucaú aided and abetted the Portuguese; likewise, Zumbi had spies scattered throughout the valley. Tactically, Zumbi needed to rid himself of Cucaú because this settlement was too close to the villages of Palmares. But there were advantages and disadvantages to this course. He had family members on both sides of the equation, and the trade between Cucaú and the neighboring towns afforded him access to guns and essential provisions; however, those who did not side with Zumbi had an intimate knowledge of Old Palmares and how to get there easily, giving the Portuguese a tremendous advantage. What great saga, rebellion, uprising, or planned insurrection has not been plagued by the disease of treachery? History has shown that many slave rebellions in Brazil were thwarted because of betrayal, mostly by Brazilian-born slaves, crioulos.

Amid the fighting between these related groups of Palmaristas, some of Zumbi's loyal cadre who had earlier conspired with Zumbi to kill Ganga Zumba—Gaspar, Cangonha, and Amaro—were captured, jailed, and beheaded; no mercy was shown. Then, in 1680, the defenseless residents of Cucaú were slaughtered or captured. Some vague and unpersuasive cries of injustice were heard from the religious community and sections of the legal community in Portugal and Pernambuco, none of which mattered enough to change the results. The sympathy was of no moment and resulted in only very rare cases of relief from re-enslavement for the survivors.

Despite this adversity, Zumbi fought on. He did not succumb to anguish over the slaughter of his compatriots in Cucaú, nor the killing of his blood brothers who had fought with him to preserve Palmares as they knew it. Zumba and Zumbi reveled in their Blackness and their Africanness as they lived in a valiant effort to retain the only freedom they could expect to find in their lifetimes. As the executioner's ax severed the heads of Zumbi's beloved friends, he could feel that slaughter reverberate in his own body. What had been done to others would certainly be done to him. Their blood was in his blood, their sacrifice his sacrifice. The hope was that one day their souls would commune in the Christian heaven he had heard so much talk about, but for now, the excruciating sorrow of this sacrifice weighed heavily on his heart. "Give me liberty or give me death" was more than a patriotic declaration; it had a literal meaning to these malungos.

Vainfas[24] recounts that Zumbi "increased the number of attacks on sugar mills and farms in Pernambuco. The colonial government did not know what else to do." Activist and writer Sueli Carneiro[25] reports that during one raid conducted by Zumbi's forces, a White woman was taken captive who had been "the wife of the Porto Calvo mill owner." She reportedly bore Zumbi children.[26]

---

24. Vainfas, "God Against Palmares," 67.
25. As cited in Cheney, 147, footnote 24.
26. Cheney, 147, footnote 25.

The skirmishes, entradas, raids, attacks, and counterattacks did not abate. In late 1681, when the frustrated Crown appointed João de Souza, a career military man, as the new governor of Pernambuco, he launched a significant attack against Zumbi's forces, without success. One of these attacks was headed by a Black commander from the Henrique Diaz Regiment. The first of two additional peace offerings was then made through de Souza.

De Souza was replaced in 1685 by João da Cunha Souto Maior, who offered settlement on behalf of Dom Pedro II. In an attempt to further divide the already divided Palmares, this new offer required the Palmaristas to "cooperate or die." According to Cheney,[27] the offer committed the king to free those Palmaristas who were "descended from white settlers and were not black or mulatto." Anyone who had been a slave before fleeing to Palmares would be returned to slavery. Any child born from a woman who was herself enslaved would remain a slave. The former residents of Cucaú who did not participate in the conspiracy to overthrow Ganga Zumba would be considered free; the rest would be regarded as traitors and punished.

Not long after, the king, on February 26, 1685, made a direct offer of peace to Zumbi through João da Cunha Souto Maior. The king had plenary power to bring this matter to a close, and he did so by acknowledging the wrongs committed against the slaves by his subjects. He was repentant, offering Zumbi and his lieutenants the opportunity to live where they wished, in freedom with their wives and children as his faithful subjects and under his protection. On its face, such a broad offer for peace seems to acknowledge that the Palmaristas had won their war of attrition. However, the fugitive slaves had little trust in the integrity of the Portuguese, deservedly so. Could these Europeans peacefully live alongside the Blacks they had enslaved for centuries?

Unlike Ganga Zumba, whom some saw as an accommodationist, Zumbi was a militant. He had long decided that war was better than

---

27. Cheney, *Quilombo dos Palmares*, 143.

relying on the oppressor to keep his word. He chose not to accept the offers of peace. By my count, from 1682 to 1686, at least three governors were appointed, and over ten different military commanders attempted to defeat Zumbi. During this time, a plague took hold in Pernambuco, and thousands died. Needless to say, the colonial authorities had been thus far outmaneuvered by the Palmaristas despite Cucaú and the wedge politics used by the Portuguese.

Cheney and Anderson[28] both write that sometime after 1686, Zumbi visited his adopted father, Friar António Melo, in Porto Calvo. By all accounts, Zumbi retained love, gratitude, and respect for Melo and enjoyed being in his presence and receiving the counsel of his adopted father. This counsel, combined with Zumbi's experience and the advice of his trusted followers, created a worthy and crafty opponent. Some have speculated that Zumbi was on the cusp of establishing a Black state in South America had events transpired differently, especially considering the Palmaristas' successes.

Zumbi's exploits appear to have been a cross between the imaginary Zorro and the real Elfego Baca, two Hispanic heroes of the late nineteenth and early twentieth centuries. Indeed, I dub him "Black Spartacus." Perhaps he was a forerunner of later heroes. And Palmares, as we discussed earlier, was the forerunner of Black towns established in North America. Though many of these towns were destroyed, just as Palmares was ultimately destroyed, the mere fact that they endured for as long as they did, under such adversity, was a tremendous accomplishment.

As previously mentioned, some of these towns do still exist, a testament to the ingenuity and perseverance of the Black people who established them.

The Indians of North America can attest to the duplicity as well as the disdain for their culture that colonial Whites and settlers of that continent displayed toward them and the treaties they negotiated and signed in good faith, later abrogated by the Whites; the Portuguese

---

28. Cheney, 157; Anderson, "Quilombo of Palmares," 560.

of Brazil showed similar behavior toward the Palmaristas. The same species of folk and their descendants were involved in both travesties.

One thing that distinguished Palmares from similar maroon communities in North and South America and gave it a cohesion that otherwise might not have existed is expressed by Funari and Carvalho:[29] "The people of Palmares had a positive sense of their community. They had a common consciousness of themselves as a rebel group. Their common enemy provided them with enough solidarity to resist several onslaughts over the seventeenth century." But the 1678 agreement dismantled this united front, and Ganga Zumba was soon poisoned—a method of regicide not uncommon in the kingdoms of Central Africa, where it was a severe form of punishment reserved for kings viewed as weak or who had abused their power and forfeited their right to leadership.

Vainfas[30] asserts that the date of Cucaú's destruction was around 1680, meaning that the residents of the Cucaú Valley only had peace for two years before being overrun and reenslaved. This caused a stir among the Catholics and the Portuguese legal community. A court case resulted, and a court order was issued on March 10, 1682, two years after the destruction of "New Palmares." Lara[31] relates the following:

> This legal text [court opinion] considered the accord of 1678 a mere "favor" conceded by the governor of Pernambuco to those that submitted themselves to royal obedience, but maintained the freedom conceded to the "blacks and mulattos, their wives and children and descendants" who had sought royal "obedience." Those who disrespected the royal concession ended up being considered traitors, lost their freedom and were condemned to death. In more general terms, the court

---

29 Funari and Carvalho, "Rebel Polity," 37.
30 Vainfas, "God Against Palmares," 59.
31 Lara, "Palmares and Cucaú."

order reiterated the principal of captivity for all those who were slaves before going to Palmares, as well as for those "children and descendants of captive women, following their birth."

As we can see from the opinion, the Portuguese did not take the 1678 treaty seriously. It was a mere artifice to gain the surrender of the Palmaristas. Furthermore, Ennes, Cheney,[32] and others have posited that the Portuguese wanted the cleared and cultivated lands in the mountain areas they had yet to settle. Immediately after they destroyed Palmares, the governor distributed the lands for planting to the victors. As we will discuss later, the *sesmarias*—the awarding of lands by the Crown to its favorite sons—took place concurrently with the Palmares negotiations.

---

32 Ennes, "Palmares Republic," 215; Cheney, *Quilombo dos Palmares*, 131-132.

CHAPTER 13

THE NEGRO NUMANTIA

There are several analogues for the final siege of Old Palmares. One is the Numantine War, which began in 153 BC and saw the Numantians fighting to their destruction against Rome during a siege that lasted over thirteen months. Another is the slave war led by the gladiator Spartacus in Rome between 73 and 71 BCE, and a third, the siege of Masada, occurred in 73 to 74 CE, during the First Jewish–Roman War between the Sicarii Jewish rebels and troops of the Roman Empire. The conflict lasted over three months.

The saga of Spartacus is known to most of us through the movie *Spartacus*. But the real Spartacus, what little is known of him, was quite different. He and his trusted lieutenants, all former slaves, fought the Romans successfully on many battlefronts before being defeated by a wealthy and ruthless Roman general. Plagued by wrongheaded decisions and by the defeat of several lieutenants, Spartacus was killed, and his army scattered.

The historian Charles E. Chapman[1] finds an exact parallel to the siege of Palmares in the defense of Numantia, a key ancient settlement on a hill outside the city of Garray in northwest central

---

1. Charles E. Chapman, "Palmares: The Negro Numantia," *Journal of Negro History* 3, no. 1 (January 1918), 29-32.

Spain, pivotal to Rome's conquest of the region. Roman legionnaires were sent to destroy the city during the third major rebellion in 143 BCE. There is much history involved in this conflict, but ultimately, the Celtiberian tribes that came together to fight the Romans were defeated. The overwhelmed inhabitants of Numantia, running low on food, weapons, and subsistence, burned their city and all that was in it to the ground. Those residents not killed by the Romans committed suicide rather than be captured. Only a small number surrendered.

The siege of Masada, about which there is much information, was the final act of the First Jewish–Roman War. Masada was a diamond-shaped mountain hideout considered to be impregnable and inaccessible. The inhabitants of Masada comprised several Jewish groups, all to some extent in conflict with the Romans. Succinctly, the Romans amassed thousands of soldiers to overtake Masada. Rather than commit suicide, in this case, the residents killed each other but chose not to burn their food. They wanted the Roman forces to know that they had chosen death rather than enslavement.

The common thread running through these unsuccessful but gallant efforts to defend countries, regions, or settlements is the undaunted willingness to sacrifice oneself in the defense of liberty. The leaders of these struggles chose self-sacrifice over capitulation and dishonor. The ignominy of defeat was not an option. And so it was for Palmares.

As previously noted by Kent,[2] "six expeditions went into Palmares between 1680 and 1686," all of them conducted by the Portuguese and costing hundreds of thousands of cruzados, the Brazilian currency at that time. In actual dollars, it is difficult to determine the cost. Needless to say, it was significant.

---

2. R. K. Kent, "Palmares: An African State in Brazil," *Journal of African History* 6, no.2 (1965): 161-175, p. 173.

According to Ennes,[3] "from the restoration of Pernambuco to the time of this Governor [João da Cunha], the expeditions against Palmares numbered more than twenty-five, with no other accomplishment than the destruction of houses, the ruining of their crops, the imprisonment or death of a certain number of Negroes."

The Brazilian historian Sebastião da Rocha Pita, in *História da América Portuguesa* (1724),[4] provides us with (rather baroque) language to describe how the Portuguese authorities viewed the ultimate battle with Palmares. He says, "The difficulty of the war makes a better victory, and the valor of the enemy—whose 'prince' with his 'most valiant warriors . . . disdaining death by our swords, elevated themselves to the highest esteem and voluntarily ran headlong into battle against us'—emphasizes the 'glory of the battle.'"

In this language, we see Portuguese heroism propagandized in the final struggle against the colonialists' archenemies: Zumbi and his Palmarista followers. On the one hand, the Portuguese wanted the battle to be elevated in the minds of the populace so that their victory would be remembered as a historic event, a heroic accomplishment, a grand finale against an epic foe. Ironically, at the same time, the Portuguese wanted to extinguish Palmares from the history of Brazil and to remove its threat from the minds of its White population. Consequently, they pretended the treaty they negotiated with Ganga Zumba was insignificant because to do otherwise would acknowledge the ordeal they underwent to defeat Palmares.

The equation that Zumbi sought to resolve was unbalanced in favor of the oppressors, as it has always been for African-descended people living in the diaspora. The Palmaristas fought courageously against the odds, but the odds became insurmountable, nirvana unattainable.

Returning to the metaphor of Palmares leaders as boat captains,

---

3. Ernesto Ennes, "The Palmares Republic of Pernambuco: Its Final Destruction, 1697," *Americas* 5, no. 2 (October 1948): 200-216, p. 203.
4. As quoted in Kent, "Palmares."

the rough seas and the flurry of storms in the recent past had shattered Zumbi's oars, as they had those of his predecessor; it was now his duty to steady the ship. He hoped to set a course to a welcoming port, a haven that would provide his people succor and a balm for wounds that remained unhealed. But was such a port on the horizon? What was his heading? Was his courageous though motley crew up to the challenge? How was this supposed to end? Where was this optimistic "best of all possible worlds" he had dreamed about, as Leibniz defined it? Or was this world rather, as Voltaire explained, a world dependent on man and his ingenuity to make it his own?

For Zumbi and his people, "the best of all possible worlds" was the one in which they lived. He was already living in his paradise: a place he had arranged and that exemplified *his* imagination and *his* values and *his* wealth, the closest to freedom and opportunity he and his people were likely to get in that part of the world and in that era. Palmares, by their judgment, was worth dying for.

Zumbi's exposure to the Catholic religion—which many in the Jesuit community thought would be unintelligible to Africans because of its abstractions—under the tutelage of his adopted father brought to mind a vision of himself as the king of a "New Jerusalem," a sublime community. He envisioned that one day, his people would bask in the manna of freedom descended from heaven because of the righteousness of their fight. But neither right nor justice are determinants of fate. He and his people would have to win this place of rest for themselves. This was the reality they confronted in a land of hostility, enslavement, and inglorious death.

The trial at Cucaú had failed, providing hard lessons about what lay ahead. But Zumbi's faith lay in a benevolent Providence that had protected him and his people thus far and guided them through much tumult over the years. As the old Negro spiritual says, "If he bought me this far, God is not through with me now." Perhaps it was not his fate, though, as he approached an existential judgment, to pass into their land of milk and honey. Was Cucaú as close to Canaan as they could get in this world? If so, only the abyss awaited them.

Perhaps Zumbi obtained his spiritual strength not from Catholicism but from the African religion of his heritage—from the Yoruba orisha Shango, a god also worshiped in the Afro-Brazilian religion of Candomlé that was still very much at play in Palmares. Shango was revered for his strength, tenacity, malleability, intractable will to resist, and aggression. These were emblematic of Zumbi's character. He called upon this orisha in this critical time of need.

Zumbi did not wax rhapsodic about the plight of Palmares, as captivating orators such as Cotton Mather, the uncompromising moralist preacher, did about politics in colonial Massachusetts. But in his own way, he preached insurrection and usurpation. I imagine Zumbi as a dismissive, analytical, Malcolm X–type leader, a fiery realist when he needed to be but reserved on most occasions; keeping his cards close to the vest yet fighting racism on all fronts; willing to upset the existing system at any costs, pierce the veil of hypocrisy the Portuguese hid behind, and trade swords for swords and arrows for arrows. He wanted to upend the orthodoxy of slavery.

Over twenty years had elapsed since he had left the comfort of his home in Porto Calvo. Wounded and in pain, still suffering the lingering ache from his leg that never healed properly, he knew there was no turning back. His struggle was between the sacred and the profane. His men had bled and suffered while he wrapped himself in the armor of Shango and relied on his vision of absolute and total freedom with no compromises. There is no compromise with death, and there was no difference between death and slavery in his eyes or the eyes of the Portuguese. So there would be no compromise with freedom: either he and his people would be free, or they would be dead.

The previous decade had been difficult and the interstices of peace rare. Zumbi was forewarned of the portentous battle to come. He thought his stores of food and munitions were adequate and his defenses sufficient to turn back the attackers. But he did not account for the creep of incompetence and betrayal, the ever-present Achilles heel of any design dependent on human beings for its success. As in the past before many attacks, and certainly before this existential one, his spies and his sentries kept him informed of his enemy's plans. After discovering the factors set against him, he knew the end was at hand.

The crescendo to this song of disquiet began with the marshaling of Portuguese military forces on March 3, 1687. The governor, João da Cunha Souto Maior, employed the services of the Paulistas, also known as bandeirantes, and backwoodsman. According to Vainfas,[5] the Paulistas had previously refused to attack Palmares around 1675 because of the success of the Palmaristas' guerrilla tactics.

The Paulistas largely emerged from São Paulo, one of the largest slave-trading centers in the Americas, and from secluded regions in the northeast. These areas were essentially backwaters of depravity and de facto slave dungeons for Indigenous and Black people. Anyone operating in this community was bereft of morality. These Paulistas fit that mold exactly: they had no scruples. Cheney[6] relates, "Their brutality was absolute." This assortment of roughnecks, miscreants, the uncouth, the irreligious, and the lowbrow isolated themselves from the main cities of Brazil, creating enclaves and a language particular to their environment and culture. They had their own social hierarchy of standard functionaries, such as soldiers, lawyers, and scribes.

In 1685, Governor João de Souza called upon a leader among the bandeirantes to wipe out Palmares. Domingos Jorge Velho and his men had distinguished themselves among the colonial authorities as "hardened Indian fighters and slavers who had been used in Bahia to

---

5. Ronaldo Vainfas, "God Against Palmares: Lordly Representations and Jesuitical Ideas," in João José Reis and Flávio dos Santos Gomes, eds., *Freedom by a Thread: The History of Quilombos in Brazil* (New York: Diasporic Africa Press, 2016), 51-71, p. 57.
6. Glenn A. Cheney, *Quilombo dos Palmares: Brazil's Lost Nation of Fugitive Slaves* (Hanover, CT: New London Librarium, 2014), 159.

open up the interior."[7] Cheney[8] remarks that Velho had "lost almost every sense of civility." Seen as a savage and a debaucher of Indian women, Velho owned a farm about a thousand kilometers (620 miles) from Recife, where he raised cattle—as well as an army composed mainly of Indians, mamelucos, and disaffected colonists—and lived among the very populations he helped oppress. He was one of the earliest settlers in that region.

Ennes[9] describes the "field marshal" and "wilderness tamer" and his irregulars as being unbreakable, indomitable, and persistent, with the mettle, strength, and heroism to get this job done. Velho entered into a contract with the governor that promised him the land occupied by the Palmaristas if he defeated them. He promised that quilombos would never again occupy these lands. Unlike other expeditions that had run out of food and supplies, lost heart, and suffered deserters, his forces would be supplied and resupplied as needed until the job was done.

The Portuguese had reached the end of their strategies to defeat Palmares. The colonial authorities scraped together the dregs of humanity from the bottom of the cask. Though modestly successful over the years, their regular military had proven inept and unable to withstand the withering environmental conditions. They needed their version of the Marines: a hardcore, quasi-amphibious, battle-tested regiment of killers who took no prisoners.

Velho accepted the contract to defeat the Palmaristas and, in preparation, traveled to Pernambuco from his base in the hinterlands of São Paulo—an arduous journey with much loss of life. But when unrest arose in the Rio Grande do Norte, the governor ordered Velho to circle back to quell it. The Janduí Indians in the northeast, in alliance with other tribes, had caused much mischief in the region

---

7. Stuart B. Schwartz, "Rethinking Palmares: Slave Resistance in Colonial Brazil," in *Critical Readings on Global Slavery*, eds. Damian Alan Pargas and Felicia Roşu (Leiden, Netherlands: Brill, 2005): 1294-1325.
8. Cheney, *Quilombo dos Palmares*, 161.
9. Ennes, "Palmares Republic."

known as the Rio Grande do Norte, killing the settlers, slaughtering their livestock, and making it impossible for them to live in peace. As a precursor of what would happen in Palmares and a reminder of what had happened at Cucaú in 1678, a truce was signed between the colonial authorities and the Janduí to settle this uprising.

The colonial authorities were fighting the Indians and the Palmaristas with only one force capable of completing either job. As in any military campaign, the generals knew the hazards of spreading an army too thin. The focus was on Palmares. What happened in Rio Grande do Norte was to some degree unexpected, a sideshow, but one that had to be dealt with.

The truce with the Janduí recognized their territorial sovereignty and granted them the right to live, plant their crops, and live peacefully under the king's protection. Sound familiar? No sooner had the ink dried on the paper and the Indians disarmed themselves than, on orders of the governor, Velho and his fearsome Indian contingent[10] slaughtered the Janduí men, women, and children alike, leaving none alive to tell the story. The Battle at Wounded Knee and the Trail of Tears provide a North American equivalent. After the massacre, Velho and his men were free to return to Pernambuco to engage in the fight against Palmares.

From 1687 to 1692, Zumbi continued what had been routine since Palmares was founded. The quilombolas attacked, raided, grew crops, traded for guns and foodstuffs, and went about their business as usual. The colonial authorities' aggravation reached a high intensity in 1690, and now a new governor was in town, the fourth since 1680. Governor Antônio Luís Gonçalves da Câmara Coutinho invited Jorge Velho back to Pernambuco "to do to the black rebels of Pernambuco what he had done to the Indian rebels of Rio Grande do Norte."[11]

Around July 20, 1690, the first assault against Palmares began but was unsuccessful. Velho's troops were already exhausted from

---

10. Cheney, *Quilombo dos Palmares*.
11. Cheney, 168.

their round-trip and, according to Ennes,[12] stymied by "the deceits, wiles and strategies of this enemy, and their total lack of knowledge of the layout of this terrain, so irregular and difficult to penetrate." The lack of supplies and these obstacles prevented the attackers from establishing a defense line. They "grew faint, and, fearing that the supplies which yet remained to them would be entirely lost, they retired again to their homes."

Like a failing automobile, this military engine sputtered on and off until 1692.

Reinforced by troops from the northeast after their initial defeat, another assault on Palmares began in 1692. From early 1692 into 1693, Velho's men bivouacked on a deserted beach some distance from Porto Calvo. Ennes[13] writes, "They were stalemated for 10 months in the situation." Then governor Melo e Castro, against the urgings of many, resupplied his field marshal, and Velho pressed his attack.

Anderson[14] imparts that in December 1693, after much back-and-forth between the various governors, the authorities mustered "the largest military force ever seen in Brazil" in Porto Calvo: more than 8,500 soldiers. Once dismissed as unnecessary, cannons were hauled up the mountains, out of range of the defenders.

The Palmaristas had abandoned some of the fortifications en route to Macaco that Velho initially fell victim to, and the fortress of Macaco, the capital, was permanent—a fortress surrounded by three layers of palisades in concentric circles, with moats and caltrops between each circle. Cheney[15] describes "a fort built by a bunch of half-breeds and Africans . . . standing in defiance of the Portuguese empire and the Catholic Church." The Palmaristas would fight where they stood: no more guerrilla warfare.

---

12. Ennes, "Palmares Republic," 208.
13. Ennes, 208.
14. Robert Nelson Anderson, "The Quilombo of Palmares: A New Overview of a Maroon State in Seventeenth-Century Brazil," *Journal of Latin American Studies* 28, no. 3 (October 1996): 545-566, p. 563.
15. Cheney, "Quilombo dos Palmares," 187.

According to Cheney,[16] these defensive designs were said "to have been inspired by a 'Moor' who escaped his chains on the coast and joined Zumbi, teaching him something about warfare and defense." The speculation was that such intricate defenses could not have been installed by a sub-Saharan Black person but rather came from the Berbers (in Arabic, Amazigh, their self-name) or an Arab of North Africa. Historians have often noted this stereotype about the deficits in sub-Saharan African culture. Make what you will of this conjecture. A letter from Governor Castro sums up the frame of mind of the Portuguese, expressing their exasperation: "The audacity of these barbarians, that they are daring enough to establish fortifications that they are able to defend with such resolution."[17]

Field Marshal Velho led several attacks. Cheney[18] relates,

> He'd failed in his first attack, then launched a second without changing tactics or waiting for reinforcements. The only time they'd gotten anywhere close to the enemy's first wall, it was a disaster. Now they were out of cannonballs, short on ammunition, low on food, running out of patience, and tending to scores of men who had been wounded by arrows, punctured by bullets, impaled on stakes, cooked like fish, scalded with water, burned like infidels. The fortress of slaves, criminals, and Indians stood unscathed. As far as anyone outside the fort knew, no one inside the fort had suffered so much as a scratch. . . . This was the second devastating defeat in a week.

Anderson[19] states that after much strategizing and with the aid of his trusted commanders, Velho "built a counter-fortification in order to move their cannon within range of the compound palisade,"

---

16. Cheney, 180.
17. Cheney, 180.
18. Cheney, 190.
19. Anderson, "Quilombo of Palmares," 563.

in what became known as an "oblique circling line." Velho chose to build this slanted line in an area undefended by the Palmaristas to provide the attackers with cover to remove the caltrops preventing their assault on the mountain.

Cheney[20] provides his interpretation of the counterfortification:

> After some cogitating, someone devised a new tactic: another stockade. This one would run at an oblique angle from the counter-wall to a corner of the fortress at the top of the cliff on the north side of the mountain. That point, seemingly inaccessible, was poorly defended, and we can surmise that there may have been only one defensive wall at the point. If invading forces built the stockade at a precise angle, the gunners in the fort would never be able to shoot anyone behind it. If the oblique wall reached the top of the cliff, a cannon could fire point-blank into the enemy wall. The safest way to do this would be to build a wall without being noticed.

In response, Zumbi "reprimanded the guard of this station and gave a tongue-lashing to the chief, saying: 'And you let the whites make this line? Tomorrow we shall be breached and slaughtered, and our women and children taken captive.'"[21]

On the eve of his ultimate demise, Zumbi assembled his closest compatriots for what amounted to a prayer meeting—not the usual prayer meeting devout Christians might anticipate but rather a prayerful introspection and a plea to God for intercession on their behalf. Zumbi knew his fate was decided, but rather than despair, he soldiered on. He could no more lose faith in his God than in himself because he knew that God and self are incorporated into each other. As written in Luke 17:21, and later affirmed by Tolstoy, "The kingdom of God is within you."

---

20. Cheney, "Quilombo dos Palmares," 191.
21. Ennes, "Palmares Republic," 209.

In such a moment of truth, he may have asked himself whether there was an inherent good in what he had done and tried to accomplish for his people, a good that might reveal itself in the progress his people would make over time. He encouraged his men to fight on, to save themselves and their families. They all summoned their courage, knowing their cause was just and their sacrifices would be transcendent. Zumbi knew instinctively that his life would be an example of love and commitment to a cause greater than himself, that a facile attention to the duty of life would not suffice; the dream of life and freedom, establishing an Afrocentric paradigm in the Americas as a bulwark against Eurocentrism, would be a preeminent worthy sacrifice.

On the day of salvation—some would say the day of deliverance—dawn broke. The air was heavy with the moisture of a recent rainfall. The verdant trees and shrubs mixed into the defensive alignment reaffirmed the fertility of the soil that sustained the slopes of the Serra da Barriga. As the early-morning sun grew hotter, the mist evaporated, the low-hanging clouds lifted, and the climate intensified. The surface of the surrounding waters undulated almost imperceptibly, as if a pebble had been dropped into them, forewarning of a more violent wave to follow.

The night before, Velho's men had encircled the mountain. Detachments of various sizes covered the west, east, north, and south to prevent all means of escape. They had built the counterfortification at night to conceal their works from the Palmarista sentries.

According to Kent,[22] "the Paulistas had to fight for two years to reduce Palmares to a single fortified site. After 20 days of siege by the Paulistas, the state of Pernambuco had to provide an additional 3,000 men to keep it going for another 22 days." Anderson[23] confirms that "when they reached the heavy fortification of the royal compound of Macaco, they laid siege for 22 days."

---

22. Kent, 174.
23. Anderson, "Quilombo of Palmares," 563.

In recounting the final battle, Ennes[24] writes that when "one of their [the Palmaristas'] sentinels was captured on the preceding night, they considered themselves as lost, supposing that he would reveal the small quantity of gunpowder which they had." The breakthrough occurred during the night of February 5, 1694. The knowledge the sentinel provided comforted Velho's commanders. Their troops would fight more fiercely, knowing the Palmaristas could not return fire. They would have to fight in hand-to-hand combat. According to Ennes,

> In this confusion, on that very night, the Negroes, in despair, threw themselves against the stockade with which we had encircled their fortifications.... A volley of muskets was fired on those who were already outside the encirclement, by which many were killed and so many were wounded that the blood which they shed as they withdrew served as a guide for the troops who followed them. They imprisoned many; and others began to gather again, but, mistaking the way, a great part of them hurtled themselves from a rock so high that they were broken into pieces.[25]

There are various accounts of the final battle, but they all essentially agree on several facts enumerated by Ennes.

Anderson[26] shares his interpretation:

> The attackers were building a counter-fortification to move their cannon within range of the compound palisade when the Palmarinos began abandoning their positions, either to attack from the rear or in order to flee through a break in the opposing fortification. In the ensuing battle on 5-6 February

---

24. Ennes, "Palmares Republic," 210.
25. Ennes, 210-211.
26. Anderson, "Quilombo of Palmares."

1694, Jorge Velho took some 400 prisoners. Another 300 died in battle, while some 200 hurled themselves or were forced from the precipice at the rear of the compound. In all, some 500 Palmarinos were killed and over 500 total were taken prisoner in the campaign.

Cheney makes the case that the sentinel's betrayal enabled the attackers to prepare for the breakout of the Palmaristas, and Velho's forces were waiting for them. In effect, they were sitting ducks. Cheney describes the Palmaristas walking in a single-file line, guiding each other through the night. Pandemonium struck when the attackers fired several volleys, striking some and missing others. The Palmaristas panicked and scattered as though a fire had broken out in a crowded room and no one knew where the exits were. In the midst of this confusion, clamoring to save life and limb, some Palmaristas gave themselves up, others committed suicide, and some fought to the death.

One can take heart, if that is your inclination, in the fact that the Palmaristas fought valiantly. They were simply outflanked, encircled, outmaneuvered, and overwhelmed by superior force. They were never going to win this battle. If they had, Brazil would be a different country today. The Portuguese equated the victory over Palmares with their expulsion of the Dutch from Pernambuco in 1654, hailing it as a great accomplishment after seventy years of fighting.

Regarding Zumbi, several different scholars describe what happened to him. I am reminded of the movie *Braveheart*, when the main character (portrayed by Mel Gibson) is betrayed, captured, beheaded, and dismembered. His head is put on a pike and displayed publicly for the subjects of the king to see and be deterred by.

Ennes[27] asserts that "as to Zumby, he received . . . only two shots. Not as a victim of disaster, nor of these wounds, but at the hands of the Paulistas, he died 22 months later, November 20, 1695." According

---

27. Ennes, "Palmares Republic," 211.

to Kent,[28] "Zumbi, taken alive and wounded, was decapitated on 20 November 1695. The head was exhibited in public to kill the legend of his immortality." Schwartz[29] elaborates, "Zumbi, wounded and in flight, was betrayed, captured, and decapitated. Palmares was no more, but as late as 1746, slaves were still fleeing to the site of Palmares and once again forming into fugitive groups." This, above all, is Zumbi's most important legacy!

In contrast to the above depictions, Cheney and Anderson, as well as Rocha Pitta (who was alive at the time of these events), tell a different story. They say, in effect, that Zumbi escaped the final battle and fought on against the Portuguese for over a year—that Zumbi had been carrying his son during the final battle, his wives had been following him, and he was anything but dead. "Palmares hadn't really been defeated," Cheney[30] says; it had only been downsized. Zumbi assembled a small group of devout compatriots and went back to doing what they had done all along to survive in this mountainous wilderness, until one of his remaining followers, a mulatto, betrayed their whereabouts to the authorities; he was then captured, killed, and decapitated.

Indeed, if Zumbi had slipped away into the darkness, he perhaps became a phantom of Palmares. Another theory is that Zumbi hurled himself from the precipice during the final assault on Macaco to avoid capture. Lara[31] proclaims "the suicide of Zumbi." I prefer this version of the final events, whether true or false. Nevertheless, all sources agree that the king was dead.

When the invaders entered Macaco, they were impressed by what they found. The spoils went to the victors, including the land Palmares occupied (preemptively awarded as a bonus to Velho and his men), the food, and other useful supplies. The Palmaristas who

---
28. Kent, "Palmares," 174.
29. Schwartz, "Rethinking Palmares," 1319.
30. Cheney, "Quilombo dos Palmares."
31. Silvia Hunold Lara, "From Singular to Plural: Palmares, Capitães-Do-Mato, and the Slave Government," in Reis and Gomes, *Freedom by a Thread*, 73.

survived were likewise divided among the victors and reenslaved.

Velho's men were taken aback to find these so-called slaves had been living better than many of them. The houses the residents occupied, which numbered in the hundreds, were neatly arranged and situated in such a way as to protect the community from fires and other naturally occurring destructive events. Velho's forces also found blacksmith shops and an abundance of water. Clearly the Palmaristas had improved their lives for a lengthy period.

What matters, I would say, is not how long you live but, how you live long. It is the quality of your life that ultimately matters.

CHAPTER 14

SESMARIAS AND THE LAW OF GOOD REASON

A predecessor to the quilombo, in a different context but similar in application, was the concept of the sesmaria: plots of land granted by the Portuguese Crown to peasant immigrants and gentry alike. These land grants allowed the Portuguese who received them to work for themselves toward their own economic success. In addition, within the European slave culture and especially in Portuguese colonies with slavery, small plots similar to gardens could be owned by slaves, enabling them to earn a small amount of cash and grow subsistence crops. Slaves worked these plots on Sundays or holidays as the slave master allowed. This sort of thing was not as common in North American slavery.

Kent[1] mentions that "the ink was hardly dry [on the 1678 treaty] when Aires de Souza Castro began to distribute some 192 leagues of land to sixteen individuals who had taken part in wars against Palmares, Carrilho alone obtaining a twenty-league sesmaria."

If one were to distill the most salient of the quilombo legacies, it would be the pursuit of land ownership by the descendants of quilombolas. Land ownership—of land their ancestors occupied and

---

1. R. K. Kent, "Palmares: An African State in Brazil," *Journal of African History* 6, no. 2 (1965): 161-175, p. 172.

grievously died for over many years—is the essential ingredient by which the descendants of slaves in Brazil retain their cultural heritage. To help accomplish this, the quilombolas and their descendants have used the historical, cultural, and legal practice, albeit short-lived, of land grants by the Portuguese Crown to its favored patrons in Portuguese colonies, specifically in Brazil.

The precedent for the extralegal possession of land was established by culture, practice, and history as early as the sixteenth century.[2] The law enacted on May 3, 1795, which came to be known as the Alvará of 1795, established a legal predicate for the continuation of this cultural norm. According to educator Marcia Maria Menendes Motta,[3] the law "sought to regulate the granting of sesmarias."

As reported by the Rapoport Delegation:[4]

> Beginning in the early 1500s, the Portuguese crown bestowed land grants in Brazil through an already-proven template worked out in earlier centuries during the Iberian "Reconquista" against the Moors. *Sesmaria* laws permitted individuals with the resources necessary to go through the formal land-granting processes and with a stated commitment to improving the land within five years to receive a land grant (or *sesmaria*) on otherwise "empty land." This legal system operated in such a way that, by the eighteenth century, vast tracts of the Brazilian frontier lay in the hands of a few entrenched, landed elites.

The primary objective of the sesmaria system was to address the food supply issue, which became a severe crisis for the Portuguese at various times in the eighteenth century. The objective of instituting

---

2. Rapoport Delegation on Afro-Brazilian Land Rights, "Between the Law and Their Land: Afro-Brazilian Quilombo Communities' Struggle for Land Rights" (report, University of Texas, 2008).
3. Marcia Maria Menendes Motta, "The Sesmarias in Brazil: Colonial Land Politics in the Late Eighteenth-Century," *e-JPH* 3, no. 2 (Winter 2005), 2.
4. Rapoport Delegation, "Law and Their Land," 12.

regulations was not to prevent the uncultivated land from being cultivated but to control how it was used. Additional goals were to (1) regulate the administration of the sesmarias, (2) prevent illegal occupation of the land, and (3) establish an "agrarian regularization," meaning to administer the farming of uncultivated land.[5] The controversy that arose in colonized Brazil as well as in the Portuguese political system concerned the colonial authorities' inability to settle land disputes between adjacent landowners, or *sesmeiros*. The disputes between these parties were numerous, mean spirited, and at times violent.

The Alvará of 1795 established a judicial system to solve these problems. It created an orderly and rational approach while purging the system of unbridled cronyism, nepotism, and patronage land grants. It also detailed the steps and the process that subjects of the Crown must follow to acquire a concession of land and enhanced the power of the land "possessor."

The legislation was an outgrowth of the deliberations of Portugal's Overseas Council (Conselho Ultramarino). Brazil was Portugal's most significant colonial territory. The husbanding of its resources and production capabilities was essential for Brazil's continued economic security. The council therefore sought to safeguard and tightly regulate its land concessions, only distributing the land to persons who ingratiated themselves to the colonial authorities or whose services furthered the acts of colonization. The ability to award sesmarias was a power possessed by only the highest colonial authority: governors of captaincies and the like.

Motta writes that the Alvará "was revoked only one year after its promulgation." Part of the reason was the law's inability to provide a mathematical mechanism for determining boundary lines for the distributed tracts of land. In North American law, land boundaries are called the "metes and bounds" of a parcel of land, usually determined by state-licensed surveyors. Though the Alvará delineated the steps

---

5. Motta, "Sesmarias in Brazil," 5.

a probable owner had to take to acquire legal possession of the land he occupied without "legal title," it did not have the "geometers" necessary to demarcate the land precisely. This was the complaint of those who opposed the law.

The Alvará of 1795 arose from the Portuguese Enlightenment period that occurred during the second half of the eighteenth century, which, among other things, sought to improve the country's law, education, and commerce. The Law of Good Reason was enacted by King Dom José on August 18, 1769. Succinctly, this law recognized custom as a subsidiary source of law; stated that national law should predominate over Roman and canon law, which formed the bedrock of Portuguese law; and determined that law adopted from other nations offered a new or more modern approach to lawmaking and should be incorporated into national law so long as those laws were not in conflict with existing law and filled in a gap with good reason.

Despite its revocation, the Alvará in effect enunciated minimal standards for what a "possessor of land" had to take to acquire legal title. Those seeking regularity of these issues saw the short-lived enactment as beneficial, moving the country forward during the Enlightenment.

Similarly, and as an aside, in North American jurisprudence, the law of real property includes the doctrine of "adverse possession." Briefly, this concept permits an untitled occupier of privately owned land to acquire legal title to that land by occupying it "adversely"— i.e., in opposition to the real, titled owner—usually for twenty years. This is done by obstructing access to the land, treating the land as if it is owned by the untitled occupier, and presenting oneself publicly as the owner of the land. This concept has origins as far back as the Code of Hammurabi around 2000 BCE and in English law in the seventeenth century. The Portuguese used this age-old legal system of political power reposed in the state for political objectives, food production, and colonization.

I bring this issue to the fore as a comparison to quilombo land acquisition in Brazil that ensued from the slave era and to show how this parallel universe of land occupation by fugitive slaves has a nexus with past legal practices and has coexisted with the colonial practice of sesmarias in colonized Brazil. However, quilombolas suffered legal disabilities unanticipated in the original construction of these ancient laws.

Many of the requirements to acquire land by adverse possession under the Code of Hammurabi, English law, and North American law were factually met by the quilombolas in Brazil. For example, as we have seen, the quilombolas certainly occupied land that was otherwise individually untitled for years. (All the land untitled individually and unoccupied by sesmeiros belonged to the king.) Consequently, they occupied land notoriously, in opposition to the Portuguese Crown, which claimed ownership by virtue of its colonial conquest of the land and in opposition to the Indigenous people living on it.

Quilombolas obstructed access to the land and, of course, used the land agriculturally, planting and raising crops and sharing some of what they produced with neighboring communities: a sesmaria requirement. For these reasons and more, they "adversely" acquired title, hence ownership of, for example, the Serra da Barriga Mountains and adjoining properties. Their land occupation lasted for three-quarters of a century—much longer than the twenty-year requirement. On that account, title to the lands of Palmares and the lands of many other quilombos should pass legally to the descendants of quilombolas. But as we know, these rules were never intended to apply to slaves or their descendants in North or South America. To deny them this right is of course a denial of "equal protection" under the Fourteenth Amendment to the US Constitution as defined in American Law.

It should be noted that when Brazil became independent in 1822, the granting of sesmarias was suspended but not eliminated. Thereafter, land could only be acquired by purchase or inheritance, making it virtually impossible for small landowners and farmers and the marginalized to acquire land. But until the enactment of the Land Law of 1850, Lei de Terras, occupation of land as aforementioned became the modus operandi of public land acquisition.

Ultimately, there is historical, cultural, and legal precedent for granting legal title to land occupied by untitled owners—lands such as those occupied by descendants of quilombolas. These precedents, both de facto and de jure, have found their way into current Brazilian law that further seeks to resolve this issue, in a template not dissimilar from that delineated in the repealed Alvará of 1795.

CHAPTER 15

THE LEGACY: I WAS BORN IN THE FOREST

Most individuals and institutions want to leave a meaningful legacy—a record that will inspire and benefit others by the actions taken or standards set. Legacy is the residue of the tangible and intangible, what remains after a life or institution no longer exists in its prior form. It is the wake of a time that has ended, like the frothy turbulence left by a ship or an airplane. A legacy is self-determinant. All acts are considered volitional, except in the case of juveniles and acts occasioned by mental illness. The law makes an exception in these cases.

Legacy by itself is not dependent on worth. A legacy can be either good or bad, healthful or unhealthful to survivors of a decedent, to those who seek to follow the example set. If the legacy is unhealthful, accomplishing something positive can be more difficult for the next generation because there is no path to follow or values to emulate. If the legacy is beneficial, the next generation's task is made easier.

Legacy is evidence of existence, either in values, material gain, or both. An accurate record is essential for proper appraisal. Yet as Richard Price[1] reminds us, "almost all of what we know about Palmares derives from the written words of its mortal enemies."

Many who have studied Palmares believe it to be the most significant quilombo in Brazil in the seventeenth century. And there can be no doubt that its symbolic value transcended its destruction. According to Funari,[2] and in other historical documents of the seventeenth century, Palmares was referred to as a "Republic," the rebel state of Palmares; a communist interpretation of Palmares would see the polity as a people's republic and Zumbi as a people's guide—a Black "Ironman" or Stalin.

The Jesuit priest António Vieira declared that if Palmares were not destroyed, it would represent a beacon of hope for the other slaves and the "destruction of Brazil." He said, in effect, that Palmares would generate other small quilombos and offer a haven for those slaves who "would escape and hide in the bushes carrying all their wealth, which is no more than their own body."[3] He was correct about Palmares generating other quilombos—it certainly did—but Vieira's vision of the African slave was only partially accurate: the African's wealth included much more than just their bodies. They had "their stock," the political culture they carried with them from Kongo before their capture and enslavement. The myopic vision of the colonial slave bureaucracy is only noteworthy for its underestimation of the culture, intelligence, and ingenuity of the slaves they imported from Kongo.

Funari[4] quotes the highly regarded Brazilian historian, writer, and diplomat Evaldo Cabral de Melo as saying ex cathedra, "Palmares

---

1. Richard Price, "Refiguring Palmares," in João José Reis and Flávio dos Santos Gomes, eds., *Freedom by a Thread: The History of Quilombos in Brazil* (New York: Diasporic Africa Press, 2016), 44.
2. Pedro Paulo A. Funari, "Conflict and the Interpretation of Palmares, a Brazilian Runaway Polity," *Historical Archaeology* 37, no. 3 (2003): 81-92, p. 87.
3. Ronaldo Vainfas, "God Against Palmares: Lordly Representations and Jesuitical Ideas," in Reis and Gomes, *Freedom by a Thread*, 51-71, p. 70.
4. Funari, "Conflict and Interpretation."

was destroyed and I prefer that it was so. It was a black polity and if it had survived, we would have in Brazil a Bantustan." Such a statement, according to Funari, manifests the feelings of the elite in Brazil about the symbolic value of Palmares as a "fight for freedom." The elite did not and do not want a Black state in Brazil—or anywhere in South or North America, for that matter.

When evaluating the situation of Palmares in its most favorable light, I cannot help but conclude that it would have taken overwhelming good fortune for this "Black polity" to have survived in the environment where it was founded. The deck was stacked against it from its inception. The obstacles that Palmares overcame for almost an entire century are exceptional and deserve our recognition and respect.

One interesting legacy of Palmares is the account related to us by Eurípides A. Funes[5] of a different mocambo in the Amazon, "located by the bank of the Curuá River in the city of Alenquer, in Western Pará, a region also known as the Lower Amazon rainforest." According to one study, 53,000 slaves were brought to this community, generally referred to as the Pacoval community, directly from Africa and through the internal trade from other adjacent slaveholding states in Brazil. Several quilombo communities formed in this area west of Palmares, further into the interior of northern Brazil and southeast of Guyana and Suriname, where the Saamaka community still survives.[6]

João Farias Guerreiro et al.[7] state,

---

5. Eurípides A. Funes, "'I Was Born in the Forest; I've Never Had an Owner': History and Memory of the Mocambo Communities in the Low Amazon Rainforest," in Reis and Gomes, *Freedom by a Thread*, 399.
6. Price, "Refiguring Palmares," 43-50.
7. João Farias Guerreiro et al., "Genetical-Demographic Data from Two Amazonian Populations Composed of Descendants of African Slaves: Pacoval and Curiau," *Genetics and Molecular Biology* 22, no. 2 (June 1999), https://doi.org/10.1590/S1415-47571999000200004.

> Following the example of other Brazilian regions and South American countries, several communities named *mocambos* or quilombos were founded in the Amazon region by escaped slaves, particularly in the State of Pará, a point of entry of African slaves to the region. Many of these communities remain relatively isolated, and much of their identity is preserved. . . . From 1770, Curiau constituted a point of convergence of escaped slaves from the region including slaves from Suriname and French Guiana.

One can question whether the existence of the Suriname quilombo had any effect on the Pacoval people of this region, considering their geographic proximity.

These mocambo settlements appeared throughout the nineteenth century and earlier, continuing for some 200 years after the destruction of Palmares, preexisting North American slavery and the American Civil War. Funes[8] relates that some 135 quilombolas were arrested in this area and subjected to an inquiry on March 28, 1876. Along with those detained was one Maria Candida. When asked by her interrogator who her owner was, she replied, "I've never had an owner as I was born in the forest." Her peers answered the same way, saying they "had no owner or they did not know who their owner was supposed to be because they were born in the Curuá forest."

Funes[9] conducted his research through the oral history of the descendants of this region's original quilombola inhabitants. He claims, "The grandparents' history is a lived history," and "the community of Pacoval, its cultural expressions, its daily routine and lifestyle, reveal its origins, which are better expressed not only by the skin color of its people, but above all by the elders' memory and remembrances of the histories told by their grandparents, which always takes us to another past." The ancestors speak through their

---

8. Funes, "Born in the Forest."
9. Funes, 399–402.

descendants. Funes also recites that these quilombo societies created a "freedom space," separate and apart from the "enslaver's world, where being free was the greatest experience."

The stories of the Pacoval quilombo communities, the memory of these people, is alive in the "grandchildren and great-grandchildren who are the guardians of the histories their ancestors have told them."[10] The culture of these quilombos has survived and transcended the attempt at their destruction by the colonial slave bureaucracy. The descendants who shared their stories ranged from seventy to ninety years old. One such narration is as follows:

> They were smart people, they were people from Africa. . . . [T]hey came from Africa, a nation of people who know everything. The Portuguese started to take their children while they were gathering whistling duck's nest in the field. They were brought to Belém [a port city and capital in northern Brazil, part of the Amazon Delta] to work, from there to Santarém, then to the Curuá village. After leaving that place too, they went up the Curuá River looking for better conditions.[11]

Funes notes that this story is the classic example of how fugitive slaves left the area where they were enslaved to find freedom in communities established in obscure, inaccessible places—the Palmares/maroon society pattern. In keeping with the traditions of the Africans who settled in this area, "a new family was created, or an existing family grew. The family institution was the base of the social organization of the mocambos and the guarantee of their reproduction."[12]

Funes[13] further elaborates that the story of these quilombos epitomizes the irrepressible legacy of what Palmares accomplished.

---

10. Funes, 401.
11. Funes.
12. Funes, 409-410.
13. Funes, 411.

Moreover, "the existence of these quilombos over such a long period, with a significant number of people, implied the presence of a power and leadership structure, which was able to guarantee some unity, in order to coordinate the resistance and assure the reproduction of the societies." Does this sound familiar?

Because the mocambeiros of the Pacoval region encountered the same treatment by colonial authorities as other quilombo residents throughout Brazil, their fates were similar, but successive generations reestablished iterations of their quilombo. Their mocambos were overtaken from time to time, the fugitive slaves recaptured, and those persons who were born in the mocambos were considered free in the latter years of the nineteenth century due to a change in the *lei do ventre livre*, the "law of the free womb."

Interestingly, the quilombolas of Pacoval and other quilombo communities became one with the forest by necessity. They used the forest as a sanctuary, a pharmacy, and a natural food restaurant. For example, according to Funes, the residents developed medicines from the forest for diarrhea and headaches and antivenin for snakebites that are still in use today. They acquired this knowledge by observing the animals in their habitat. They hunted, fished, and grew crops—and, of course, just as the Palmaristas did, they maintained a "parasitic economy" between themselves and neighboring communities.

The Africans shared space with the Indigenous people whose natural habitat was the forest. Mutual coexistence was their tacit understanding, for the most part. The term *bichos do mato*, meaning "forest beast," heretofore applied only to the Indigenous people as an epithet, came to refer to the Blacks who lived with them in the forest. In the words of a descendant: "Thus, we also call our mother forest our mother because you could say it is from her that we take everything . . . What I mean is, our mother forest is life."[14]

As the White man encroached further into the forest,

---

14. Funes, 413.

[it] forced the indigenous population to retreat further into the remote areas, especially those who had escaped the actions of the missions. Once there, freed from the effects of civilization, they were able to maintain their identity and rebuild their territorial presence. It would be these remote regions that would also be occupied by black people escaping from slavery. The encounter between these "two pariahs of society" was marked by moments of conflict and alliance.[15]

This is what the fight has been all along: one waged by Indigenous people and other groups disfavored by the Whites, usually people of color, against White encroachment onto their lands and into their neighborhoods. A fight to maintain their culture, to live freely and protect their families from laws and social policies enacted to suppress them. To paraphrase James Baldwin, Black folks just want White folks to get out of the way.

Funes goes on to say, "Together with the natives, they learned the secrets of the forest, became familiar with the footpaths through the forest and kept in touch with the quilombolas from Suriname."[16] And even though the communication with the fugitive slaves in Suriname was sporadic, infrequent, and haphazard, the groups were aware of each other and knew where the others were. Hence, after an attack, the quilombolas had a place to flee.

The Portuguese authorities were clearly aware of this cross-border connection and intersection with Indigenous tribes. Funes[17] relates the words of an Obidos deputy in 1858:

> There are the Indians on this side of the Tremubitaque mountain range and on the other side of the same mountain range there are three independent republics of black people that undoubtedly

---

15. Funes, 415.
16. Funes, 416.
17. Funes, 416-417.

must communicate with the people from here using Indians as intermediaries.... The republics that I told you of before were recognized by the Dutch in 1809.... Because of the numerous runaways that occur every day and if no action is taken, certainly very soon we will be without any slaves.

Funes quotes one of his interview subjects as saying,

If the mocambeiros from Cuminá-Panema [quilombos of the Pacoval region] did not go, the ones from Trombetas [a large river and area in the region] opened a connection with the north and the Dutch colony because of commerce, and so these people rise up little by little and the communication increases more and more; not just black people but many Indians too.

The possibility of relocating to the Dutch colony was not lost on the Pacoval quilombo community. Funes mentions that the quilombolas threatened to flee to the Dutch colony (where slavery was not practiced) if they were not granted certain rights and freedoms after the Paraguayan War. I have discussed how slaves have used cross-border conflicts to their advantage (such as in the US Revolutionary War and the Paraguayan War). Here we see that the proximity of the Dutch colony to the Pacoval quilombo community gave the Pacoval inhabitants leverage in dealing with the Portuguese slave bureaucracy, which they used. The Suriname quilombo communities were less than 200 miles from the Brazilian quilombos, still a good distance away by foot but very much within reason if life or limb depended on it. The coordination of vital interests between the cross-border quilombos allowed those of the Pacoval region "to survive for the entire period of slavery."[18]

When the Pacoval quilombos were destroyed over time in one place or another, they regenerated because the fuel of slavery and

---

18. Funes, 418.

igniting force of its abuses were as yet unextinguished and would continue until 1880. They responded much as a plant cut off at the ground whose roots remain alive—watered by a rain that continues to fall—renews itself and brings forth its fruit and blossoms again.

The mocambeiros who survived the onslaught of incessant attacks, the remaindermen, came back to the safety they knew, not the life of slavery they abhorred. They returned to the forest, a habitat that had provided them sustenance, refuge, and family.

As the indomitable spirit of the mocambeiros prevailed not only in this region but throughout Brazil during this era, a false anthropological orthodoxy of White supremacy dominated regarding the characterization of the people who lived "in the forest." Because these Africans could not be suppressed or extinguished permanently, they had to be denigrated, debased, and defamed so that they would be seen as less than human. The classic demonization of an indefatigable foe provided a convenient rationale for their destruction. The Africans cared little about these mischaracterizations of their humanity. They focused on their freedom.

What the Africans themselves thought about their characterization as "Bush Negroes," "animals," "slave refugees," and *bichos do mato*, "forest beasts," is explained in the Funes[19] interview with Barbosa Rodriguez in 1875, when speaking to a "White" about this condition:

> I saw the love of freedom personified there. Two black people, two brothers, Antônio and Miguel, walking skeletons, with white hair showing their age of more than seventy years old, naked, working but not being able to, being in danger when crossing waterfalls, always restless, choosing an unfortunate life he enjoys with tranquility and rest rather than feeling they have to earn power from under the owner. Advising them to come back to their families that they abandoned, that they would be

---

19. Funes, 427.

guaranteed their freedom, they answered to me "We prefer the life of a free animal to the well-being of a life in captivity."

Given such an unappealing choice, I too would choose to live in the forest. The price of regaining the freedoms to which African and African-descended people were always entitled has been high, but those freedoms are invaluable and indispensable.

Palmares represents the resilience of African-descended people in their ability to obtain and maintain their freedom. "Running away" and marooning themselves represented the highest form of resistance to slavery, more costly to the slave owner than any other means. The fact that Palmares remained independent for most of the seventeenth century is astounding. Africans built a heterogeneous society in a foreign land that was resistant to its existence in the extreme. Think about the costs to the slave bureaucracy of that kind of endurance. Think about the cunning and prowess displayed amid the torrent of attacks and adversity. The quilombo's success defied the grand strategies of the slave owners, leaving them with no choice but to destroy the settlement, lest it betoken the destruction of the fabricated edifice of racism, capitalist exploitation, incompetence, and White supremacy erected to rationalize dehumanizing Africans and African-descended people.

CHAPTER 16

PRESENT-DAY QUILOMBOS: THE 1988 CONSTITUTION, THE ENDOWMENT

The Portuguese custom of sesmarias dating from the fourteenth century, the ill-fated Alvará of 1795, and the subsequent Land Law of 1850 all formed a historical basis for Article 68 of the 1988 Brazilian Constitution. These approaches to awarding parcels of land to various recipients are firmly rooted—though politically toxic—in the history of Brazil. In today's world, these land grants to quilombolas are a de jure award similar to a sesmaria, a throwback. Through the process of land entitlement, a labyrinthian scheme designed to delay and deny, Afro-Brazilians have nonetheless obtained a form of reparations thus far unachieved by African Americans in North America.

It took more than a century after the abolition of slavery in Brazil for the Brazilian government to recognize the right of enslaved Africans to own the land they historically occupied. Article 68 of the Transitory Disposition of the Brazilian Constitution (ADCT), enacted on October 5, 1988, reads: "Final title shall be recognized for the remaining members of the former fugitive slave communities who are occupying their lands, and the State shall grant them the respective deeds."¹

Accompanying Article 68 are two additional articles, Articles 215 and 216, which, among other things, enshrine into law the endowment of Indian and Afro-Brazilian cultural rights, obligating the country to protect the expressions of these cultures. They further specify that "all documents and sites bearing historical reminiscences of the old hideouts for fugitive slaves are declared to be historical monuments." Together, these articles indicate that quilombo lands are to be considered "Afro-Brazilian Cultural Territory and should be protected as a national public good."²

Without the tireless efforts of Afro-Brazilian activists, this legislation would not have come into being. Josilene Brandão da Costa, interviewed by scholar Merle Bowen,³ asserts that Maranhão, a northeastern state near the Pacoval community, "has the country's largest number of rural black communities identified as quilombos. It was the first place where the Brazilian Black Movement began.... The Black Movement and the quilombo movement have the same African roots . . . and suffer from the same social problem: racism."

The Bernard and Audre Rapoport Center for Human Rights and Justice reports that "in 1995, on the three hundredth anniversary of the execution of Palmares's iconic quilombos leader Zumbi, the Brazilian State finally began to respond to calls for the effective implementation of Article 68 of the ADCT."⁴ Still, the Brazilian government moved at a snail's pace to implement this law. Delay is another common political weapon. The Rapaport Delegation

---

1. Rapoport Delegation Report on Afro-Brazilian Land Rights, "Between the Law and Their Land: Afro-Brazilian Quilombo Communities' Struggle for Land Rights" (report, University of Texas, 2008), 2.
2. Rapoport Delegation, 15.
3. Merle L. Bowen, "The Struggle for Black Land Rights in Brazil: An Insider's View on Quilombos and the Quilombo Land Movement," in Fassil Demissie, ed., *African Diaspora in Brazil: History, Culture and Politics* (London: Routledge, 2014), 133-154, p. 135.
4. Rapoport Delegation, "Law and Their Land."

reports, "In the twenty years since the passage of Article 68 ADCT, the story of the titling of quilombo lands has been one of undue delay, unfulfilled promises, and constant creation of new barriers to title."[5] Bowen summarizes, "It took more than a decade for Article 68 of the ADCT to be codified and regulated."[6]

In 2003, 2005, and 2007, the requisite laws and regulations were finally legislated to enforce Article 68. Under the left-leaning presidency of Luiz Inácio Lula da Silva, on November 20, 2003, Presidential Decree 4.888/2003, Article 2 of Normative Instruction 20, was put in place to implement Article 68. Lula was the founder and leader of the Workers' Party (PT) and president of Brazil from 2003 to 2010. He was born in Pernambuco.

Bowen elaborates, "In 2007, President Lula signed decree 6.040/2007, instituting the national policy for traditional peoples. This decree defines traditional peoples and communities as groups that see themselves as culturally unique, have distinct forms of social organization; use land and its natural resources for their cultural, religious, ancestral, and economic reproduction; and have a tradition of transmitting and receiving knowledge orally."[7]

On the international front, on July 25, 2002, Brazil ratified International Labour Organization Convention No. 169, accepting and recognizing this convention as applicable to quilombo lands. The International Labour Organization is an agency of the UN, and ILO 169 set a standard for the protection of Indigenous and tribal peoples, quilombo land, and the cultural rights of quilombo communities. Bowen explains, "The quilombos are trying to guarantee their rights through this convention, linking their cultures and identities to collective territorial and cultural rights within the nation-state."[8]

Gradualism remains the watchword for the issue of quilombo

---

5. Rapoport Delegation, 4.
6. Bowen, "Struggle for Black Land Rights," 136.
7. Bowen, 137.
8. Bowen, 136.

land rights. The "fierce urgency of now" is not a consideration. As an aside, parallels exist between Brazil's approach to this issue and that of Southern governments in the US that proceeded "with all deliberate speed" after the 1954 *Brown v. Board of Education* Supreme Court decision to integrate public schools. This ruling took over twenty years to be fully implemented in the South. Brazilian government agencies assigned to implement Article 68 moved slowly and were not adequately funded to discharge their legal obligation under the articles. Jurisdictional disputes and turf wars developed between government agencies assigned to regulate the law, namely the National Institute of Colonization and Land Reform (INCRA) and the Palmares Cultural Foundation (PCF), hindering the strained and overtaxed system.

Clearly, the Brazilian government intentionally dawdled and deferred action in this area because, as diaspora scholar Fassil Demissie, the Rapoport Delegation, and Luiz Fernando do Rosário Linhares agree, "the amount of territory these communities occupy is enormous. According to some studies, the sum of *quilombo* territory corresponds to about one-third of the Brazilian land mass. Da Costa explains that '[t]his is too much land for just one ethnic group!'"[9] Estimates are that "there are currently about 5,000 *quilombos* communities in Brazil."[10] Other authorities estimate between 3,000 and 5,000. Linhares[11] reports that in the year 2000, the Palmares Cultural Foundation found that there were 743 communities, with a population of two million, occupying an area of 30.5 million hectares, approximately 76.25 million acres of land, and "another inventory, completed in December 2002, recorded 1,296 kilombos communities, spread throughout 22 Brazilian states." Only forty-two were given title deeds between 1995 and 2002 by the Palmares

---

9. Bowen, "Struggle for Black Land Rights," 137.
10. Bowen, 138.
11. Luiz Fernando do Rosário Linhares, "Kilombos of Brazil: Identity and Land Entitlement," *Journal of Black Studies* 34, no. 6 (July 2004): 817-837.

Cultural Foundation. More recent statistics aver that as of 2008, "of the over 3,550 quilombos currently recognized by the Brazilian government, only 87 of them (consisting of 143 communities) had received titles as of May 2008."[12] Most of these were issued by land agencies at the state level (see appendices B and C).

There is ample constitutional authority domestically and sufficient international legal authority for the land rights of quilombolas to be recognized. It is not a question of law; it is simply a question of politics. An underclass of people, i.e., African-descended people—the least appreciated and the most disenfranchised people—are demanding vast amounts of irreplaceable and valuable land that they have a legal, historical, and cultural claim to; this challenges the whole basis of Indo-European White supremacy in a capitalist economy, a situation that is untenable to the ruling White classes.

It is not enough to have a law on the books. How that law is implemented by government agencies, interpreted by the public, construed by the courts, and enforced by the executors is pivotal. These factors determine the breadth, spirit, and application of a law. In the case of Article 68, a controversy arose regarding the narrow interpretation of that statute and the clarity and explanation of language (some would say) in applying the "colonial" definition of quilombos. Those seeking land grants must prove that they occupy the land of their ancestors, who were either enslaved or who escaped from slavery. In effect, they must be "fugitive-slave descendant communities"[13] able to trace their past to before the abolition of slavery in 1888.

Activist Josilene Brandão da Costa explains to Merle L. Bowen[14] that "the legislation excludes those rural black communities that cannot prove that they are authentically rooted run-away slave societies."

---

12. Rapoport Delegation, "Law and Their Land," 2.
13. Bowen, "Struggle for Black Land Rights," 138.
14. Bowen, 138.

You will recall that the Alvará of 1795 had twenty-nine articles that laid out a procedure for awarding sesmarias. In 2003, Lula's government limited the authority of the Palmares Cultural Foundation to issue quilombo certification of self-identification (a prerequisite to obtaining titling from the Institute of Colonization and Land Reform [INCRA]) and assigned the duty of administering land titles to INCRA itself, an agency more equipped than any other to carry out this function. In 2005, INCRA published a seventeen-step procedure for implementing decree 4.887/2003, a process to "identify, recognize, delimit, demarcate, and title *quilombo* territory"—a modern resurrection of the Alvará of 1795.

Succinctly, according to Linhares,[15] the procedure requires "a simple statement of their existence in an inventory, mapping, official identification or recognition, and issue and official registration of the title deed." The residents of the quilombos would have to hire experts and consultants to meet these requirements. For example, the inventory identifies the community by its name, county, and state. The residents must provide research that describes their history, cultural underpinnings, economic means, and social relationships. Also, the residents must provide demographic and geographic data, genealogies, history, and information on economic production, such as handicrafts, agriculture, and other commercial activities. And the documentation must include their social organization and religion.

The groups obviously cannot afford engineers and consultants to do this work. In most cases, they rely on volunteers from local, state, and federal agencies. An interagency review is required, as well as a contestation period, within which private individuals who oppose or want to obstruct the pending application can file objections, resulting in more hurdles to overcome.

When the process concludes, a "final report is issued and published in the daily federal legal compendium."[16] This is the

---

15. Linhares, "Kilombos of Brazil."
16. Linhares.

last administrative action required by the regulations before a last determination is made as to whether the group qualifies as a quilombo and is entitled to a deed. If so, titles are issued in the community's name, reflecting the historical African communal style of living. No land titles are granted to individuals.

Some of the lands the quilombolas seek to acquire are in environmentally protected areas or may have military, scientific, or priority government uses. In these cases, "special use" permits are issued rather than land titles. All of this is quite complex and extends beyond the scope of this chapter.

The politics of this issue have resulted in a process designed to be complicated and to act as a disincentive and control mechanism to ward off frivolous claims of quilombo status. When Black Movement activists in 1987 sought to enter language protecting quilombo land entitlement into the 1988 constitution, they made concessions, a compromise in the scope of the language that reserved its benefits and rights to a specific class of people: those communities that fall within the ambit of the Palmares example. A throbbing source of frustration in the Black Brazilian activist community has to do with the exclusion of "rural Black communities" from the definition of quilombos.

Courts of law and government bureaucrats charged with implementing Article 68, as Linhares recounts, "prefer to restrict their understanding of quilombos to the classic concept of fugitive runaway slave, rebellion, or escape communities, because they believe that an updated definition would extend property rights to many 'rural black communities.'" In essence, this is the problem the drafters of Article 68 anticipated would be created by the language in the law: opening "Pandora's box" to allow any group of African-descended people who live in rural Black communities to claim they are entitled to the land they occupy because their heritage is the same and sprang from the same injustices that have yet to be remedied; they are de facto quilombos, having acquired their land for the same reasons as lineage quilombos, but not in the same chain of title.

The pervasive and intractable effects of past and present racial intolerance deserve a remedy. A liberal interpretation of the law, perhaps, can make an earnest deposit on a remedy. Some would have the definition of quilombos extended to include the preservation of natural resources and the longevity of land tenure. These even broader definitions have run into conservative and right-wing opposition that threatens to repeal existing laws and regulations. Overreach by overzealous advocates of an expansive interpretation of the law must be reined in to protect the gains already made and to secure and perfect existing laws.

It is important to observe that the quilombos represent African heritage in the communal sense. Africans were used to being in their communities together, working for the common good, and protecting each other from external threats. Josilene Brandão da Costa[17] expounds on the topic of Black land rights in Brazil, saying,

> The quilombos share a collective view of land ownership. Our African identity is very important. We cannot conceive of *quilombos* without this connection to the continent—we did not start from here but came from another place. When African people were brought as slaves to Brazil, they resisted slavery, and we were born as a result of that resistance. Previous generations came from this historical process. We are Brazilians, but our origin is Africa, and we can never make that break.

According to Linhares,[18] the spirit and psyche of Afro-Brazilians are manifested in the national calendar, which promotes November 20 as National Black Consciousness Day, the creation of the Zumbi Memorial in 1980, and a National Pole of African-Brazilian Culture and Emancipation that "succeeded in expropriating the lands of Palmares at Serra da Barigga, State of Alagoas."

---

17. Bowen, "Struggle for Black Land Rights," 142, 147.
18. Linhares, "Kilombos of Brazil," 826.

The legacy of Palmares is embodied in modern Brazilian law. First, the Federal Constitution of Brazil has incorporated the land rights of quilombolas. Second, numerous government agencies have been formed to implement this law, including the Palmares Cultural Foundation (PCF) and the National Institute of Colonization and Land Reform (INCRA). Third, numerous other regulations, administrative rules, and provisional measures have been authorized by the Brazilian government and its subagencies, all charged in one way or another with sorting out the issue of quilombo land entitlements. All of this and more can be attributed to the Quilombos dos Palmares.

There also resides a legacy of Palmares in international law. You may recall that Palmares would have had a better chance of surviving had other viable quilombos existed nearby. The anthropologist Richard Price introduced us to the quilombos in Suriname, about 200 miles from the Pacoval region. The Inter-American Commission and Court of Human Rights entered judgment on March 29, 2006, affirming the right of Indigenous people to possess their traditional property and resources they have occupied and used that are necessary for their physical and cultural survival. This decision, along with a companion decision concerning an Indigenous community in Paraguay, imposed an obligation to protect and guarantee the communal property rights of lands traditionally occupied by the Saamaka people. These decisions are binding on the Brazilian government via its ratification in 2002 of Convention 169 on Indigenous and Tribal Peoples and were implemented in Brazil by decree in 2004.

CONCLUSÃO

A PERSPECTIVE

"I was born exiled."
—Abdias do Nascimento[1]

The symbolism of Palmares transcends its history, such symbols can be found in the assault on the colonial mindset, the indefatigable will to survive attitudes about the racial, ethnic, and cultural inferiority of people of color, the perceived lower caste of this world, the subaltern condition imposed by the colonizer. Palmares forces us to consider by what defenses a subjected people repel their assailant's physical, mental, and cultural attacks. If the quintessence of a society is ethnocentrism, why wouldn't the other prongs of that society, e.g., its religion, media, politics, economics, law, and education, embrace the same principles? What separates them? Each of these segments operates to fulfill the mission of the whole.

Psychiatrist Frances Cress Welsing[2] notes that symbols have more staying power than a statute, legal opinion, or constitution, depending on how people interpret and embrace them. Symbols resonate with the people who benefit from them as well as those who

---

1. Dawn Duke, "In Poetic Memory of Zumbi's Palmares and Adbias do Nascimento's Quilombismo. In Homage to Abdias do Nascimento (1914-2011)," *Aletria Revista de Estudos de Literatura* 28, no. 4: 11, doi:10.17851/2317-2096.28.4.11-29.
2. Frances Cress Welsing, *The Isis Papers: The Keys to the Colors* (Washington, DC: C.W. Publishing, 1991).

oppose them. The Confederate symbols strewn across the Southern US are a classic example.

The symbol of Palmares galvanizes the downtrodden, timid, disbelieving, ignorant, and naysayers; those who feel defeated before they even begin to fight; those who feel the odds are impossible to overcome; those populations struggling to throw off the yoke of oppression.

The history of Palmares is inspiring to those who can appreciate its history, purpose, and message. From time to time, we need such inspiration to lift us from the doldrums of complacency and exhaustion that characterize the unending pursuit for humanness and equality. Palmares is an aspirational example to those who want to build upon that symbolism as the Black Movement in Brazil seeks to, to become architects of tomorrow's equality. Palmares symbolizes the Black person's state of mind in the Western world. Symbolism matters! So does historiography.

In the diaspora of Africanity and Blackness, what does the personage of Zumbi mean? It all goes back to a deep and abiding appreciation for what our ancestors, parents, and family members have striven to accomplish under adverse conditions and against overwhelming odds. The story of Zumbi connotes a refusal to relent, a steadfast determination to in no way be assuaged from the absolute pursuit of freedom—as defined by African-descended people, not the vision of other populations. This fight against deculturation takes place every day. We would do well to abide by this approach and trust that our sojourn will ultimately end in freedom, though this is something I struggle to do. After all, Jesus tells us, "In my father's house are many mansions; if it were not so, I would have told you."[3]

In the pantheon of African heroes and leaders who fought physical battles against Black subjugation, enslavement, and colonization, Zumbi and Palmares must rank near the top because of the complexity, creativity, and bravery required of them.

---

3. John 14:1-3, KJV.

Consider again African-descended heroes such as François-Dominique Toussaint Louverture, leader of the Haitian Revolution in Saint-Dominque in 1804; Menelik of Ethiopia, who defeated the Italians at Adwa in 1896; Nelson Mandela in South Africa in 1952; and Dr. Martin Luther King Jr. in the United States in 1955. These men fought heroic battles against injustice toward people of African descent. Consider them the kingpins of the African diasporic struggle.

Regarding Menelik, G. F. H. Berkeley declares in *The Campaign of Adwa and the Rise of Menelik* (1902), writing about the Ethiopian defeat of the Italians, "This is the first revolt of the Dark Continent against domineering Europe."[4]

According to Bahru Zewde,[5] in *A History of Modern Ethiopia 1855-1991* (1991),

> The racial dimension was what lent Adwa particular significance. It was a victory of blacks over whites. Adwa thus anticipated by almost a decade the equally shattering experience to the whites of the Japanese victory over Russia in 1905. The symbolic weight of the victory of Adwa was greater in areas where white domination of blacks was most extreme and marked by overt racism, that is, in southern Africa and the United States of America. To the blacks of these countries, victorious Ethiopia became a beacon of independence and dignity.

Palmares has assumed that place in the minds of Afro-Brazilians and other persons informed of the African diaspora.

Afropessimism is an additional factor to consider from a symbolistic perspective. Frank Wilderson authored a book entitled *Afropessimism* in which he suggests that there is no redemption for Black people in the world as we know it—no way to solve an insoluble problem. I

---

4. As cited in Bahru Zewde, "From Adwa to Maychaw 1896-1935," in *A History of Modern Ethiopia 1855-1991* (Ohio University Press, 2002), 81-149.
5. Zewde, *History of Modern Ethiopia*.

confess that I belong to the Afropessimism club. Wilderson discusses having undergone clinical treatment for a nervous breakdown brought on by an inability to cope with and accept a contrived racist system that misled him into thinking that if he did everything right and played by the rules, he would be successful. Such an effort by a Black man has never been enough. Ignorance about the corrupt foundations of a political system designed to perpetuate inferiority translates to being unsuitable, uncompetitive, not good enough. Puzzlement, naivete, and shock engender neurosis in vulnerable people of color. Frances Cress Welsing practiced psychiatry along these lines and sought through her practice to alleviate the mental anguish of Black people poisoned by this hoax.

An Afropessimist, in my view, believes that the plight of Black people will never be resolved favorably in non-Black areas of the world; the idea is a veritable chimera. There is plenty of historical evidence of White obstinance with regard to this objective. Racism is endemic in the United States of America, as intrinsic to the cloth that drapes society as marrow is to the bone. Before its founding and afterward, America incorporated racism into its value system, as evidenced by the compromises required to reach, write, and ratify a constitution by the White founding fathers, most of whom were slave owners, most notably Thomas Jefferson and George Washington. None of this is new information. Even in modern society, when progress seems to hover on the horizon, this scourge persists, rears its ugly head, and resurfaces; it ebbs and flows like the currents of the seas, never permanently still, just waiting for the next breeze to stir.

In those areas of the world that did not practice African slavery or otherwise attest to the alleged inferiority of Black people in the founding or governance of society, racist stereotypes promoted by Western-inspired media have still polluted the narrative. Africans and African-descended people are usually behind the eight ball, working, for the most part, from a disadvantage. And God forbid a crisis arises—then the going really gets rough. This is a tiresome, exhausting, and life-shortening position to be in. Is the price Black people pay for second-class citizenship in the Western world worth the bargain? Racism is an albatross around the necks of colored people. Life itself is difficult for all people regardless of color, but the overlay of racism, an unnecessary fiction made real, adds additional weight.

Having sampled a variety of cultures around the world, I have found to some extent a tolerance, accommodation, or tortured nonchalance toward Blackness. Blackness in the White world, and in countries influenced by that world, is alien. Color adds a veneer or patina of alieniy to White, Black, and Asian person-to-person familiarity. A tincture of the "other" is always at play. In fact, what I have observed in the Americas and in Europe is that the darker the hue, the heavier the burden, whereas in Africa and the Caribbean, the opposite is true: the darker the hue, the more authentic you are perceived to be and the less likely your DNA has been miscegenated.

Despite its history, on a net positive basis, America probably is the best home of choice for African Americans, as many Black leaders from the past and present have argued. There is no panacea for Black people. The US breaks your heart. Many places are nice to visit and perhaps even stay a while, including Africa and the Caribbean, but America is my home, as I wrote in *The Last Train from Djibouti* (2019)—nonetheless acknowledging that you must keep your fists clenched, be vigilant, and stay in the fight, because relaxation is an unaffordable luxury. This is the lesson gleaned from the story of Palmares.

The people of Palmares were always on a war footing; that stance was the only way they survived for close to a century. We are a "hybrid people," as Baldwin writes. We have invested and endured too much to surrender to passivity. To do so would be the equivalent of defaulting on a mortgage when the house is almost paid for, thereby losing our hard-earned equity in American society.

Pessimism about the future of Afro-Americans in the Americas and Europe is not unrealistic. This view has been with us for a long time. In 1866, Henry McNeal Turner expressed optimism about the future of Blacks in America only to repudiate his earlier optimism in 1905 with a harsh critique of the American flag regarding its meaning to Black people.[6]

In 1940, Du Bois spoke of his pessimism in *Dusk of Dawn*, urging Black Americans to fight on without much hope of success. Activist Marcus Garvey saw the writing on the wall and sought unsuccessfully to economically enfranchise African Americans. Other prominent Black writers, including Cornel West, have also expressed an unoptimistic view about the future of Black people in America.

Should hope be kept alive? Of course. Can one imagine an end to anti-Blackness, or shall we conclude, as the psychologist Kenneth B. Clark, an African American whose testimony was pivotal in the case of *Brown v. Board of Education*, said, "Reluctantly, I am forced to face the likely possibility that the United States will never rid itself of racism and reach true integration. . . . I am forced to recognize that my life has, in fact, been a series of glorious defeats"?

Harvard Law professor Randall Kennedy has written on the issue in his book *Say It Loud* (2021). He now appears to have succumbed to Afropessimism in light of recent trends in elections and American politics. And we cannot forget the continuous tragedy of unarmed Black people being killed by White police officers, the most prominent of whom, most recently, was George Floyd. The future of African-descended people in the Western world has been a cause for much philosophical thought by Black academics for decades. Progress has surely been made, but the root of racism is very much alive.

As for me, I see a recurring retrenchment on the part of White people every time society progresses on Black issues. Numerous examples of this persist throughout the nineteenth and twentieth centuries in America. There is always a recoil. For example, after the O. J. Simpson acquittal, there were immediate calls for undoing

---

6. Daniel Fryer, "A Scholar of Race Relations Says He's Now Less Optimistic," *Washington Post*, September 10, 2021.

policies of affirmative action. When Barack Obama became president in 2008, the Tea Party political group immediately arose. Culturally, there is a concerted effort to limit Black progress and to ensure that White people do not pay a price for what little is permitted. Affirmative action and similar government programs are relentlessly attacked for denying equal protection to White folks under the Fourteenth Amendment to the United States Constitution. In fact, White people *should* be the ones paying the price, for it is they who profited from 500 years of enslaved Black labor.

The system of descent and distribution in American law and in other Western countries has enabled the profits to flow from the scarred bleeding backs, stolen uteruses, and sweaty brows of enslaved labor down to generations of corporate as well as individual proprietorship in perpetuity. It is not enough to say, "*I* did not do that," "*I* am not responsible," or "That happened generations before my birth; it's not *my* fault." In this case specifically, White society is the beneficiary of the law of descent and distribution that makes no exception for later generations who did not participate in the accumulation of wealth via slavery. *Non es here nisi superstes testator*: "You are not an heir unless you survive the testator" is a Latin expression in the law of wills and trusts. One need only be an heir to the slave master, corporate founder, shareholder, plantation owner, or sugar mill planter and survive them to benefit from that plunder. Descendants of these privileged classes have received the benefits of this wealth, as has their society. By law, inheritance is a legally protected birthright; it is affirmative action purchased by slavery, fruit from that unsavory tree.

Every time a bag of sugar, a bag of coffee, a bale of cotton, a hogshead of tobacco, or a pack of cigarettes is sold in the Western world, descendants of African slaves should receive a royalty check. African slaves built those industries. They were indispensable to the flourishing of these industries and their ancillaries. Yet slaves were paid only in brutality, poverty, and mistreatment. How likely are economic reparations? So, yes, I am in the camp of Afropessimists. What has been stolen will not be repaid in equal measure.

What I describe above is not an indictment against White people. Quite the contrary. There are many well-meaning Whites in this world. The conflict occurs because Black folks cannot be successful without well-meaning Whites. These people are largely a neutralizing influence—advocates for change and a bridge over the polarity that separates the races.

The achievements of White people and the societies they have constructed (with the aid of others) and that we enjoy and have become accustomed to are gratifying and essential to our daily lives. White society has brought benefits, pleasures, and ease, so long as class status within that society provides access to these benefits. Moreover, the accomplishments of White people are laudatory but were not achieved alone. The accusation against White society lies in how these successes were accomplished—in the absence of atonement for the inhumanity and dehumanization exacted upon people of color and the exploitation of their labor, genius, and culture. This unsettled debt has enabled the construction and maintenance of these societies without acknowledging the price and contribution of non-White actors and without sharing the profits from their labor.

There is indeed an overdue need for atonement, reconciliation, and, yes, reparations for this indebtedness long in default. Why is there still such resistance to these truths? The history is real and indisputable.

On the question of reparations: the following is a prescription that begins to address the race disease that afflicts America. These are general concepts for the payment of reparations. The details will need to be filled in by experts.

Within a degree of mathematical certainty, a value should be placed or determined for the African lives lost in the middle passages that began in 1441 and lasted until 1904 when slavery was abolished in British East Africa. In addition, a value should be placed on all the African and African American lives lost during slavery from mistreatment, murder, state-sponsored killing, and other deprivations. A value must also be placed on the unpaid labor from the enslavement of African-descended people until slavery was ended around 1865. These values should be determined by actuaries and cost accountants, using methods similar to those used to determine the value of a human life in a wrongful death lawsuit.

Next, a government agency should be established with adequate funding to help African Americans trace their genealogy to a slave ancestor, if any exist, should they desire. Credentialed genealogists should be employed to research applicants for reparations to determine their eligibility. In addition to government funding, reasonable fees based on the ability to pay should be charged for the genealogy service, reimbursable to the applicant if the service discovers an enslaved African ancestor. If a family can determine such genealogy without government assistance, a tax deduction shall be permitted up to a specified dollar amount for actual costs incurred. All fees collected by the government for this purpose shall be paid to a trust as described below.

Determination of ancestral slave heredity shall thereby enable that person to establish their eligibility for the reparations program. Authenticity—that is, being able to trace through a credible process a family's ancestral link to an enslaved ancestor—shall be a prerequisite to receiving benefits from this program. This requirement is similar to the quilombolas' requirement in Brazil to gain title to land occupied by quilombola ancestors. Economic status of African-descended people is not a disqualifying criterion; had race not been a factor in the lives of Black people in the Americas and Europe, their status would be enhanced from their current state wherever they fall on the scale in the economic system.

I propose using historically Black colleges and universities (HBCUs) as the payment mechanism for reparations. As a graduate of one of these very fine universities, I can attest to the benefit of graduating from one of them. Every Black high school graduate who desires to attend a four-year or junior college or trade school should be guaranteed admission to an HBCU, junior college, or vocational training facility of their choice, all expenses paid. Black students may apply to attend any White university they choose. However, if such a school was built by slaves or endowed with funds derived from the slave trade in any manner whatsoever, that student who is accepted and meets the eligibility standards of descendancy from a slave ancestor shall have their tuition, room, and board paid by the university or by the trust established as described herein. Several prominent universities—Georgetown University, most notably—have taken modest steps in this direction.

A trust should be established much like the Indian Trust Fund, which is managed by the Bureau of Indian Affairs in the Department of the Interior, funded as aforementioned by the United States government to pay the fees and costs, including room and board, books, and incidentals, for any eligible student who can establish descendancy from a slave ancestor.

This trust should be managed by trustees appointed by a branch of the federal courts, preferably a federal appeals court such as the United States Court of Appeals for the District of Columbia Circuit, because appeals from this appellate court may go directly to the United States Supreme Court. Trustees shall have rotating tenures of four years and backgrounds in finance, economics, budgeting, sociology, and education. Trustees shall not be paid a salary but shall have their expenses reimbursed. To serve on the board of trustees should be an honor and a privilege for those selected, not sought after for remuneration.

The Descendants of Enslaved Peoples Fund (DEPF), the trust, should act and serve as a de jure endowment for HBCUs. Black faculty and scholars employed by these institutions should be supported with grants and stipends from this fund to further their study and research. And a nonprofit organization should be formed to strengthen the academic offerings, standards, research, teaching methods, libraries, laboratories, and administration of these schools. This will enable them to maintain a high standard of competitiveness and academic excellence in all aspects of their operations without the need to be concerned with their economic viability. The mission of this nonprofit should be to make these schools equal to and competitive with, if not better than, any White university in the United States.

Every Black descendant of a slave who wants to work and is physically able to do so should be guaranteed a job in accordance with their skills and abilities. Black people with professional degrees shall not be guaranteed a job but given assistance to find a suitable position. Five hundred years of enslavement without pay ought to equal guaranteed employment with pay for another five hundred years.

The Small Business Administration and the Department of Agriculture shall be engaged to make loans and provide management assistance and technical services to Black businesspeople and farmers to facilitate the retention and expansion of Black farms and businesses and to enable capital formation. By statute, these as well as the educational component shall be immune from attack on equal protection grounds.

African and Caribbean countries that have been the recipients of predatory lending from the Americas or Europe shall have their loans forgiven. And grants, not loans, from these same countries and continents shall be the means of finance for African countries, administered by an international governmental agency similar to the World Health Organization, until this international organization determines that proper governance and financial integrity are in place in recipient African countries.

Globally, every European country that colonized or seized or traded slaves from an African or Caribbean country or enslaved its people, exploited its minerals and resources, and exploited political divisions should be made to pay royalties and fees to those African countries so colonized. The royalties shall be paid on the end value of the products and added value these resources made to the products produced or moneys added to their treasuries.

Citizenship shall be offered by colonizer countries to people in North and South America and North Africa who can prove an ancestral tie to an enslaved ancestor seized by that European country. Tuition and fees and preferential admission to a college or university in Europe or North America, depending on ancestral ties, shall be awarded to students from these African and Caribbean countries who can prove eligibility as aforementioned.

The United Nations shall monitor and annually report on compliance with these mandates.

These countries should make grants, not loans, for capital improvements in schools, roads, hospitals, leadership institutes, and overall infrastructure. Some Caribbean countries—members of Caricom, of which there are sixteen—have already started agitating for these kinds of reparations.

Affirmative action in education, employment, healthcare administration, policing and law enforcement, and other sectors of the economy should be made public policy through law. Brazil sought to implement an affirmative action program during the Lula administration between 2003 and 2010.

How long should all this last? For 246 years: as long as slavery and Jim Crow existed in North America and in Europe.

All of this, of course, is a wish list in the "best of all possible worlds," probably a Leibniz-style optimism.

Here is an analogy to explain why such reparations should be made: In the federal criminal court system, a defendant must first "accept responsibility" for their crimes before the court will consider a sentence reduction. Often, a plea agreement entered into by a criminal defendant acknowledges this acceptance. This is a bedrock principle in federal sentencing. What then prevents the United States and Europe from accepting responsibility for their crimes against the humanity of Black people? This failure is an indictment of Western democratic values, a blatant hypocrisy for all to witness. These hypocrisies are not lost on competing world government systems and ideologies, which have used them in propaganda battles against Western countries, particularly the United States. To many, this self-inflicted contradiction is palpable and repugnant. And until there is a substantive resolution of this centuries-old cancer, progress toward a more perfect union will be minimal and slow.

Though structural racism is endemic to the Americas and Europe, it is imperative that a work-around be found. As I've mentioned, James Baldwin often wrote on the theme that most Black people just want White people to get out of the way; give us our rights unbounded by race, and we will make our own way. We are a self-reliant people.

Modern African-descended people must apply the lessons of Palmares and build a figurative palisaded enclosure around our communities. For example, we should do away with self-inflicted wounds, such as a failure to grasp and understand how to matriculate successfully within the existing system, as flawed as it may be, in the legal, educational, and economic spheres. We should also end the commission of senseless crimes: Black-on-Black murders and other self-destructive criminal behavior.

Some of our people, especially our young people, operate like they have no idea about the consequences of their actions or are oblivious to the system's desire to rid itself of them—making it easy for the system to throw them away in prison for ten, twenty, or thirty years. Only after a sentence for the crime is levied do they realize the gravity of their wrongful behavior and the heavy price the system will exact from them individually, as well as the cost to their families and community. When people of color leave their fates to biased courts, racist judges and prosecutors, and incompetent lawyers, they have defaulted on their obligations to themselves and to their people. The closest thing to justice Black people will ever receive in this society, as it is presently constituted, is the justice they get for themselves by solving their own problems as best they can. Anything else is at worst a misadventure and at best a lark.

Moreover, we need to eliminate the crab barrel mentality of pulling each other down rather than lifting each other up; we need to place importance on knowing, learning, and appreciating our history; we need to put an end to discrimination within the race and the petty jealousies that exist in some of our communities. These are improvement opportunities that will otherwise work against us. Fortunately, there are many exceptions. All populations have similar problems, but we, as a beleaguered people living in a hostile environment, can least afford them, and we must work hard to overcome them.

Lastly, Black people must take advantage of existing opportunities and leave no crumbs on the table. Every Black student should carry a knapsack full of books and a sleeping bag under one arm—so that they will keep their heads in the books, read and keep reading, and can spend the night in the schoolhouse. I believe the only salvation for Black people is education and entrepreneurship. Learn a skill or trade so that you are useful to other people. Make something you can sell, or start a business. As the old folks used to say (and my dad loved this expression), "Root hog or die poor." There are numerous examples of populations that apply this formula.

These are some of the defenses that need to be applied in African American communities—nothing new here—to ensure the best opportunity to survive and prosper. Remember, the people of Palmares not only grew crops for their own subsistence, but they also produced enough to trade with neighboring communities. And they worked together to protect each other and their community from harm. They were united in their fight against the Dutch and Portuguese because their very lives, and the lives of their children, depended on their ingenuity. They took pride in their community. They had a fortress mentality.

We have a vested interest in keeping America moving forward, helping it to evolve into that "more perfect union," to be better than it is, and to live up to its heralded creed. America was founded, in part, on lofty principles—ideals and wish fulfillment, as Freud would say—none of which included people of color or the Indigenous. The Constitution was amended, as you know, to protect the rights of those it originally excluded. Hence, the Reconstruction Amendments: the Thirteenth, Fourteenth, and Fifteenth Amendments, and other civil rights acts enacted from 1866 through 1968. Nonetheless, the fault line in American democracy is the denial of equal protection under the Fourteenth Amendment to people of color and its obtuse application to Whites when Black folks are favored in laws and social practices. For us, the ideals, principles, and lofty proclamations are not self-executing. They must be fought for every day to make them real and alive, as the Palmaristas had to fight every day for their right to freedom, dignity, and self-respect as equal human beings.

Understanding how the system we operate in works is essential for survival. For instance, America is not a true democracy, because of the Electoral College, voter suppression, gerrymandering, and the use of the filibuster rule in the Senate. True democracies are ruled by political majorities, not political minorities. In the United States, political minorities often rule more substantially, depending on how shrewd their manipulations are. We must work with and understand that.

America is indeed a republic, where the people exercise power through their elected representatives. According to Runciman,[7] the American form of democracy is impregnated with hypocrisy, as are other democracies worldwide. There are only two types of politicians in democratic politics: an honest hypocrite who exercises "reserve or holding back in the spirit of avoiding untruths" and the "sincere liars. . . . [B]oth wear masks." Runciman gives examples of each and provides names to match, but I shall not do that here. Suffice it to

---

7. David Runciman, *Political Hypocrisy: The Mask of Power, from Hobbes to Orwell and Beyond* (Princeton University Press, 2008), 194-238.

say "there is a certain honesty to this: after all, that is where the main business of politics has always been done, even in democracy." Finally, Runciman says, "People preferred the liar to the hypocrite because the liar was simply trying to deceive them. The hypocrite was patronizing them, which is worse." But "the liar cannot govern without becoming a hypocrite." Runciman reaffirms that "hypocrisy *in* democracy is both inevitable and, in many ways, essential. But hypocrisy *about* democracy can be fatal."

There is a system within the system. Nothing is what it appears to be on paper. Ganga Zumba and his cohorts learned that lesson the hard way in 1678. The Palmaristas did not understand how the Portuguese system worked, nor did they perceive or understand the fraud embodied in the agreement they signed. Ganga Zumba believed the Portuguese intended to grant them some form of sovereignty over the Cucaú region. Because it would have violated the Portuguese's supreme law and doctrine, this was not legally possible, yet the Portuguese chose to patronize them. A pledge to grant some form of sovereignty was a lie and a hypocrisy.

Brazil is a school for understanding color consciousness, with its many varieties of skin tone and treatment according to shade. We can understand a lot about race in North America by understanding more about Afro-Brazilian culture and history.

Barry Goldwater, the former Republican senator from Arizona, uttered the phrase "Extremism in defense of liberty is no vice" at the 1964 Republican Convention. Though he did not write these words, he has come to be identified with them. African-descended people can apply the thrust of that language in our struggle by saying, "Extremism in defense of Black rights is no threat, except to those who seek to do us harm."

In furtherance of that view, John Hope Franklin[8] writes in his memoir, "There are hundreds of instances, many of which must be

---

8. John Hope Franklin, *Mirror to America* (New York: Farrar, Straus and Giroux, 2005).

known to you, where achievements and contributions [speaking of Black achievements in the United States] ... were not the result of civil rights but were, indeed, in spite of the denial of civil rights." He goes on to say, "I am afraid that I cannot 'tidy up' the history that Americans themselves have made.... The past cannot be sacrificed ... for the sake of the present.... The history of the Negro and civil rights in the United States is not a pretty picture."

And on the same subject, Franklin declared to the BBC that "the struggle for equality in the United States seems never-ending."

There may or may not be a God or a benevolent Providence, but there is nature, reality, and truth. As poet and writer Heinrich Heine[9] has said, "We will leave heaven to the angels and the sparrows." Black people must understand that in this competitive world, our fate is in our own hands. In the words of Dawn Duke,[10] discussing work by the poet Aberlardo Rodrigues, Zumbi's example "pushes forward today[,] sustaining a state of warrior readiness and the conviction that the battle is not over." The attainment of freedom, equal rights under the law, and first-class citizenship in its fullest dimensions, immunities, privileges, and protections cannot be left to chance.

Roderick Bush[11] embraces the view of historian John Henrik Clarke, who claims, "History is not everything ... but it is the starting point. History is a clock that people use to tell their time of day. It is a compass they use to find themselves on the map of human geography. It tells them where they are, but more importantly, what they must be." I agree. I can always think of things I am not: I prefer to think about what I am.

Nevertheless, for millennia, the world has been the White man's

---

9. Heinrich Heine, quoted in Sigmund Freud, *The Future of an Illusion* (New York: W. W. Norton & Company, 1989), 63-64, note 4.
10. Dawn Duke, "Beyond the Quilombo? The State of Zumbi's 'Palmares' According to the Poets," *Obsidian: Literature in the African Diaspora* 13, no. 1 (2012).
11. Roderick D. Bush, *The End of White World Supremacy: Black Internationalism and the Problem of the Color Line* (Philadelphia: Temple University Press, 2009), 7.

oyster. Only now is the pearl being slowly revealed to be shared by people of color. I said earlier that this slog was akin to a chimera. Yes, it is a dream yet unfulfilled, a political desideratum, but perhaps actually more like a unicorn: highly prized but improbable.

Inshallah!

ACKNOWLEDGMENTS

I want to acknowledge the ever-present and enduring support of Dr. Michelle Palmer Lee for her willingness to review, comment, and edit portions of the manuscript. Without her very able contribution, this project would not have realized its full potential.

In addition, I want to thank the residents of the Quilombo do Campinho da Independência outside of Paraty for their very warm and gracious hospitality when Michelle and I visited them on February 23, 2012. It was their story that energized me to undertake this project.

Special thanks especially to "Sky" Schuyler Foerster, whose suggestions enhanced the clarity and organization of the manuscript, and Robert B. Toplin and Norman C. Hill for their very meaningful comments and suggestions, all of which helped to strengthen and tighten the manuscript.

APPENDIX A

Quilombo Communities with Title as of May 2008

Source: The Bernard and Audre Rapoport Center, University of Texas at Austin; Comissão Pro-Indio de São Paulo, CPI-SP https://law.utexas.edu/wp-content/uploads/sites/31/2016/02/brazil-eng.pdf

Quilombo Territory	Community	Families	Size (hectares)	Municipality	State	Titling Agency	Year Awarded Title
Boa Vista	Boa Vista	112	1.125, 0341	Oriximina	PA	Incra	1995
Água Fria	Água Fria	15	557, 1355	Oriximina	PA	Incra	1996
Pacoval	Pacoval	115	7.472, 879	Alenquer	PA	Incra	1996
Trombetas	Bacabal, Aracuan de Cima, Aracuan do Meio, Aracuan de Baixo, Serrinha, Terra Preta II, Jarauacá	138	80.887, 0941	Oriximina	PA	Incra; Iterpa	1997
Erepecuru	Pancada, Araçá, Espírito Santo, Jauari, Boa Vista do Cuminá, Varre Vento, Acapú	154	221.044, 2605	Oriximina	PA	Incra; Iterpa	1998 2000
Itamoari	Itamoari	33	5.377, 602	Cachoeira de Piria	PA	Incra	1998
Abacatal - Aurá	Abacatal - Aurá	53	308, 1991	Ananindeua	PA	Iterpa	1999
Campinho da Independência	Campinho da Independência	59	287, 9461	Parati	RJ	Secretaria de Assuntos Fundiários do Rio de Janeiro	1999
Curiau	Curiau	108	3.321, 8931	Macapa	AP	Fundação Cultural Palmares	1999
Eira dos Coqueiros	Eira dos Coqueiros	35	1.011, 8271	Codo	MA	Iterma	1999
Mocorongo	Mocorongo	24	162, 6254	Codo	MA	Iterma	1999
Rio de Contas	Bananal, Barro do Brumado	148	1.339, 2768	Rio de Contas	BA	Coordenação de Desenvolvimento Agrário	1999
Santo Antônio dos Pretos	Santo Antonio dos Pretos	102	2.139, 55	Codo	MA	Iterma	1999

Quilombo Lands with Title in Brazil							
Quilombo Territory	Community	Families	Size (hectares)	Municipality	State	Titling Agency	Year Awarded Title
Cabeceiras	São José, Silêncio, Matar, Cuecê, Apui, Castanhaduba	445	17.189, 6939	Obidos	PA	Fundação Cultural Palmares	2000
Castainho	Castainho	206	183, 6	Garanhuns	PE	Fundação Cultural Palmares	2000
Conceição das Crioulas	Conceição das Crioulas	750	17.845, 0015	Salgueiro	PE	Fundação Cultural Palmares	2000
Furnas da Boa Sorte	Furnas da Boa Sorte	52	1.475	Corguinho	MS	Fundação Cultural Palmares; Idaterra	2000 2006
Furnas do Dionísio	Furnas do Dionísio	92	1.031, 8905	Jaraguari	MS	Fundação Cultural Palmares	2000
Gurupá	Jocojó, Flexinha, Carrazedo, Camutá do Ipixuna, Bacá do Ipixuna, Alto Ipixuna, Alto do Pucuruí, Gurupá-mirin	300	83.437, 1287	Gurupa	PA	Iterpa	2000
Kalunga	Kalunga	600	253.191, 72	Monte Alegre de Goias / Teresina de Goias / Cavalcante	GO	Fundação Cultural Palmares	2000
Mangal/Barro Vermelho	Mangal	295	7.468, 9643	Sítio do Mato	BA	Fundação Cultural Palmares	2000
Maria Ribeira	Maria Ribeira	32	2.031, 8727	Gurupa	PA	Iterpa	2000
Mata Cavalo	Mata Cavalo	418	14.748, 3413	Nossa Senhora do Livramento	MT	Fundação Cultural Palmares	2000
Mocambo (SE)	Mocambo (SE)	113	2.100, 54	Porto da Folha	SE	Fundação Cultural Palmares	2000
Porto Corís	Porto Coris	21	199, 3001	Leme do Prado	MG	Fundação Cultural Palmares	2000
Rio das Rãs	Rio das Rãs	300	27.200	Bom Jesus da Lapa	BA	Fundação Cultural Palmares	2000
Santana (RJ)	Santana (RJ)	25	828	Quatis	RJ	Fundação Cultural Palmares	2000
Laranjituba/África	Laranjituba, África	48	118, 0441	Moju	PA	Iterpa	2001
Maria Rosa	Maria Rosa	20	3.375, 6582	Iporanga	SP	Itesp	2001
Pilões	Pilões	51	5.908, 6824	Iporanga	SP	Itesp	2001
São Pedro (SP)	São Pedro (SP)	39	4.558, 1986	Eldorado / Iporanga	SP	Itesp	2001
Bailique	Bailique Beira, Bailique Centro, Poção, São Bernardo	112	7.297, 691	Oeiras do Para / Baião	PA	Iterpa	2002

APPENDIX A

Quilombo Lands with Title in Brazil							
Quilombo Territory	Community	Families	Size (hectares)	Municipality	State	Titling Agency	Year Awarded Title
Bom Remédio	Bom Remédio	116	588, 167	Abaetetuba	PA	Iterma	2002
Camiranga	Camiranga	39	320, 6121	Cachoeira de Piria	PA	Iterpa	2002
Cipó dos Cambaias	Cipó dos Cambaias	124	2.440	Sao Joao do Soter	MA	Iterma	2002
Guajará Miri	Guajará Miri	70	1.024, 1954	Acara	PA	Iterpa	2002
Icatu	Icatu	80	1.636, 6122	Mocajuba / Baiao	PA	Iterpa	2002
Igarapé Preto	Igarapé Preto, Baixinha, Panpelônia, Teófilo, Varzinha, Campelo, Cupu, França, Araquenbaua, Carará, Costeiro, Igarapezinho	565	17.357, 0206	Baiao / Oeiras do Para / Mocajuba	PA	Iterpa	2002
Ilhas de Abaetetuba	Campopema, Jenipaúba, Acaraqui, Rio Tauaré-açu, Arapapu, Alto Itacuruça, Baixo Itacuruça, Igarapé São João (Médio Itacuruça)	701	11.458, 532	Abaetetuba	PA	Iterpa	2002
Jenipapo	Jenipapo	74	589	Caxias	MA	Iterma	2002
Jurussaca	Jurussaca	45	200, 9875	Tracuateua	PA	Iterpa	2002
Santa Fé/Santo Antônio	Santa Fé, Santo Antônio	28	830, 8776	Baiao	PA	Iterpa	2002
Santa Rita de Barreira	Santa Rita de Barreira	35	371, 3032	Sao Miguel do Guama	PA	Iterpa	2002
São José de Icatu	São José de Icatu	80	1.636, 6122	Baiao	PA	Iterpa	2002
Alto Trombetas	Abuí, Paraná do Abuí, Tapagem, Sagrado Coração, Mãe Cue	182	138.788	Oriximina	PA	Iterpa	2003
Itancuã Miri	Itancuã Miri	96	968, 9932	Acara	PA	Iterpa	2003
Ivaporunduva	Ivaporunduva	82	672, 2844	Eldorado	SP	Itesp	2003
Pedro Cubas	Pedro Cubas	40	2.449	Eldorado	SP	Itesp	2003
Santa Maria do Mirindeua	Santa Maria do Mirindeua	85	1.763, 0618	Moju	PA	Iterpa	2003
Santo Cristo	Santo Cristo	52	1.767, 0434	Moju	PA	Iterpa	2003
Bela Aurora	Bela Aurora	32	2.410, 2754	Cachoeira de Piria	PA	Incra	2004
Paca e Aningal	Paca, Aningal	22	1.284, 2398	Viseu	PA	Incra	2004
Altamira	Povoado Altamira		1.220, 9398	Pinheiro	MA	Iterma	2005

Quilombo Lands with Title in Brazil							
Quilombo Territory	Community	Families	Size (hectares)	Municipality	State	Titling Agency	Year Awarded Title
Jamari dos Pretos	Jamari dos Pretos	162	6.613, 063	Turiacu	MA	Iterma	2005
Nossa Senhora da Conceição (PA)	Nossa Senhora da Conceição (PA)	54	2.393, 0559	Moju	PA	Iterpa	2005
Olho D'água do Raposo	Olho D'água do Raposo		187, 3333	Caxias	MA	Iterma	2005
Santa Maria do Tracateua	Santa Maria do Tracateua		833, 3833	Moju	PA	Iterpa	2005
São Manoel	São Manuel	68	1.293, 1786	Moju	PA	Iterpa	2005
São Sebastião dos Pretos	São Sebastião dos Pretos	62	1.010, 2186	Bacabal	MA	Iterma	2005
Agrical II	Agrical II		323	Bacabeira	MA	Iterma	2006
Bom Jesus dos Pretos	Bom Jesus dos Pretos		216, 3937	Candido Mendes	MA	Iterma	2006
Carananduba	Carananduba		644, 5477	Acara	PA	Iterpa	2006
Centro Ouro	Bom Jesus Centro Ouro, Nossa Senhora das Graças, São Bernardino		5.243, 1409	Moju	PA	Iterpa	2006
Conceição do Macacoari	Conceição do Macacoari	30	8.465, 471	Macapa	AP	Incra	2006
Imbiral	Povoado Imbiral		46, 4981	Pedro do Rosario	MA	Iterma	2006
Jacunday	Jacunday		1.701, 5887	Moju	PA	Iterpa	2006
Jussaral	Santa Helena		345, 4331	Itapecuru Mirim	MA	Iterma	2006
Lago Grande	Lago Grande		906, 8315	Peritoro	MA	Iterma	2006
Olho D'água dos Pires	Olho D'água dos Pires		623, 839	Esperantina	PI	Interpi	2006
Parateca e Pau d'arco	Pau D'Arco, Parateca	500	41.780	Malhada / Palmas de Monte Alto	BA	Secretaria de Patrimônio da União	2006
Queluz	Queluz		256	Anajatuba	MA	Iterma	2006
Rio dos Peixes	Povoado Rio dos Peixes		54, 2234	Pinheiro	MA	Iterma	2006
Santa Izabel	Povoado Santa Izabel		837, 6155	Candido Mendes	MA	Iterma	2006
Santana (MA)	Povoado Santana		201, 1171	Santa Rita	MA	Iterma	2006
Santo Inácio	Povoado Santo Inácio		1.363, 4178	Pinheiro	MA	Iterma	2006
Sítio Velho	Sítio Velho	92	92.335	Assuncao do Piaui	PI	Interpi	2006
Usina Velha	Usina Velha		1.160, 9576	Caxias	MA	Iterma	2006
Galvão	Galvão	32	2.234, 33	Eldorado / Iporanga	SP	Itesp	2007

Quilombo Lands with Title in Brazil							
Quilombo Territory	Community	Families	Size (hectares)	Municipality	State	Titling Agency	Year Awarded Title
Jatobá (BA)	Jatobá (BA)	69	14.496, 152	Muquem do Sao Francisco	BA	Secretaria de Patrimônio da União	2007
Mel da Pedreira	Mel da Pedreira	25	2.600	Macapa	AP	Incra	2007
Porto Alegre	Porto Alegre	54	2.597	Cameta	PA	Iterpa	2007
Volta do Campo Grande	Volta do Campo Grande	103	10.800	Isaias Coelho	PI	Interpi	2007
Jacarequara	Jacarequara		1.602, 9725	Santa Maria do Para	PA	Iterpa	2008
Matias	Matias	60	1.479, 6824	Cameta	PA	Iterpa	2008
Menino Jesus	Menino Jesus (São Miguel do Guamá)		306, 5891	Sao Miguel do Guama	PA	Iterpa	2008
Santa Luzia (Macapazinho)	Santa Luzia (Macapazinho)			Santa Isabel do Para	PA	Iterpa	2008
Tipitinga	Tipitinga		1.624, 1271	Santa Luzia do Para	PA	Iterpa	2008
87	143	8.874	1.171.579				

APPENDIX B

Quilombo Rights/Observatory
Source: https://cpisp.org.br/direitosquilombolas/
Accessed March 2023

With the aim of contributing to guaranteeing the rights of quilombola communities, the São Paulo Pro-Indio Commission is dedicated to researching and disseminating how these rights have been recognized in legislation, implemented by the government and interpreted by the Judiciary.

206 TITLED LANDS

159 lands titled by state governments
41 lands titled by the federal government
4 lands titled by state and federal governments
2 lands titled by municipal government

1,803 LANDS WITH OPEN PROCESS AT INCRA

3 identification reports published in 2022
4 recognition and declaration ordinances published in 2022
0 expropriation decrees published in 2022

LEGISLATION

Access the national and international repertoire, treaties and conventions related to the rights of quilombola communities at https://cpisp.org.br/direitos-quilombolas/legislacao/

JUDICIARY IN FOCUS

Check out relevant jurisprudence for the effectiveness of the rights of quilombola communities at https://cpisp.org.br/direitos-quilombolas/jurisprudencia/

Source: https://cpisp.org.br/
Accessed March 2023

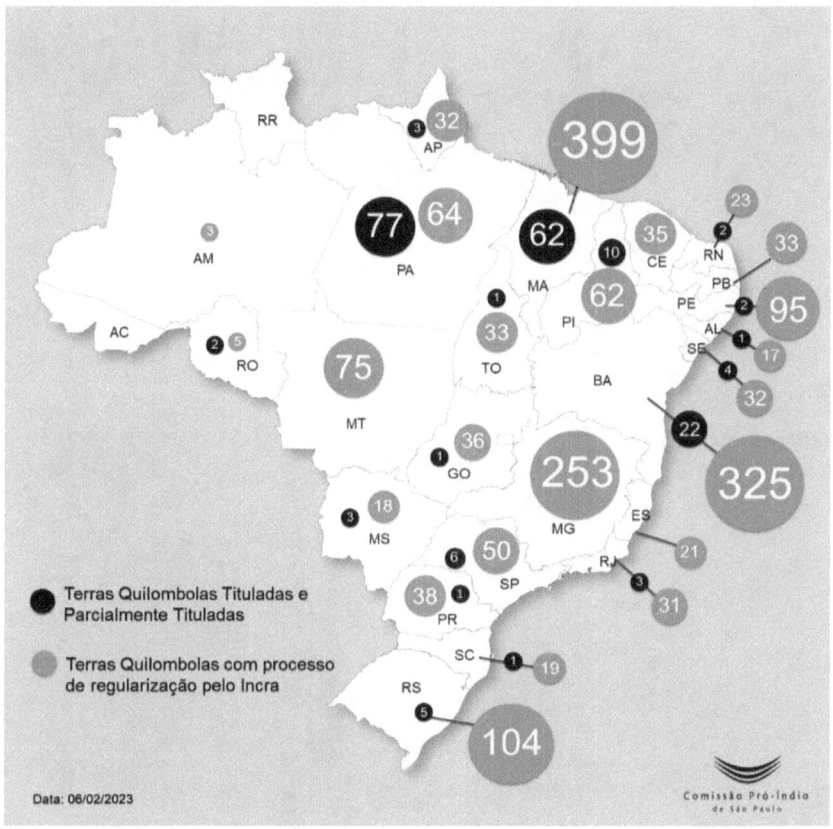

Since 2004, we have been monitoring the implementation of the land regularization policy for Quilombola Lands in Brazil.

1803
Open regularization processes

84 %
lands under identification

148
Regularized Quilombola Lands

58
Partially titled Quilombola lands

APPENDIX C

Thirty years ago, the constitution recognized quilombo rights.
Source:https://cpisp.org.br/ha-30-anos-constituicao-reconhecia-os-direitos-quilombolas/
Accessed March 2023

It was only in the 1988 Constitution that quilombola communities were assured the right to own their lands. However, to date, only 9 percent of quilombola communities live in titled areas.

Photo: Lucia Andrade

DEGREE SCOREBOARD

175 territories where 265 communities live in 16 states.
Total regularized dimension: 1,012,124.6116 hectares

The current scenario does not allow for optimism regarding the advancement of titles. There are 1,696 processes underway at INCRA; 44 percent of them have been open for more than ten years. Most of the processes (85 percent) do not even have the Technical Report of Identification and Delimitation, an initial phase that identifies the limits of the quilombola territory to be titled.

The 1988 Brazilian Constitution, in Article 68 of the Transitory Constitutional Provisions Act (ADCT), grants quilombola communities the right to own their lands. Article 68 textually states: "To the remnants of the quilombo communities that are occupying their lands, definitive ownership is recognized, and the State must issue them the respective titles."

• • •

QUILOMBOLA RIGHTS IN THE CONSTITUTION

The proposal was brought to the debates of the Constituent Assembly by Black Movement entities also responsible for the inclusion of a similar device in some state constitutions, such as those of Pará, Maranhão, and Bahia. The proposal was formalized by then deputy Carlos Alberto Caó (PDT-RJ) and presented under the rubric of popular amendment on August 20, 1987.

While the Indians' rights to own their lands have been guaranteed in all Brazilian constitutions since the 1934 Constitution, it was only in the 1988 Constitution that quilombolas' rights were recognized. The inclusion of this constitutional precept repairs a historical injustice committed by the Brazilian slave society against the Black people, a reparation that materializes through the recognition of the rights of communities of descendants of former slaves, allowing them, finally, access to ownership of their lands.

Quilombola communities were also guaranteed the right to maintain their own culture through Articles 215 and 216 of the

Constitution. The first provision determines that the State protects Afro-Brazilian cultural manifestations. Article 216, on the other hand, considers Brazilian cultural heritage—to be promoted and protected by the public power—goods of a material and immaterial nature (which include forms of expression, as well as ways of creating, doing, and living) of different groups makers of Brazilian society, among which are undoubtedly the Black communities.

Read also: "Quilombola Rights – History of regulations" at https://cpisp.org.br/direitosquilombolas/regularizacao-historico-regulamentacoes/

GLOSSARY

African Weltanschauung: African worldview. The cultural values of African-origin people and African-descended people. Philosophies encompassing God, life, faith, death, and more.

Aldeias: Indian villages.

Amancebaria: Concubine, mistress.

Amerindian: Indigenous tribes in the Americas

Aquilombodos: Quilombo refugee.

Bandeira: Expedition.

Bandeirantes: Flag carriers and slave catchers who roamed the frontiers, claiming lands for the Portuguese Crown and capturing runaway slaves. Ruthless adventurers. Include slave hunters from São Paulo, also known as Paulistas.

Batuques: Drumming, an African dance, often performed with an instrument or voice.

Bichos do Mato: "Forest beasts." A term usually applied to Indigenous people living in the forest. Later also used to refer to Black people living in the forest. A pejorative.

Brancos: Whites.

Cabas: Mixed-breed Blacks.

Caboclos: A Brazilian of mixed White and Indigenous or Black and Indigenous ancestry. A country person.

Cabores: Person of mixed Indian and African blood.

Cabra: A person of "Black and mulatto" derivation.

Caburé: A descendant of an Indigenous and a Black person.

Cachaça: Liquor distilled from sugarcane.

Calhambolas: A pejorative term for runaway slaves.

Calundu: A generic term for African Brazilian religious practice; in contemporary Brazil, the term means "bad mood."

Calundus: Trance dancing.

Candomblé: A polytheistic religious ritual practiced by Afro-Brazilians; a dance of the gods.

Cantos: Groups of slaves who worked in the cities and urban areas.

Capitão do Mato: "Captain of the forest," slave catchers.

Carijó: Culturally related Indigenous peoples of South America. They are distinguished from the related Tupi Indians by their use of the Guarani language.

Catachós: Indigenous groups.

Cerrado: Tropical wetland, savanna.

Charqueadas: A dried meat farm worked by slaves. Large cattle ranches centered on dried meat production.

Cidades: City or town.

Cimarrón: Spanish word meaning "wild thing" or "untamed." Enslaved Africans who escaped from Spanish slave masters and lived together in the forest of Panama. They helped to defeat the Spanish in their conquest of Panama.

Classe Média: A member of the Portuguese middle class. Bourgeoisie.

Coffles: A train of slaves fastened together.

Coiteiro: One who gives asylum, a free man (Black) who managed a quilombo, who worked with and lived with the runaway slaves, especially in agriculture. Quilombo Oitizeiro was known to provide habitation to coiteiros.

Comarca: A judicial district; the *comarca* of the north (the state of Tocantins) and the *comarca* of the south (the state of Goiás).

Cafuso: Offspring of Indian and Negro.

Cooper: A maker of casks, crates, and barrels. My grandfather Patrick was a cooper from South Boston, Virginia. He made hogsheads—tobacco barrels.

Conterminous: Having the same area, context, or meaning; within the same boundary.

Crioulos: People of African descent not born in Africa, living in Brazil.

Cultigen: A plant species with no known wild ancestor. Fugitive slaves were responsible for growing several edible plants of this nature.

Entrada: An expedition into unexplored territory. A Spanish exploration or conquest expedition in the Americas.

Escravos: Slaves.

Escravo de Ganho: A wage-earning slave, equivalent to a hired-out slave in America.

Espertos: An intelligent individual, used in the same context as *ladino*.

Faute de Mieux: For lack of something better or more desirable.

Fazenda: A large plantation, farm, or estate.

Fidalgo: A Portuguese nobleman or gentleman.

Ganga Zumba: "Great lord."

Gente de Cor: Colored people.

Gentio: A heathen.

Gentio da Terra: Indigenous people in colonial Brazil who were non-Jews.

Grand Marronage: Escapes of fugitive slaves for long periods of time, vs. *petit marronage*, individual escapes, usually temporary.

Grog Shop: A place where alcoholic beverages were served or sold.

Griffe: A person of mixed Black and American Indian blood. A term used by slave owners when referring to escaped male slaves.

Guinea Negroes: Any newly arrived Black slave. A newly arrived African from the coast of Guinea.

Guerra do Mato: "War of the woods."

Hostlers: One who takes care of the horses or mules. A job often performed by the enslaved.

Inconfidência: An uprising against Portuguese rule.

Irmandades: African-based ethnic organizations.

Kilombo: Kimbundu in Angola; a male initiation camp, a male military camp. Portuguese pronunciation is *quilombo*. A hidden camp.

Kith: One's friends, acquaintances, and relations.

Ladeiras: Another Portuguese name for runaway slave communities.

Ladino: A Westernized Spanish-speaking Latin American. Some slaves acquired enough learning to be labeled a *ladino*, learning Christianity and earning a livelihood.

Libambo: A long, heavy chain with rings that locked around the captured Africans.

Macaco: The capital of Palmares. A term that also means, in Portuguese, "monkey."

Makanda: Plural "kanda," a term that often relates to kinship but which can also refer to any faction or categorical grouping.

Malungos: In the case of the peoples of the Bantu language group, Africans who made the passage together from Angola and Central Africa to Brazil to be enslaved. African comrades. A travel partner in the journey toward *calunga*, the land of the dead from whence the White people came. African slaves who crossed the Atlantic together.

Mamelucos: Mix of the Indigenous population and the Portuguese.

Mambises: Cuban slaves, Blacks, and mulattos who fought independently against the Spanish in the Ten Years' War.

Maroons: runaway slaves.

Mato Grosso: "Great forest."

Mestiço: People primarily of mixed European and Indigenous Angolan African lineages.

Mestizos: Of mixed European and Indian descent

Métis: People of mixed European and Indigenous ancestry.

Minas Gerais: "General mines."

Moradores: Residents.

Mouro: A Moor, a diffuse ethnic group with applied darkness of skin. Muslims who invaded Europe.

Mustees: A person of Black ancestry, the offspring of a White person and an octoroon or quadroon.

Negroes da Terra: "Blacks of the land."

Ngola Janga: Palmares.

Nzumbi: Associated with a Bantu priestly and military title in Angola.

Nègress Sauvages: "Wild negroes" who escaped rather than serve the Spanish.

Orisha, Orixá: An African conception of a deity.

Ouvidors: The royal judges.

Palenques: "*Cumbes*" in Spanish America; runaway slaves.

Pardos: Mixed-breed Blacks and Whites.

***Paulistas*:** Inhabitants of São Paulo and south central Brazil. They also formed an informal army that was used to attack Palmares.

***Pedestres*:** Indigenous person who had been assimilated and lived in religious missions. Effective frontiersmen.

***Pelotas*:** The village of São Francisco da Paula, the main center for dried meat production.

***Pelourinho*:** A nine-night flogging until the whip drew blood. A pillory or whipping post. A slave auction location. Now a historic location in Bahia, Salvador, Brazil.

***Petit Marronage*:** Rest stops along the way for runaway slaves. Escapes of short duration.

***Pretos*:** Blacks.

***Plausible*:** A term used by slave owners to describe runaway slaves to indicate that the slave may be cunning or able to convince authorities that they were who they purported to be. Defined as superficially fair, reasonable but often specious; superficially pleasing or persuasive; appearing worthy of belief.

***Pousada*:** An inn, in Portuguese. A more intimate facility than a hotel.

***Provenience*:** The place of origin or discovery or source.

***Quilombos/Mocambos*:** In Brazil, runaway slave communities.

***Quilombolas/Calhambolas/Mocambeiros*:** Members of runaway slave communities.

***Race Identifiers*:** Mainly in Portugal but also in other European states, Africans, Black people, and people of color were categorized by the circumstances of their birth. Blacks born in Brazil were *crioulos*. A *mameluco* was the child of a White man and an Indian woman. A *brasileiro* (one who works with the Brazil tree) was an Indian or *mameluco*. A *banda-forra* was the offspring of a White male and a Black slave. A mulatto was the product of any Black and

White persons. A *pardo* was a mulatto or someone with brown skin. A *terceirao* was the offspring of a White and a new mulatta. A *curiboca* was the offspring of a Tupi and a White. A *cafuzo* was the offspring of a Black and a Tupi or Indian. The French in San Domingo, with the Negro Code of 1685, divided the offspring of White and Black and intermediate shades into 128 categories.

***Rigor de Cativeiro*:** "Rigor of captivity."

***Santidade*:** Runaway natives who had escaped slavery and religious conversion. The true ancestors of the quilombos on Brazilian soil.

***Saamaka*:** A maroon society of Africans in Suriname that exists today.

***Sawyer*:** One who saws.

***Scamp*:** A person, especially a child, who is mischievous in a likable way. A term used by slave masters to describe slaves; in one case, an elderly Black person.

Senzalas: A slave camp in colonial Brazil. Black slave residence.

***Sertao*:** Hinterland, backcountry, an arid region of scrub.

***Sesmarias*:** Plots of land assigned to settlers by the Portuguese monarchy for agriculture.

***Skiff*:** A flat-bottomed rowboat. Various kinds of small boats.

***Swidden*:** The process of clearing land by slashing and burning existing vegetation for the purpose of further cultivation. This approach was often used by the fugitive slaves to plant crops.

***Thaumaturge*:** A performer of magic or miracles. Often used in regard to Catholic personages who performed miracles for Brazilian settlers.

***Uma Guerra dos Pretos*:** "Blacks' War."

Umbanda: Afro-Brazilian religion that blends African traditions, Roman Catholicism, spiritualism, and Indigenous religious practices and symbols.

Wench: A young woman, girl. A female servant, a lewd woman, or a prostitute. The term was often used by slave owners to refer to young Black women.

Zumbi: The last and most influential leader of Palmares.

BIBLIOGRAPHY

Anderson, Robert Nelson. "The Quilombo of Palmares: A New Overview of a Maroon State in Seventeenth-Century Brazil." *Journal of Latin American Studies* 28, no. 3 (1996): 545-566.

Antognazza, Maria Rosa. *Leibniz: A Very Short Introduction.* Oxford, 2016.

Anushiem, Chidera. "10 Traditional African Hairstyles and Their Origin." *African Vibes Magazine,* July 26, 2022. https://hair.africanvibes.com/10-traditional-african-hairstyles-and-their-origins/.

Aptheker, Herbert. "Maroons Within the Present Limits of the United States." *Journal of Negro History* 24, no. 2 (1939): 167-184.

Araújo, Ana Lucia. "Zumbi and the Voices of the Emergent Public Memory of Slavery and Resistance in Brazil." *Comparative* 22, no. 2 (2012): 95-111.

Assis, Odete, and Jennifer Tristan. "Dandara, Aqualtune e Luiza Mahin: Mulheres Negras na Luta Contra a Escravidão no Brasil." *Esquerda Diário,* July 25, 2018. https://www.esquerdadiario.com.br/Dandara-Aqualtune-e-Luiza-Mahin-Mulheres-negras-na-luta-contra-a-escravidao-no-Brasil/.

Bastide, Roger. "The Other Quilombos." In Price, *Maroon Societies,* 191-201.

Bennett, Jack. "Maroon State: Slave Community and Resistance in Palmares, Brazil." *Retrospect Journal,* 2020.

Bergad, Laird W. *The Comparative Histories of Slavery in Brazil, Cuba, and the United States: New Approaches to the Americas.* New York: Cambridge University Press, 2007.

Bethell, Leslie. *Brazil: Essays on History and Politics.* University of London Press, 2018.

Bowen, Merle L. "The Struggle for Black Land Rights in Brazil: An Insider's View on Quilombos and the Quilombo Land Movement." In Demissie, *African Diaspora in Brazil,* 133-154.

Browne-Marshall, Gloria J. "1619 to 1819: Tell Them We Fought Back, A Socio-Legal Perspective." *Phylon* 57, no. 1 (2020): 37-55.

Bush, Roderick. *The End of White World Supremacy: Black Internationalism and the Problem of the Color Line.* Temple University Press, 2009.

Campbell, Joseph. *Historical Atlas of World Mythology.* New York: Harper & Row, 1998.

Carvalho, Marcus Joaquim M. "The Quilombo of Malunguinho, the King of the Forest of Pernambuco." In Reis and Gomes, *Freedom by a Thread.*

Cha-Jua, Sundiata Keita. *America's First Black Town: Brooklyn, Illinois, 1830-1915.* Chicago: University of Illinois Press, 2002.

Chapman, Charles E. "Palmares: The Negro Numantia." *Journal of Negro History* 3, no. 1 (January 1918), 29-32.

Cheney, Glenn A. *Quilombo dos Palmares: Brazil's Lost Nation of Fugitive Slaves.* Hanover, CT: New London Librarium, 2014.

da Costa, Maria Suely. "Representações de Luta e Resistência Feminina na Poesia Popular." III Conedu, Congresso Nacional de Educação.

Dain, Bruce. "Beyond Black and Red: African-Native Relations in Colonial Latin America, and: To Intermix with Our White Brothers: Indian Mixed Bloods in the United States from Earliest Times to the Indian Removals (review)." *Journal of the Early Republic* 27, no. 1 (2007): 180-184.

Davidson, Basil. *The Black Man's Burden: Africa and the Curse of the Nation-State.* New York: Three Rivers Press, 1992.

de Carvalho, Aline Vieira. "Archaeological Perspectives of Palmares: A Maroon Settlement in 17th Century Brazil." *African Diaspora Archaeology Newsletter* 10, no. 1 (2007): article 5.

de Mello e Souza, Laura. "Violence in Frontier Lands." In Reis and Gomes, *Freedom by a Thread*.

de Tavares, Julio Cesar. "Deconstructing Invisibility: Race and Politics of Visual Culture in Brazil." in *African Diaspora in Brazil: History, Culture and Politics*, edited by Fassil Demissie, 5-14. London: Routledge, 2014.

de Souza, Yvonildo. *Grandes Negros do Brazil*. Livraría São José, 1963.

Demissie, Fassil, ed. *African Diaspora in Brazil, History, Culture and Politics*. London: Routledge, 2014.

Diegues, Carlos, and Coco Fusco. "Choosing Between Legend and History: An Interview with Carlos Diegues." *Cinéaste* 15, no. 1 (1986): 12-14.

Diggs, Irene. "Zumbi and the Republic of Os Palmares." *Phylon* 14, no. 1 (1953): 62-70.

Du Bois, W. E. B. "Criteria of Negro Art." *The Crisis* 32 (October 1926): 290-297.

Duke, Dawn. "Beyond the Quilombo? The State of Zumbi's 'Palmares' According to the Poets." *Obsidian* 13, no. 1 Special Issue: Afro-Brazilian Literature (2012): 37-60.

Duke, Dawn. "In Poetic Memory of Zumbi's Palmares and Adbias do Nascimento's Quilombismo. In Homage to Abdias do Nascimento (1914-2011)." *Aletria Revista de Estudos de Literatura* 28, no. 4: 11. doi:10.17851/2317-2096.28.4.11-29.

Ennes, Ernesto. "The Palmares Republic of Pernambuco: Its Final Destruction, 1697." *Americas* 5, no. 2 (October 1948): 200-216.

Escrita, Manu. "Tereza de Benguela." *illustrated Women in History* (January 3, 2018). https://illustratedwomeninhistory.com/this-weeks-illustrated-women-in-history-was-7/.

Fogel, Robert William, and Stanley L. Engerman. *Time on the Cross: The Economics of American Negro Slavery.* Boston: Little, Brown and Company, 1974.

Franklin, John Hope. *Mirror to America.* New York: Farrar, Straus and Giroux, 2005.

Franklin, John Hope, and Loren Schweninger. *Runaway Slaves: Rebels on the Plantations.* New York: Oxford University Press, 1999.

French, Jan Hoffman. "Buried Alive: Imagining Africa in the Brazilian Northeast." *American Ethnologist* 33, no. 3 (2006): 340-360.

Freud, Sigmund. *The Future of an Illusion.* New York: W. W. Norton & Company, 1989.

Freyre, Gilberto. *The Masters and the Slaves: A Study in the Development of Brazilian Civilization.* Berkeley: University of California Press, 1986.

Fryer, Daniel. "A Scholar of Race Relations Says He's Now Less Optimistic." *Washington Post*, September 10, 2021.

Funari, Pedro Paulo A. "Conflict and the Interpretation of Palmares, a Brazilian Runaway Polity." *Historical Archaeology* 37, no. 3 (2003): 81-92.

Funari, Pedro Paulo A., and Aline Vieira de Carvalho. "Palmares: A Rebel Polity through Archaeological Lenses." In Reis and Gomes, *Freedom by a Thread*, 288-325.

Funes, Eurípides A. "'I Was Born in the Forest; I've Never Had an Owner': History and Memory of the Mocambo Communities in the Low Amazon Rainforest." In Reis and Gomes, *Freedom by a Thread.*

Gomez, Michael A. *Reversing Sail: A History of the African Diaspora, New Approaches to African History.* New York: Cambridge University Press, 2005.

Guerreiro, João Farias, Ândrea Kely Campos Ribeiro-dos-Santos, Eduardo José Melo dos Santos, Antonio Carlos Rosário Vallinoto, Izaura Maria Vieira Cayres-Vallinoto, Gilberto Ferreira de Souza Aguiar, and Sidney Emanuel Batista dos Santos. "Genetical-Demographic Data from Two Amazonian Populations Composed of Descendants of African Slaves: Pacoval and Curiau." *Genetics and Molecular Biology* 22, no. 2 (June 1999). https://doi.org/10.1590/S1415-47571999000200004.

Guimarães, Carlos Magno. "Mining, Quilombos, and Palmares: Minas Gerais in the Eighteenth Century." In Reis and Gomes, *Freedom by a Thread.*

Lara, Silvia Hunold. "From Singular to Plural: Palmares, Capitãos-Do-Mato, and the Slave Government." In Reis and Gomes, *Freedom by a Thread.*

Lara, Silvia Hunold. "Palmares and Cucaú: Political Dimensions of a Maroon Community in Late Seventeenth-Century Brazil." Paper presented at the 12th Annual Gilder Lehrman Center International Conference at Yale University: "American Counterpoint: New Approaches to Slavery and Abolition in Brazil," October 29-30, 2010.

Lara, Silvia Hunold. "O Território dos Palmares: Cartografia, História e Política." *Afro-Ásia*, no. 64 (2021): 12-50.

Levine, Robert M., and John J. Crocitti, eds. *The Brazil Reader: History, Culture, Politics.* Durham: Duke University Press, 1999.

Linhares, Luiz Fernando do Rosário. "Kilombos of Brazil: Identity and Land Entitlement." *Journal of Black Studies* 34, no. 6 (July 2004): 817-837.

Karasch, Mary. "The Quilombos of Gold in the Captaincy of Goiás." In Reis and Gomes, *Freedom by a Thread*, 203-222.

Kent, R. K. "Palmares: An African State in Brazil." *Journal of African History* 6, no. 2 (1965): 161-175.

Kennedy, Randall. *Say it Loud.* New York: Knopf Doubleday, 2021.

Maestri, Mário. "Black Plains: Quilombos in Rio Grande do Sul." In Reis and Gomes, *Freedom by a Thread*.

Martins, Vinicius. "Aqualtune, a Luz de Palmares." *Alma Preta* (July 21, 2017). https://almapreta.com.br/sessao/cotidiano/aqualtune-a-luz-de-palmares/.

Mott, Luiz. "St. Anthony, the Divine Capitão-Do-Mato." In Reis and Gomes, *Freedom by a Thread*, 94-120.

Motta, Marcia Maria Menendes. "The Sesmarias in Brazil: Colonial Land Politics in the Late Eighteenth-Century." *e-JPH* 3, no. 2 (Winter 2005).

Nogueira, André. "De Princesa Africana a Escravizada em Solo Brasileiro: Aqualtune, a Avó de Zumbi." *Aventura na História*. https://aventurasnahistoria.uol.com.br/noticias/reportagem/de-princesa-africana-escravizada-em-solo-brasileiro-aqualtune-avo-de-zumbi.phtml/.

Orser, Jr., Charles E. "Toward a Global Historical Archaeology: An Example from Brazil." *Historical Archaeology* 28, no. 1 (1994): 5-22.

Orser, Jr., Charles E., and Pedro P. A. Funari. "Archaeology and Slave Resistance and Rebellion." *World Archaeology* 33, no. 1 (2001): 61-72.

Price, Richard, ed. *Maroon Societies: Rebel Slave Communities in the Americas*. 3rd ed. Baltimore: John Hopkins University Press, 1996.

Price, Richard. "Refiguring Palmares." In Reis and Gomes, *Freedom by a Thread*.

Ramos, Donald. "The Quilombo and the Slave System in Eighteenth Century Minas Gerais." In Reis and Gomes, *Freedom by a Thread*.

Rapoport Delegation on Afro-Brazilian Land Rights. "Between the Law and Their Land: Afro-Brazilian Quilombo Communities' Struggle for Land Rights." [Report.] University of Texas, 2008.

Reis, João José. "Slaves and the Coiteiros in the Quilombo of Oitzeiro, Bahia, 1806." In Reis and Gomes, *Freedom by a Thread*.

Reis, João José, and Flavio dos Santos Gomes, eds. *Freedom by a Thread: The History of Quilombos in Brazil*. New York: Diasporic Africa Press, 2016.

Reis, João José, and Flavio dos Santos Gomes. "Quilombo: Brazilian Maroons During Slavery." *Cultural Survival Quarterly Magazine*, April 28, 2010. www.culturalsurvival.org/publications/cultural-survival-quarterly/quilombo-brazilian-maroons-during-slavery/.

Runciman, David. *Political Hypocrisy: The Mask of Power, from Hobbes to Orwell and Beyond*. Princeton University Press, 2008.

Russell, Jr., Broderick. "Zumbi & Dandara." *Honest Media Blog* (December 7, 2019). https://honestmediablog.com/2019/12/07/zumbi-dandara/.

Said, Edward. Culture and Imperialism, *1994*.New York: Alfred A. Knopf. Inc. 1993.

Schwartz, Stuart B. "The Mocambo: Slave Resistance in Colonial Bahia." *Journal of Social History* 3, no. 4 (1970): 313-333.

Schwartz, Stuart B. "Rethinking Palmares: Slave Resistance in Colonial Brazil." In *Critical Readings on Global Slavery*, edited by Damian Alan Pargas and Felicia Roşu, 1294-1325. Leiden, Netherlands: Brill, 2005.

Skidmore, Thomas E. *Brazil: Five Centuries of Change*. New York: Oxford University Press, 1999.

Smallwood, Arwin D. "A History of Native American and African Relations from 1502 to 1900." *Negro History Bulletin* 62, no. 2/3 (April-September 1999), 18-31.

Thomas, Hugh. *The Slave Trade: The Story of the Atlantic Slave Trade: 1440-1870.* New York: Touchstone, 1997.

Thornton, John K. "Afro-Christian Syncretism in the Kingdom of Kongo." *Journal of African History* 54, no. 1 (2013): 53-77.

Thornton, John K. "The Art of War in Angola, 1575-1680." *Comparative Studies in Society and History* 30, no. 2 (1988): 360-378.

Thornton, John K. "Elite Women in the Kingdom of Kongo: Historical Perspectives on Women's Political Power." *Journal of African History* 47, no. 3 (2006): 437-460.

Thornton, John K. "The Kingdom of Kongo and the Thirty Years War." *Journal of World History* 27, no. 2 (2016): 189-213.

Thornton, John K. "Legitimacy and Political Power: Queen Njinga, 1624-1663." *Journal of African History* 32, no. 1 (1991): 25-40.

Thornton, John K., and Linda Heywood. *Central Africans, Atlantic Creoles, and the Foundation of the Americas, 1585-1660.* University of Cambridge Press, 2007.

Tyler, Ronnie C. "Fugitive Slaves in Mexico." *Journal of Negro History* 57, no. 1 (1972): 1-12.

van der Puye, Franz. "Media and the Preservation of Culture in Africa." *Cultural Survival Quarterly* 22, no. 2 (1998). https://www.culturalsurvival.org/publications/cultural-survival-quarterly/media-and-preservation-culture-africa/.

Vainfas, Ronaldo. "God Against Palmares: Lordly Representations and Jesuitical Ideas." In Reis and Gomes, *Freedom by a Thread*, 51-71.

Viswanathan, Gauri. *Outside the Fold: Conversion, Modernity, and Belief.* Princeton: Princeton University Press, 1998.

Volpato, Luiza Rios Ricci. "Quilombos in Mato Grosso: Black Resistance in a Border Area." In Reis and Gomes, *Freedom by a Thread*.

Walton, James L., ed. *Asian & African Systems of Slavery*. Berkeley: University of California Press, 1980.

Weik, Terry. "The Archaeology of Maroon Societies in the Americas: Resistance, Cultural Continuity, and Transformation in the African Diaspora." *Historical Archaeology* 31, no. 2 (1997): 81-92.

Welsing, Frances Cress. *The Isis Papers: The Keys to the Colors*. Washington, DC: C.W. Publishing, 1991.

Wilderson, Frank. *Afropessimism*. New York: Liveright, 2020.

Zewde, Bahru. "From Adwa to Maychaw 1896-1935." In *A History of Modern Ethiopia 1855-1991*, 81-149. Ohio University Press, 2002.

INDEX

1619 Project 9
    New York Times

A

Aboriginal peoples (Australia) 18
ADCT (Transitory Disposition of the Brazilian Constitution) 219–221
    Article 68 221–223, 225
African religions 149–151
    Candomblé
    Jurema
    Vodun (Voodoo)
Afro-Brazilian culture 1, 8
Afropessimism 230–231
    Wilderson, Frank
Alagoas 47
Alfonso I, King 145
Alvará of 1795 204–206, 219, 224
Amazon 48
Ambrosio (quilombo) 55
    Minas Gerais
American Revolution 90, 117, 169, 176
Anderson, Robert Nelson 7, 18–19, 45, 67–68, 72, 77, 84, 180, 184, 195–196, 198–199, 201
Andrew, King of Hungary 144
Angola 4, 40, 45–46, 49–50, 54, 61, 65–66, 69, 71–72, 84–85, 114, 123, 150, 154, 163
António I, King (Kongo) 66, 80
António Melo, Friar 72–75, 77, 162, 184
    Porto Calvo
Anushiem, Chidera 166

Aptheker, Herbert 90, 93, 95, 97, 99
Aqualtune 65–66, 70–71, 80, 127–129, 137, 167
Aranha, Filippa Maria 135
Araújo, Ana Lucia 7–9
Asad, Talal 151
Attucks, Crispus 117
    American Revolution
    Boston Massacre

B

Baca, Elfego 184
Bahia 23, 25–26, 28, 44, 54, 192
Baldwin, James 38, 215, 232
Bandeira 115
Baptista, João 150
Bastide, Roger 44, 134–135, 148
Batista, João 63
Battell, Andrew 49
Battle at Wounded Knee 194
batuque 134
Berbers 196
Bergad, Laird W. 15, 67, 147–148
Berkeley, G.F.K. 230
    The Campaign of Adwa and the Rise of Menelik
Berlin, Ira, Dr. 34
Bernard and Audre Rapoport Center for Human Rights and Justice 220
Beyond Black and Red 111
    Restall, Matthew
Black diaspora 1, 12, 17, 24, 26, 36–37, 43, 69, 80, 105, 229
Black Lives Matter 5
Black power movements 5

Black settlements 103–108
blacksmiths 55
bloco-Afro 27–28, 31, 224, 228
    see Olodum
Boston Massacre 117
    American Revolution
    Attucks, Crispus
Bowen, Merle 220–221, 223
Bradford, John 77
Brazil 1–3
Brazilian Black Movement 27–28, 31, 224, 228
    see Olodum
Brazilian Constitution (1988) 219–220
Brazilian cuisine
    moqueca 30
    caipirinha 30–31
Brown v. Board of Education 5, 18–19, 222, 233
Browne-Marshall, Gloria J. 163
Buraco de Tatú 168
Bush, Roderick 10, 244

C

Cabral, Pedro Alvarez 62
Campbell, Joseph 7
Camuanga (Zumbi) 87–88
Candida, Maria 212
Candomblé 83
Cão, Diogo 61
capitalism 2
Carlota quilombo 119
Carlyle, Thomas 153
Carneiro, Edison 50, 59, 65, 67
    O Quilombo Dos Palmares
Carnival troupes 27–28
    Olodum
    Ilê Aiyê
    Malê Debalê
    Timbalada
Carnival 25–31, 32
Castro, Melo e 195–196
Catholicism 74, 77, 110, 143–146, 148, 157, 164, 190–191, 195
Cerrado 48
Cha-Jua, Sundiata Keita 102, 103–105
Chapman, Charles E. 187
Cheney, Glenn 49–51, 62, 72, 74, 80–81, 84, 152–153, 156, 168, 183–184, 186, 192–193, 195–197, 200–201
Christianity 110–114, 126, 143–164
Cisplatine War, Uruguay 100
Civil Rights Act of 1964 18
Civil War 91, 106, 117, 176
Clark, Kenneth B. 5, 233
    Brown v. Board of Education
Clarke, Henrick 10, 244
coconut palm 48–49
Code of Hammurabi 206–207
coiteiros 54
colonial (state of mind) 2
Columbus, Christopher 43
Congo 61
Council of Trent 147, 156, 158
crioulos 181

D

da Costa, Josilene Brandão 220, 222–223, 225
da Cunha Souto Maior, João 183, 192
da Rocha Pita, Sebastião 189
    História da América Portuguesa
Dain, Bruce 111
Dandara 129–130, 138
    Nagó 129
Davidson, Basil 15
de Almeida, Luis Brito 44
de Almeida, Pedro 171–172
de Ayllon, Lucas Vazquez 91
de Benquela, Tereza (Queen) 130–132
de Carrilho, Fernão 167, 177, 203

de Carvalho, Aline Vieira 13–14, 19, 87, 151, 185
de Mello e Souza, Laura 112
de Melo, Evaldo Cabral 210–211
de Silverira, Duarte Gomes 109
de Souza e Castro, Aires 171, 181
de Souza, João 183, 192, 203
de Souza, Yvonildo 8
de Tavares, Julio Cesar 4–10
    "Deconstructing Invisibility: Race and Politics of Visual Culture in Brazil"
de Zurara, Gomes Eanes 43
Demissie, Fassil 54–55, 222
Department of Agriculture 238
Dias, Henriques 175
Diegues, Carlos 19–22
    Quilombo
Diggs, Irene 54, 64–65
Divinus Antonius 143–144, 158–160
    St. Anthony of Lisbon
    Fifth Crusade
do Nascimento, Abdias 15–16
Dom João II, King (Portugal) 62
Dom João III, King (Portugal) 62
Dom José, King 206
    Law of Good Reason
Du Bois, W.E.B. 3, 16, 108, 233
    The Philadelphia Negro 108
    Dusk of Dawn 233
Duke, Dawn 16, 22, 244
Dutch authorities 56–58
Dutch–Portuguese War 72

E

engenhos 54
Engerman, Stanley 107–108
Ennes, Ernesto 44–45, 53, 86–87, 168, 186, 189, 195, 199–200

F

Fabian, Johannes 144
Fanon, Frantz 16

favela 26, 30, 33–34
Fifth Crusade 144
    Divinus Antonius
    Pope Innocent III
    St. Anthony of Lisbon
Floyd, George 233
Fogel, Robert 107–108
François-Dominique Toussaint Louverture 88
    Haiti
Franklin, John Hope 74, 92–93, 96, 99–102, 121, 243–244
    From Slavery to Freedom 121
Freitas, Décio 84, 180
French and Indian War 117
French, Jan Hoffmann 13, 17
Freyre, Gilberto 3, 20–21, 52–53, 58, 62, 79–80, 88, 111–112
Funari, Pedro 13, 87, 120, 144, 185, 210–211
Funes, Eurípides A. 211–217

G

Galvão, Manuel Lopes 180–181
Gandhi, Mahatma Karamchand 6
Ganga Zona 65, 70, 84, 128
Garcia II, King 125–126
Garvey, Marcus 233
Giddings, Joshua R. 99
Golden Law 33
    Princess Isabel
Goldwater, Barry 243
Gomes, Flavio dos Santos 44, 46, 51, 55, 58–60, 64, 84
Gray, Thomas 37
    "Ode on a Distant Prospect of Eton College"
Groot Desseyn 61, 72, 123
guerra da floresta 65, 86
Guerreiro, João Farias 211–212

H

Haiti 88

Revolution 106
Handelmann, Gottfried Heinrich 44
HBCUs 236–238
    Historically Black Colleges and Universities
Heine, Heinrich 244
Henry, Patrick 169
Herbert, Lord (Baron of Cherbury) 151
historicity (unbiased history) 2
Hobsbawm, E.J. 52
Honorius III 144

I

Ilê Aiyê 27
    see Carnival troupes
Imbangala 45, 49, 66
    see Jaga
Incas 18
Indians 109–122
    Aimoré 110
    Akroá 110
    Apinajé 110, 120, 133
    Bororo 110
    Botocudos 110
    Cabixes 110
    Canoeiro 110
    Cariris/Kiriri 110
    Cayuga 116
    Iroquois 116
    Janduí 193–194
    Karajá 110
    Kayapó 110, 118
    Krahô 110, 118
    Mohawk 116
    Onandaga 116
    Oneida 116
    Santidade 113–114
    Seminole 116–117
    Seneca 116
    Tupi 47, 110, 114–115, 118
    Tupinambá 113–114
    Tuscarora (Iroquois) 116–117
    Xavante 110, 118, 134
indigenas brasileiros 56–57
Indigenous movements 5
Indios 51
Inter-American Commission and Court of Human Rights 227
International Labour Organization Convention No. 169 221

J

Jackson, Michael 34
Jaga 45, 66
    see Imbangala
Jefferson, Thomas 231
Jesuits 72, 76, 110, 119, 143, 145, 147, 156–157, 163
Jesus Christ 6
Jobim, Carlos Antonio 32
    bossa nova

K

Karasch, Mary 118–119, 133
Kennedy, Randall 233
    Say It Loud
Kent, R.K. 11, 19, 23, 46, 53, 55, 57, 59, 65, 85, 146, 148, 171–172, 178, 188, 198, 201, 203
kilombo 45
Kimani, Martin 15
King, Jr., Martin Luther 6, 154, 230
Kongo 4, 61, 66–67, 69, 70, 79, 94, 123

L

L'Ouverture, François Dominique Toussaint 165, 230
Land Law of 1850 208, 219
    Lei de Terras
Lara, Silvia Hunold 59, 185, 201
Law of Good Reason 206
    King Dom José
law, civil 2

law, criminal 2
Lei de Terras 208, 219
    Land Law of 1850
Leibniz, Gottfried 164
Linhares, Luiz Fernando do
    Rosário 222, 224–225
Lula da Silva, Luiz Inácio 221

M

Macaco 59, 65, 173, 195, 198, 201
Makandal 150
Malê Debalê 27
    see Carnival troupes
malunguinho 64–65
mameluco 113, 115
Mandela, Nelson 6, 230
Māori people 18
Maranhão 23
maroon communities 42, 47,
    49–50, 55, 58, 72, 88, 93–94,
    98–102, 103–108
    Saamaka 88, 178, 211
Maroon Societies 52
    Price, Richard
Martins, Vinicius 128
Marx, Karl 162
Masada 187–188
Mather, Cotton 191
matriarchy 134
Mauro 81
    Moors
Mbantu language 40
media bias 2
Menelik of Ethiopia 230
    Berkeley, G.F.K.
    *The Campaign of Adwa and
    the Rise of Menelik*
Mill, John Stuart 153
missionaries 3
mocambo 44, 47, 65
Moors 81
    Mauro
Mott, Luiz 146, 152, 158–159, 164
Motta, Marcia Maria Menendes
    204
Moura, Clóvis 134

N

Nascimento, Elisa 22
National Council of La Raza 5
National Institute of Colonization
    and Land Reform (INCRA)
    222, 224, 227
Ndongo 61
    Angola
New Palmares 53
Njinga, Queen of Ndongo 71,
    124–127
    Angolan War 125–126
Numantia 187–
Nzinga, King 145

O

Obama, Barack 234
Oitizeiro 54
Old Palmares 53
Olodum 27–28, 31, 224, 228
    bloco-Afro
    see also Carnival troupes
Orser, Jr., Charles E. 11, 13, 120
Our Lady of the Rosary of the
    African Blacks 161–164

P

Pacoval 213–214, 216, 220
Palmares cidades (settlements),
    mocambos 53–54
    Zumbi
    Arotirene
    Tobacas
    Dombabanga
    Subupuira
    Osenga
    Amaro
    Andalaquituche
Palmares Confederation 59
Palmares Cultural Foundation
    (PCF) 222, 227

Palmares 1–3
Pantanal 48
Pará 23
Paraty 32, 34–41
Paulistas 192
pedestres 119
pelourinho 77
Pereira, Astrojildo 88
Pernambuco 41, 42–60, 62–63, 66, 71–73, 78, 109, 128, 170–171, 173–176, 183–184, 193, 198
petit marronage 90
    Price, Richard
    Aptheker, Herbert
Pinto, Edgar Roquette 111–112
Piolho, José 130–131
Pitta, Rocha 201
polyandry 134
polygamy 65, 134
Pope Innocent III 144
    Fifth Crusade
Porto Calvo 73–82, 84, 175
    António Melo, Friar
    Calabar, Domingas
Portuguese authorities 57
Preta Vitória 132
pretas 30
    see favela
Price, Richard 52, 90–91, 114–115, 17,2 175, 210, 227
    Maroon Societies 52

Q

Quartitere 130–131
Quechua 18
quilombismo 16
Quilombo do Campinho da Independência 38, 41
Quilombo do Campinho da Independência 70
Quilombo dos Palmares 1–2
Quilombo Malunguinho 64

R

Ramos, Donald 161
Rangers 120
Rapoport Delegation 204, 222
Recife 87
Reijmbach, Jurgens 148
Reis, João José 44, 46, 51, 55, 58–60, 64, 84
religion (politicization) 2
Restall, Matthew 111
    Beyond Black and Red
Rethinking Palmares 73, 168
    Schwartz, Stuart B.
Rio de Janeiro 32–34
    Copacabana beach 32
    Ipanema beach 32
    Christ the Redeemer statue 33
    Sugarloaf Mountain 33
Rio Grande do Norte 194
Rodrigues, Aberlado 244
Rodrigues, Nina 53, 171
    Os Africanos no Brazil 53
Rodriguez, Barbosa 217
Runciman, David 242–243
Russell, Broderick, Jr. 129

S

Sabina 70–72, 74, 128
Said, Edward 3, 152
Salvador 23, 25–30
samba 28, 31
São Paulo 192
Schwartz, Stuart B. 49, 73, 109, 161, 168, 173
    Rethinking Palmares
Schweninger, Loren 74, 92–93, 96, 99–102
sesmaria 203–208
Simpson, O.J. 233–234
slave rebellions
    New York Slave Revolt (1712) 91

Stono Rebellion (1739) 91
Hope slave ship revolt (1764) 91
German Coast uprising (1811) 91
Nat Turner's Rebellion (1831) 91, 98
Amistad slave ship revolt (1839) 91
Denmark Vesey rebellion (1822) 96
slavery 2
Small Business Administration (SBA) 238
Smallwood, Arwin 81, 113, 116, 120
Spartacus 187
St. Anthony of Lisbon 143–144, 158–160
    Divinus Antonius
    Fifth Crusade
sugarcane 4, 23, 31, 49–50, 54, 56–59, 110–111, 114, 147, 152, 156–157, 182, 234
Suriname 215–216, 227

T

The Philadelphia Negro 108
    Du Bois, W.E.B.
Thirty Years' War 61
Thomas, Hugh 43
Thornton, John K. 66, 70–71, 126–127, 145, 148, 172
Timbalada 27
    see Carnival troupes
Torres Strait islanders 18
Trail of Tears 194
Tubman, Harriet 174
Turner, Henry McNeal 233
Tyler, Ronnie C. 92–93

V

Vainfas, Ronaldo 56–57, 122, 147, 153, 156, 163, 172, 182, 192

van der Puye, Franz 124
vegetation
    Brazil nut tree 50
    liana vines 52
    oleander plant 52
    wolf's bane 52
    Dracula plant 52
    Palm of Christ (castor oil plant) 52
Velho, Domingos Jorge 192–202
Vieira, António 143–144, 152–158, 210
    "Children of God's Fire" sermon 154
Viswanathan, Gauri 144, 151, 153
Volpato, Luiza Rios Ricci 131
von Clausewitz, Carl 2–3

W

Walton, James L. 14
Washington, George 6, 231
Weik, Terry 12–13, 46, 51–52, 100, 106–107, 109–110
Welsing, Frances Cress 228. 231
West, Cornel 233
White supremacy 2, 90, 223
Wilderson, Frank 230–231
    Afropessimism

Z

Zewde, Bahru 230
    A History of Modern Ethiopia 1855-1991
Zumba, Ganga 1, 40, 57, 61–69, 70, 79–80, 83–88, 111, 127–130, 139, 150, 155–156, 160, 165–172, 174–183, 243
    Toculo 64
    Acaiene 64
    Zambi 64
Zumbi (Francisco) 1–2, 7–8, 21–22, 27, 40, 70–82, 83–88, 111, 127–129, 141, 150, 157, 162, 166, 169–172, 175–176,

180–184, 189–191, 194,
196–198, 200–201, 210, 220,
229, 244

www.ingramcontent.com/pod-product-compliance
Lightning Source LLC
LaVergne TN
LVHW091627070526
838199LV00044B/975